DEER HUNTER'S &
LAND MANAGER'S POCKET
REFERENCE

DEER HUNTER'S & LAND MANAGER'S POCKET REFERENCE

A Database for Hunters and Rural Landowners Interested in Deer Management

J. WAYNE FEARS

Skyhorse Publishing

Table of Contents

SECTION 1

WHITE-TAILED DEER PROFILE

White-Tailed Deer Profile

Common name: White-tailed deer

Scientific name: Odocoileus virginianus

U. S. White-tailed deer population when first Europeans arrived: 23–34 million
   By 1900 – 300,000
   Current – 30 million

Number of subspecies: 38total—17 in U. S. and Canada and 21 from Mexico south to Peru

Height at shoulders: 36 – 40 inches

Buck weight (average): 150 pounds, however it can range from almost 400 pounds in the far north to 50 pounds in the tropics. A buck may loose 25% of his body weight during the rut.

Doe weight (average): 100 pounds, 50 to 250 pounds depending upon where located

Life expectancy: 3-5 years in the wild, 20 years in captivity

Breeding date: October to February

Doe estrus cycle: 21 to 29 days, recycle up to seven times

Heat period: 24 hours

Gestation period: 190 to 210 days

Weight at birth: 4 to 8 pounds

Sexual maturity, doe: 1½ years. Under good nutritional conditions as high as 60% of 6-month old doe fawns will breed.

Sexual maturity, buck: 1 ½ years

Daily food intake: 4 to 6 pounds of food per 100 pounds of body weight.

Food variety: deer feed on over 600 different varieties of plants in the U.S.

Stomach: deer have four chambers in their stomach

Water intake daily: average 1.5 quarts

Home range: from 1 sq. mile to an elongated range that may be as much as 5 miles

Glands: Seven external glands that are part of the communication system of deer

1. tarsal gland on the inner surfaces of the hind leg

2. metatarsal gland on the outer surfaces of the hind legs

3. interdigital gland between the hooves

4. preorbital gland in the corners of the eyes

5. preputial gland inside the buck's penile sheath

6. nasal gland inside the nostrils

7. forehead gland between the eyes and the antler bases

Sense of smell: can detect a hunter from ½ mile away. Their sense of smell is at least 10 times more acute than man. Also, they have a vomeronasal organ in the roof of their mouth which allows them to taste odors in the air.

Eyesight: 310 degrees of vision around their head, can detect the slightest motion, excellent night vision. They can see more than black and white, as once thought, but can see a wide range of colors.

Hearing: Large ears form sound funnels. Their hearing is several times greater than humans.

Attention span: deer have a short attention span, about 3 minutes. However they can be conditioned to react to human activity and even change their movement patterns.

Hair: the hair on a deer is hollow giving it great insulating value

Droppings: deer defecates about 12 times every 24 hours.

Teeth: 32 teeth. They do not have front teeth on the upper jaw.

Running speed: 36 miles per hour

Jumping ability: 7 feet from a standing start, 8 feet with a running start.

Fawn spots: loses its spots at 3 months of age

Fawn odor: fawns are odorless the first month of life

Fawns are weaned at 4 months

Rubs: a mature buck may make as many as 300 rubs on trees each fall. Older bucks usually make rubs first in the fall.

Swimming: deer are excellent swimmers

Vocalization: deer make at least 15 distinct vocalizations

Antlers: are shed annually after the rut. New antlers are grown from late spring until early fall.

Approximate annual U.S. deaths due to deer/auto collisions: 150

Deer/vehicle collisions in U.S. annually: 1.5 million collisions cost in property damage $1.1 billion.

White-tailed Deer Subspecies
U. S. & Canada

borealis – northern woodland white-tailed deer

clavium – Key deer, Florida

carminis – Carmen Mountains white-tailed deer, Texas & Mexico

couesi – Coues / Arizona white-tailed deer

dakotensis – Dakota white-tailed deer

hiltonensis – Hilton Head white-tailed deer, South Carolina

leucurus – Columbian white-tailed deer, Oregon & Washington

macrourus – Kansas white-tailed deer

mcilhennyi – Avery Island white-tailed deer, Louisiana

nigribarbis – Blackbeard Island white-tailed deer, Georgia

ochrourus – Idaho white-tailed deer

osceola – Florida coastal white-tailed deer

seminolus – Florida white-tailed deer

taurinsulae – Bulls Island white-tailed deer, South Carolina

texanus – Texas white-tailed deer deer

venatorius – Hunting Island white-tailed deer, South Carolina

virginianus – Virginia white-tailed deer

Deer Management/Hunting Glossary of Terms

Abomasum
The fourth, or digesting, chamber of the stomach of a white-tailed deer. Biologist often use an abomasal parasite count as an index of deer condition and density relative to carrying capacity.

Aerial photo
An aerial view of a property for use in making land management decisions. Aerial photos are available for purchase from the NRCS and for free on-line viewing at www.msrmaps.com or www. googleearth.com.

Age class
Deer in the same age range. Since deer are usually born in the early summer and harvested in late fall their ages are usually discussed by biologists in ½, 1 ½, 2 ½, 3 ½, etc. age class as they are aged when harvested. A 2 ½ year age class buck is two and one-half years old.

Albino Deer
A genetic anomaly where deer lacks skin pigmentation. They have completely white coats, pink hooves and red eyes.

Antler
The branched bony growth on the head of any animal of the deer family. They are shed and re-grown annually.

Bawl

A sound made by a deer that has been injured or scared. Bawls are given by deer of all ages in situations of distress and is an alarm call.

Base camp

The central or main camp within a hunting territory.

Beam

The main branch of an antler from which tines grow. It is commonly called the main beam.

Bed

A place were a deer has laid down. A depression in grass or laves.

Bedding Area

Areas where deer take refuge. Bedding areas are often in areas that allow the deer to see and hear approaching danger. It is usually thick cover such as young planted pines, broom sedge fields, cane breaks, cedar swamps, or thickets of saplings and vines.

Bleat

A sound made by fawns to stay in contact with their mother. This sound may also be made by disturbed fawns.

Browse

Twigs, forbs, and tender woody growth that deer eat when traveling in their territory.

Brow tine
The first fork of the antler on a deer. On trophy score sheets it is the G-1 tine.

Buck
A male deer.

Buck: doe ratio
The ratio of bucks to does on a given tract of land. If a property has 20 bucks and 100 does the buck:doe ratio is said to be 1:5. If a property has 42 bucks and 126 does the ratio would be 1:3.

Calling
The hunting use of calls, imitating deer vocalizations, or rattling antlers to attract deer.

Carrying capacity
The number of deer a tract of land can support year-round. A carrying capacity of 1 deer per 20 acres means that it takes twenty acres of land to support one deer.

Clear-cut
A tract of forested land that has had all the trees harvested. In many areas even after the land has been replanted in trees it is referred to as a clear-cut by hunters.

Coniferous Trees
Trees that are cone-bearing, leaves needle-like, evergreens. They include pines, spruces, and firs.

County agent (Cooperative Extension Service)
Each state has a land grant university that offers an extension advisory service to landowners. An office is usually located in each county seat throughout the state and wildlife management advice is a part of their service.

Deer management cooperative (co-op)
Hunting clubs or landowners who do not have enough land to carry out quality deer management or trophy deer management programs may join with like-minded neighbors to form a deer co-op and manage the combined acreage as one unit.

Dibble
A tool used to hand plant tree seedlings.

Deciduous trees
Trees which shed their leaves at the end of the growing season. Hardwoods such as oak and beech are deciduous trees.

DNR
Each state has a Department of Natural Resources (DNR) to manage its wildlife resources. They offer free deer management assistance to landowners and hunting groups.

Dominant Buck

A male deer that establishes a territory and right to breed does in that territory by fighting and intimidation of smaller male deer.

Drop Tine

An antler point or tine that grows straight down from the main beam on the antlers of a mature whitetail buck.

Estrus

The period in which a female animal is in a state of sexual excitement during which the female is most receptive to mating. About 24 hours for a doe.

Estrus cycle

Does that do not become pregnant will come into estrus again 28 days later.

Fawn

An infant deer. It will have spots for the first three to four months of its life.

Firebreak

A plowed strip of land around young timber or other area that fire is to be kept out of during prescribed burning or during wild fire season. Often these strips are planted in deer food and serve as a food plot.

Field dress

To gut or eviscerate a deer in the open soon after it has been killed.

Food plot
A tract of land that is farmed specifically for the production of deer food.

G-2 tine
The first tine growing off the main beam of an antler after the brow tine (G-1). The G-2 is often the longest tine.

Gestation period
The length of time it takes a fawn to develop in the womb from conception to birth, about 200 days.

Grunt
A grunt given by bucks during courtship of a doe in estrus. This can be an effective call for hunters to use for calling bucks.

Herbivore
Any animal, including deer, which eats only plant materials.

Home Range
The area in which a deer spends most of its life. It may leave the home range during courtship but will usually return.

Hunting lease
A legal arrangement, usually written, where a landowner turns over the hunting rights of his property to a hunter or group of hunters.

Interdigital Gland
A scent gland located between a deer's hooves that leave a scent trail.

Introduced plant species
Plants may have been growing wild in the area for years. One of the best known introduced plants that deer enjoy is the Japanese honeysuckle.

Jaw puller
Extracting the lower jaw for aging purposes. It is a valuable tool for deer managers.

Loin (backstrap)
The meat found on either side of the backbone and along the top of the back of a deer. It is usually cut into chops or filets.

Logging road
A forest road that is built to haul out timber when a forest is harvested. Old logging roads often make good food plots and are good locations for finding scrapes and rubs during the hunting season.

Log landing (decks)
An open area in a forest, adjacent to a logging road where logs are loaded on trucks when the forest is cut. Old log landings often make good food plot sites.

Longhunter Society
The trophy division of the National Muzzle Loading Rifle Association. It is the official trophy hunting organization for muzzle loading rifle hunters.

Metatarsal gland
A small scent gland on a deer that is located on the outer surfaces of the hind legs, just above the dew claw.

Mineral lick
A man-made "salt lick" that is filled with mineral supplements.

Native plant species
Plant species that naturally occur in an area.

Non-typical antlers
A term referring to antlers on a deer that are not symmetrical and often have points growing off other points on the antlers.

NRCS
The Natural Resources Conservation Service, a branch of the U. S. Department of Agriculture. They have local offices in most counties to offer land, soil, wildlife and pond management assistance. To find an office near you go to http://offices.sc.egov.usda.gov/locator/app?agency=nrcs

Odocoileus Virginianus
The genus and species of the white-tailed deer

Pedicel

Pedicels are the part of the buck's skull from which antlers grow

Preorbital gland

A tear gland in the corner of a deer's eye used to leave scent on branches and twigs rubbed by the deer.

Piebald

A genetic anomaly or congenital defect that causes a deer's coat to have large patches of white hair with brown or dark spots or patches. The deer may be deformed.

Poacher

An illegal hunter who may trespass on one's land to hunt.

Pope and Young

The official organization for scoring and recording trophy big game harvested by archery hunters.

Prescribed/controlled burn

A highly controlled burn, usually in coniferous forest, to remove the forest litter to allow the sun to reach the mineral soil. It is an ideal way to improve some lands for deer management.

Rattling

A buck calling technique were antlers are rattled together by a hunter simulating two buck fighting. Under certain circumstances it can attract other bucks who hear the commotion.

Rub
The rubbing of a buck's antlers on trees and saplings during the rut.

Safari Club International (SCI)
One of the world's best known conservation and hunter education organizations. It has its own method of scoring and recording big game trophies.

Salt lick
A naturally occurring deposit of salt or one that is man-made to attract deer.

Scouting
The search for deer sign and prime areas to hunt before or during deer season.

Scrape
A means deer have of communicating. Bucks paw the ground under an overhanging limb and will urinate in the pawed out area and rub facial glands on the overhanging limb. This is to establish territory during the mating period. Female deer ready to mate may find the scrape and wait for the buck to breed her.

Snort
It is the best known sound made by deer, a short blast of air given to express alarm.

Soil testing

A means of measuring the pH of soil so that it can be determined if lime is needed to be added to the soil. It is a valuable tool for deer managers to use in planting food plots or trees.

Spike

A buck with just two main beams and no tines. Usually they are very short in length.

Supplemental feeding

The feeding to deer of additional food other than what is grown on the property. The supplemental food may be enriched to encourage bigger antlers or body weight.

Tarsal gland

A gland located on the inside of the deer's hind leg. It produces a scent unique to individual deer and are involved in rub-urination marking behavior.

Tenderloins

Two exceptionally good cuts of meat that are found just in front of the hams and under the rear of the backbone of a deer.

Topo (topographical) map

A color map made by the USGS that shows land features to scale. An ideal map for hunting use or managing land for deer.

Typical rack

Antlers grown on a buck that are somewhat symmetrical and do not have extra tines or points growing off the sides.

Velvet

A fuzzy layer of blood enriched skin that covers bucks antlers while the antlers are growing.

Venison

Meat from a deer.

Deer Management Strategies

There are four strategies a white-tailed deer manager can choose from for managing his deer population:

1. **Do Nothing Strategy**
   Maintain the existing deer density and physical condition. Little or no population or habitat management.

2. **Maximum Deer Strategy**
   Develop higher deer density – many deer on the property but physical condition of deer and habitat usually below average. This is often associated with no-doe harvesting.

3. **Quality Deer Management (QDM)**
   Improve antler development and physical condition of both the deer and habitat. This usually requires 1000 or more acres and is often done by forming a deer cooperative with neighbors who are dedicated to QDM. This strategy requires a commitment to five areas:

   - Deer population management – harvesting an appropriate number of does to balance the deer population with the habitat, and improving buck age structure by protecting young bucks.

   - Hunter management – educating hunters so they fully understand the benefits and costs of QDM before they become active participants. Ongoing education helps committed hunters continue the QDM objectives.

- Habitat management – providing abundant forage and cover. The two most common methods include natural vegetation management and food plots.

- Deer population monitoring – Collecting harvest and observation data to track progress, document QDM success and fine-tune future harvest strategies.

- Strategy monitored by a wildlife biologist.

- (For more information on QDM go to www.qdma.com)

4. **Trophy Management Strategy** - maintain a low deer density with a good portion of the bucks being large antlered bucks in above average physical condition and the habitat in excellent condition. This usually requires 5000 or more acres and is sometimes done by forming a deer cooperative. This strategy requires a commitment to:

- Fully mature bucks with large antlers being the focus

- Controlling hunter pressure

- Only hunters with above average field judging skills and self-control

- low deer density

- aggressive doe harvest

- intensive habitat management

- strategy designed and monitored by a wildlife biologist

White-tailed Deer Track

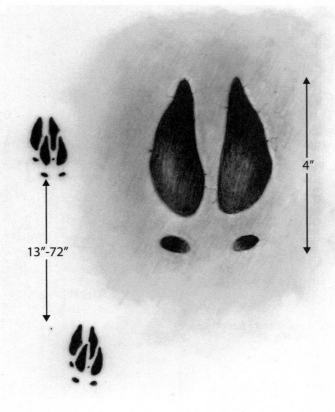

13"-72"

4"

White-tailed Deer Range

Range of White-Tailed Deer

SECTION 2

Deer Harvest

Recording Harvest Data

Harvest data, kept annually, over a period of years gives the deer manager facts to use in making long-term management recommendations for a given tract of property. Accurate harvest records allow the deer manager to evaluate such characteristics as deer body condition, antler quality, age structure, and reproductive performance of the deer population on the property.

Data from harvested deer are written on a jaw tag, which is then attached to the jawbone by a wire. Information from all tags is transferred to a deer-harvest form.

Here is what should be recorded from each deer taken:

- **Deer Number** - Assign consecutive numbers to harvested deer. Write the number on the jawbone taken from the deer. This keeps the correct jaw with the matching tag.

- **Record state tag number** – If the state Game & Fish department requires a deer tag record the number.

- **Sex of deer** – male or female

- **Date of kill**

- **Weight of deer** – Most deer managers like to get live weight if possible. Keep a good quality scale available to obtain accurate weights.

- **Antler measurements** – right and left main beam circumferences, right and left main beam lengths, inside spread, and number of points 1-inch long or longer.

- **Age of deer** – use jawbone to age deer.

- **Doe lactation** – if doe, cut into udder to see if milk is present.

- **Name of hunter**

Deer Harvest Record

| Deer # | Tag # (If Req.) | Date | Sex | Antler Data (inches) | | | | | | Weight (lbs) | | Age | Doe Lactating | Hunter's Name |
				Inside Spread	No. of Points	R. Beam Length	L. Beam Length	R. Base Circ.	L. Base Circ.	Live	Field Dressed			

A full-sized version of this form is available for download from www.protoolindustries.net

Measuring Antlers for Harvest Records

Most deer harvest data forms call for six antler measurements –
inside spread, number of points (over 1-inch), right main beam
length, left main beam length, right base circumference, and left
base circumference. These are measurements for management
purposes and not for trophy scoring. For trophy measurements see
the section of this book on trophy scoring.

Tools needed: harvest data form, ball-point pen, cloth measuring tape

Measurements needed: (all measurements to the nearest 1/8-inch)

- Base circumference – the distance around the main beam just
  above the hairline, between the burr and the brow tine.

- Main beam length – the distance from the burr to the antler
  tip, along the outside of the main beam.

- Inside spread – the longest inside distance between the two
  main beams.

- Number of points – the number of tines 1-inch or longer off
  each of the main beams. This should be done at right angles to
  the center line of the skull.

These are important measurements for the evaluation of your deer
management program so make all measurements carefully. Record
them clearly on the harvest data form.

Antler measurement illustration

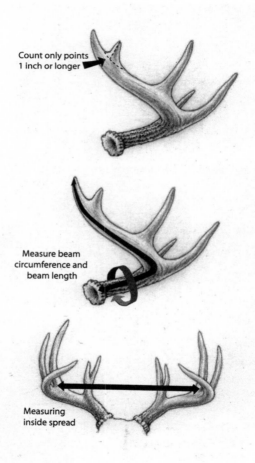

Count only points
1 inch or longer

Measure beam
circumference and
beam length

Measuring
inside spread

Pulling a Deer Jaw for Aging

Tools needed: Jaw extractor, lopping shears, deer hunting knife, jaw tag with wire and ball point pen.

Step 1. Place the back of the deer's head on a firm surface and open the deer's mouth by inserting the small end of the jaw extractor from the side of the deer's mouth between the front teeth and the first jaw teeth. Rotate the extractor 90 degrees.

Step 2. Next insert the smaller, rounded end of the extractor between the jaw and cheek to break loose membrane and muscle. Push the extractor downward as far as it will go.

Step 3. Hold the deer's mouth wide open using the short end of the extractor. Insert the lopping shears, through the opening in the extractor, with the blunt edge on the cheek side. Tilt the handle of the lopping shears toward the top of the head, and then cut the jawbone. Make sure you are cutting above the jaw teeth. Withdraw the lopping shears and extractor. (illustration S-2-4)

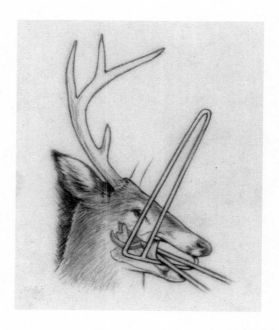

Step 4. Insert the narrow end of the jawbone extractor into the deer's mouth and back to slip over the jawbone where the cut was made. With the deer's head held down firmly, give the extractor a hard jerk. It should slide along the jaw and break loose all muscle, freeing the jaw. That side of the jaw will separate from the opposite jaw near or in the middle of the front teeth. Only the molars and premolars are used in aging so the front teeth have no value for this purpose. (illustration S-2-5)

Step 5. Using a deer hunting knife, clean all the flesh and tissue off the jaw. Using a fine wire, attach a jaw tag for recording the data. Place in a safe, well ventilated location to store. A wire fish basket hung up at the butcher area is a good place to store deer jaws for aging.

Note: When properly done, this process of extracting a buck's jaw does not affect the quality of the cape for mounting.

Make a Deer Jaw Extractor

Tools needed: welder, vise, and heavy-duty hammer, 12-inch section of old garden hose and a 52-inch section of 3/8-inch cold roll steel or rebar. Cold roll steel makes the best jaw extractor. (Illustration S-2-7 jaw puller plan)

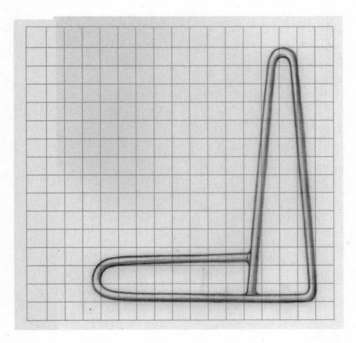

Step 1. Following the plan shown above, use a vise and hammer to bend the bar into shape. Three bends are required. Be sure to make all the openings in the bar to the dimensions in the plan.

Step 2. Weld the two ends to close the opening.

Step 3. To make the extractor easier to use when wet, slice an old garden hose section and snap over the shorter section of the extractor.

DEER AGING CHART

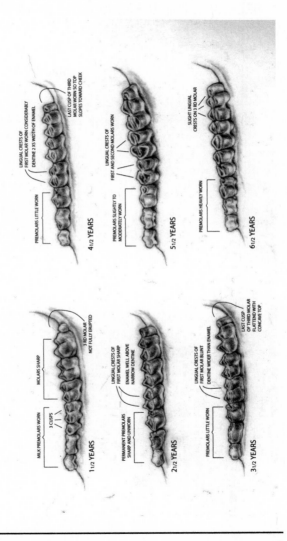

MILK PREMOLARS WORN

MOLARS SHARP

3 CUSPS

3 RD MOLAR NOT FULLY ERUPTED

1½ YEARS

PERMANENT PREMOLARS SHARP AND UNWORN

LINGUAL CRESTS OF FIRST MOLAR SHARP

ENAMEL WELL ABOVE NARROW DENTINE

2½ YEARS

PREMOLARS LITTLE WORN

LINGUAL CRESTS OF FIRST MOLAR BLUNT

DENTINE WIDER THAN ENAMEL

LAST CUSP OF THIRD MOLAR FLATTEND WITH CONCAVE TOP

3½ YEARS

PREMOLARS LITTLE WORN

LINGUAL CRESTS OF FIRST MOLAR WORN CONSIDERABLY DENTINE 2 XS WIDTH OF ENAMEL

LAST CUSP OF THIRD MOLAR WORN SO TOP SLOPES TOWARD CHEEK

4½ YEARS

PREMOLARS SLIGHTLY TO MODERATELY WORN

LINGUAL CRESTS OF FIRST AND SECOND MOLARS WORN

5½ YEARS

PREMOLARS HEAVILY WORN

SLIGHT LINGUAL CRESTS ON 3 RD MOLAR

6½ YEARS

DEER WEIGHTS WHEN A SCALE IS NOT AVAILABLE

Using a flexible tape, measure the deer's girth just behind the front legs.

Girth (inches)	Live weight (pounds)	Field-dressed (pounds)	Edible meat (pounds)
28	77	59	34
29	82	64	36
30	90	70	39
31	98	74	42
32	102	80	45
33	110	87	50
34	118	91	54
35	126	99	57
36	125	104	61
37	146	115	66
38	157	126	71
39	169	135	74
40	182	144	80
41	195	156	88
42	210	170	94
43	228	182	103
44	244	198	110
45	267	214	120
46	290	233	130
47	310	251	139

Field Dressing a Deer

Step 1. Get your deer on a fairly level spot, where you have plenty of room to walk around the animal. Turn the animal on its back so that its underside is facing upward with its head slightly uphill, if possible. Put on rubber gloves.

Step 2. If a buck, cut off the testicles, but not the penis, by grasping them in one hand and cutting them completely free. Then cut the skin from around the penis where it protrudes from the body without cutting the organ or the intestinal wall.

Step 3. Cut around the anus, and vaginal opening if a doe, under the base of the tail being careful not to puncture the anal tube. Cut like coring an apple. Cut it free from the tail and legs. Pull the anus outside the body and tie a string around it to keep contents inside.

Step 4. Next, cut down through the tendons between the legs above the pelvic bone. You will feel the legs relax and this will help make the rest of the work easier.

Step 5. Now stand straddling the deer and face the head. Slowly begin to cut the skin towards the chest. Cut very shallow. Be particularly careful not to cut into the intestines or the stomach paunch. As soon as you have enough of an opening into the body cavity, place two fingers into the opening. Guide the knife between the two fingers, as you cut up the deer's abdomen, while holding the intestines and paunch away from the blade. Do not go too deep with the knife blade. Continue cutting slowly up the center of the ribs, being careful not to puncture any innards. Cutting the centerline ribs will take some effort. Stop when you reach the point near the brisket.

Step 5. Reach up inside the upper body cavity to the neck and cut the gullet and windpipe as near the head as possible. The first spoilage in a deer occurs in the windpipe, so be sure to get as much out as possible.

Step 6. Now move to where the upper and lower body cavity meets. Cut the diaphragm, the strong layer of tissue attached to the ribs that separate the chest cavity from the abdominal cavity.

Step 7. Reach inside the rear cavity and slowly pull the anus tube to the inside, carefully using your knife to cut away any tissue that prevents it from sliding through. Be careful not to cut the bladder or allow any of the contents to spill.

Step 8. Roll your deer on its side and pull out the innards. Drain out as much blood as possible. Prop the body cavity open with sticks to allow full air movement. Be careful to keep hair, leaves, dirt, etc. from getting inside the deer.

Step 9. As quickly as possible, wash out the body cavity with a solution of 1 tablespoon of white vinegar in one gallon of water.

Step 10. Get to a cooler quickly or hang the deer outside if the temperature is 40 degrees or cooler. Use a mesh bag to keep insects at bay.

Carcass Care

The quality of your venison, to a great extent, depends on how you treat the carcass between field dressing and butchering.

- It is important for the deer carcass to be cooled, below 40 degrees, as quickly as possible. Heat induces rapid spoilage.

- Keep the meat clean and cool while field dressing and transporting. If you don't, the meat may become contaminated with a pathogenic organism. This can be done by the meat coming in contact with fecal material or contents of the stomach or intestines. If any content of the gut or fecal material comes in contact with the meat or the hunter's hands, or in contact with the tools used while dressing the meat, bacteria can contaminate the meat. The same for a butcher shop or slaughterhouse.

- If you are not set up at your camp to keep a carcass under 40 degrees, take the carcass to a commercial meat handling facility. Have one located before the hunt.

- If you plan on being in camp several more days, hang your carcass in the shade where the temperature will not go over 40 degrees.

- Prop the body cavity open to allow continued cooling.

- If flies are present, cover the carcass with a mesh bag.

- Transport the carcass in such a manner that it will stay below 40 degrees.

- Off-flavored or bad tasting venison is usually a result of poor carcass care.

Finding Hit Deer

It is the responsibility of all hunters to make every effort to find hit deer. Here are tips to make the search go easier.

- Make a mental note of the location the deer was standing when you shot and the direction of the escape. Be able to find both locations on the ground.

- Listen when the deer runs out of sight. Often you can hear him thrashing in the brush and get a good location as to where he may be found.

- Pay attention to the posture of the tail of the hit deer as he escapes. A deer that has been solidly hit will often run-off with its tail drooping. If it is a clean miss, the tail may be held high.

- Wait for at least 30 minutes before starting the search. Give the deer time to lie down and expire.

- While waiting you may want to get a friend to help you trail the hit deer. More than three trailers are too many and may walk over valuable sign. Also, try to get a helper that is not red-green color blind as many men are. They will have a difficult time finding blood sign.

- Use your GPS while tracking.

- After waiting 30 minutes, go to the location of the deer when hit and locate any blood, hair, or tissue.

- Blood that is dark maroon indicates a hit in the heart, arteries, or liver. Blood from a flesh wound will be light red. Lung blood can be pink foam or blood with little bubbles. A stomach or intestine hit will be blood that is light red, mixed with greenish bile or digestive material.

- Blood from a running deer will often be splattered on rocks, trees, or leaves and will point to the direction the deer is running.

- Hair from various sections of the body is distinctively different and gives you an idea as to where the animal was hit.

  Long, dark guard hairs – found on the heart area which may be gray in color on older deer.

  Long, dark-tipped, hollow hairs – found in the spinal area.

  Curly, dark hair – found on the brisket area.

  Long, wavy two-toned hair – found on the tail area.

  Coarse, light-tipped hair- found on the stomach area.

A close examination of a deer rug prior to hunting may serve as a good learning tool. Also, deer in different areas have different colorations.

- If no blood is found at the hit site, look for tracks that might show that the animal spun from the impact. Many hit deer do not start losing blood for several yards or more along their escape route.

- If night tracking is necessary be sure to know the regulations in your state about night trailing and carrying a firearm or bow. Use reflective tape to mark the blood trail and use a Coleman gas lantern as it makes the blood shine in the dark.

- During the day have toilet tissue or bright orange flagging tape to mark the blood trail. Mark each spot of blood found. This will give you a good back trail to help line up the direction the deer is going.

- Look for blood on branches, bushes, rocks, weeds, tree trunks. A high wound may spray blood higher than you expect.

- If blood becomes hard to find, a piece of toilet tissue wrapped around the hand will pick up the smallest trace of blood when wiped in grass or leaves.

- Deer under stress will sometimes double back and be found near where they were hit. Also, they will often go to water, a creek or beaver swamp.

- As you search for blood watch for scuff marks made by the stumbling deer's feet. Also, be alert to broken branches or other signs of a struggle.

- If you lose the blood trail, search for the deer by walking in a concentric circle using the last blood sign found as the center of the circle.

- If all else fails, return to the start point and re-trail the deer. We owe it to ourselves and the deer to exhaust every effort to find hit deer.

APPROACHING DOWNED DEER

- Approach all fallen deer as though they might still be alive. Both hit bucks and does have seriously hurt hunters when they suddenly "came back to life."

- Quietly move up on the deer from the rear and be ready to take another shot if necessary. Keep other hunters behind you.

- Observe the deer for any signs of breathing. Watch the chest carefully for signs of movement.

- Next ease up to where you can see the eye(s). It should be open and if it has been some time since it died the eye will have a glazed-over look.

- Standing behind the deer's back, use your bow or rifle barrel and touch the deer to see if there is any movement.

- Once you have confirmed the animal is dead, unload and attach your tag.

Field Judging Bucks by Age Class

Yearling – 1/2-year age class

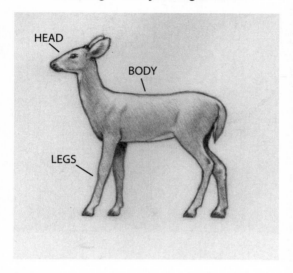

Head – short nose, large ears, protruding dark colored bumps where the antlers are located, flat forehead.

Body – smaller than most accompanying deer.

Legs – appear long, tarsal gland white

Body language – May be the first deer to appear in a food plot or opening. Often runs in alone.

1 ½-year age class

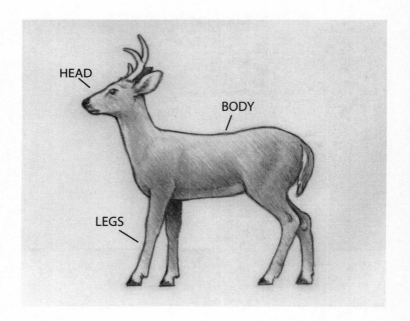

Head – face has a baby look, neck thin, antlers well inside ears.

Body - slightly sway backed with high rump, lack of brisket

Legs – appear long, tarsal glands lack color.

Body language – not as wary as other deer.

2 ½-year age class

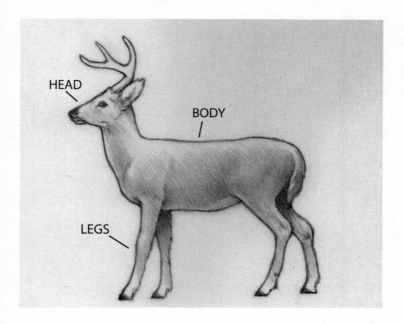

Head – antlers thin and nearing ear width, facial skin tight, eyes round, head will appear long.

Body – straight back, slightly developing brisket, belly flat,

Legs – appear long for body, tarsal somewhat dark.

Body language – appear somewhat awkward in movements.

3 ½-year age class

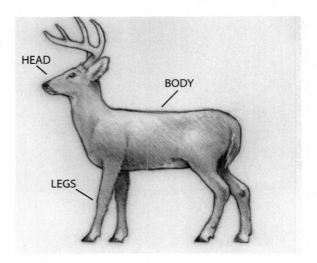

Head – antlers as wide as or wider than ears, broad nose, eyes round.

Body – flat back and stomach, slightly muscular neck and deeper chest with brisket becoming separate from neck, full rump. From side, chest beginning to appear larger than rump.

Legs – appear to go with body, tarsal gland still small but dark.

Body language – more wary, walks with attitude.

4 ½-year age class

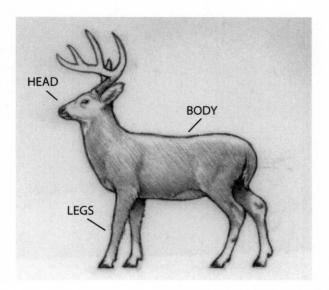

Head – antler tine length and mass increase, non typical points may appear, jaw skin tight, eyes slightly squinting.

Body – body thicker, fuller, rump rounded, muscular neck with well defined brisket.

Legs – look proportionate to body, tarsal gland large dark.

Body language – looks and acts large, always cautious.

5 ½-year age class

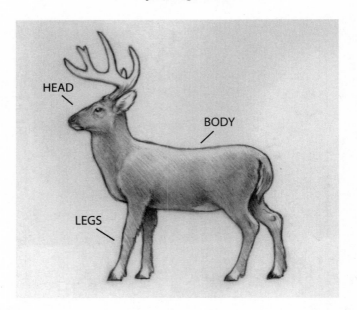

Head – eyes with more squint, wrinkled face skin around eyes, darker hair around forehead.

Body – large with slight sag to back and stomach, rump begins to appear small, brisket pronounced, large neck and shoulders.

Legs – will appear to be short, tarsal gland large and black.

Body language – walk as every move has a purpose. Extremely wary.

6 ½-year age class

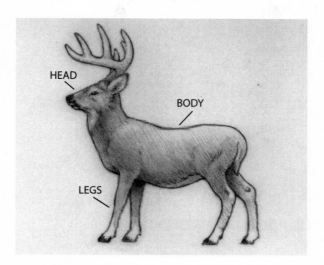

Head – face will appear small, darker and wrinkled forehead, jaw may slightly sag, antlers heavy.

Body – heavy, well muscled neck and shoulders, brisket well defined, sway back and stomach with sag, body will have a rippled look.

Legs – short looking, very dark tarsal glands.

Body language – walks with swagger, deliberate movements, always cautious.

Boone & Crockett Score Sheets

Typical

Records of
North American
Big Game

250 Station Drive
Missoula, MT 59801
(406) 542-1888

BOONE AND CROCKETT CLUB®
OFFICIAL SCORING SYSTEM FOR NORTH AMERICAN BIG GAME TROPHIES

	MINIMUM SCORES				KIND OF DEER (check one)
	AWARDS	ALL-TIME	TYPICAL		☐ whitetail
whitetail	160	170	WHITETAIL AND COUES' DEER		☐ Coues'
Coues'	100	110			

Abnormal Points	
Right Antler	Left Antler
SUBTOTALS	
TOTAL TO E	

Detail of Point Measurement

SEE OTHER SIDE FOR INSTRUCTIONS		COLUMN 1	COLUMN 2	COLUMN 3	COLUMN 4
A. No. Points on Right Antler	No. Points on Left Antler	Spread Credit	Right Antler	Left Antler	Difference
B. Tip to Tip Spread	C. Greatest Spread				
D. Inside Spread of Main Beams	SPREAD CREDIT MAY EQUAL BUT NOT EXCEED LONGER MAIN BEAM				
E. Total of Lengths of Abnormal Points					
F. Length of Main Beam					
G-1. Length of First Point					
G-2. Length of Second Point					
G-3. Length of Third Point					
G-4. Length of Fourth Point, If Present					
G-5. Length of Fifth Point, If Present					
G-6. Length of Sixth Point, If Present					
G-7. Length of Seventh Point, If Present					
H-1. Circumference at Smallest Place Between Burr and First Point					
H-2. Circumference at Smallest Place Between First and Second Points					
H-3. Circumference at Smallest Place Between Second and Third Points					
H-4. Circumference at Smallest Place Between Third and Fourth Points					
	TOTALS				

ADD	Column 1		Exact Locality Where Killed:		County:	State/Prov:
	Column 2		Date Killed:	Hunter: (Legal Name)		
	Column 3		Trophy Owner: (Legal Name)		Telephone #:	
	Subtotal		Trophy Owner's Address:			
SUBTRACT Column 4			Trophy Owner's E-mail:		Guide's Name:	
FINAL SCORE			Remarks: (Mention Any Abnormalities or Unique Qualities)		OM I.D. Number	

Boone & Crockett Score Sheets

Non-Typical

Records of
North American
Big Game

250 Station Drive
Missoula, MT 59801
(406) 542-1888

BOONE AND CROCKETT CLUB®
OFFICIAL SCORING SYSTEM FOR NORTH AMERICAN BIG GAME TROPHIES

NON-TYPICAL WHITETAIL AND COUES' DEER

MINIMUM SCORES	AWARDS	ALL-TIME
whitetail	185	195
Coues'	105	120

KIND OF DEER (check one) ☐ whitetail ☐ Coues'

Abnormal Points	
Right Antler	Left Antler
SUBTOTALS	
E. TOTAL	

Detail of Point Measurement

SEE OTHER SIDE FOR INSTRUCTIONS		COLUMN 1	COLUMN 2	COLUMN 3	COLUMN 4
A. No. Points on Right Antler*	No. Points on Left Antler*	Spread Credit	Right Antler	Left Antler	Difference
B. Tip to Tip Spread*	C. Greatest Spread*				
D. Inside Spread of Main Beams	SPREAD CREDIT MAY EQUAL BUT NOT EXCEED LONGER MAIN BEAM				
F. Length of Main Beam					
G-1. Length of First Point					
G-2. Length of Second Point					
G-3. Length of Third Point					
G-4. Length of Fourth Point, If Present					
G-5. Length of Fifth Point, If Present					
G-6. Length of Sixth Point, If Present					
G-7. Length of Seventh Point, If Present					
H-1. Circumference at Smallest Place Between Burr and First Point					
H-2. Circumference at Smallest Place Between First and Second Points					
H-3. Circumference at Smallest Place Between Second and Third Points					
H-4. Circumference at Smallest Place Between Third and Fourth Points					
	TOTALS				

ADD	Column 1		Exact Locality Where Killed:		County:	State/Prov:
	Column 2		Date Killed:	Hunter:		
	Column 3		Trophy Owner:	Telephone #:		
	Subtotal		Trophy Owner's Address:			
SUBTRACT Column 4			Trophy Owner's E-mail:	Guide's Name:		
	Subtotal		Remarks: (Mention Any Abnormalities or Unique Qualities)			
	ADD Line E Total					
	FINAL SCORE				OM I.D. Number	

*A, B, and C do not add into the score.

COPYRIGHT © 2010 BY BOONE AND CROCKETT CLUB®

55

Safari Club International Score Sheets

Typical

SAFARI CLUB INTERNATIONAL

FIRST FOR HUNTERS

Method 17-T Entry Form

For white-tailed deer with typical antlers. Antlers that have one or more non-typical tines may be measured as typical at the owner's request, but only the typical tines will count in the score. Any non-typical tines are to be recorded as supplemental information.

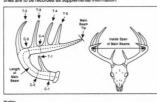

Hunter _____
How you want your name to appear in the Record Book

Membership No. _____ e-mail _____

Address _____

_____
City   State   Zip   Country

Ph. ( ) _____ ( ) _____ ( ) _____
Home   Business   Fax

I certify that, to the best of my knowledge, I took this animal without violating the wildlife laws or ethical hunting practices of the country or province in which I hunted. I also certify that, to the best of my knowledge, the laws of my country have not been violated by my taking or importing this animal.

Free-ranging ❑ Yes ❑ No

Signature _____
The acceptance or denial of all entries are at the discretion of Safari Club International, its Board and committees. Entries are subject to review by the Trophy Records Committee of SCI at any time. All photos and entries submited to SCI become SCI's property.

Submit to: Safari Club International
4800 W. Gates Pass Rd., Tucson, AZ 85745 USA.
❑ **$35** Record Book processing fee
❑ **$55** Medallion Award processing fee *(Walnut plaque)*
includes shipping & handling
❑ **$80** Record Book & Medallion Award processing fee
includes shipping & handling

To enter Record Book and/or Medallion:
1) Add the appropriate entry processing fees together as necessary.
(Medallion fee includes shipping & handling.)
2) All entries must be complete, signed by hunter and accompanied by fees and a photograph of the trophy.
3) Please clearly label back of photo with name of hunter, name of animal, and score of animal, and date taken.
❑ For simple horns and unbranched antlers: include 1 photo
❑ For animals with branched antlers: include enough photos so that all tines can be clearly seen.

Checks on U.S. banks only. Credit cards preferred. Entry fees are valid for 12 months from date of form located in lower right hand corner.
We Accept: ❑ MC ❑ Visa ❑ AMX ❑ Discover ❑ Diners Club

_____
Card Number   Expiration Date

Animal _____

Remeasurement? ❑ Yes ❑ No Former Score _____ Record No. _____

Date Taken _____
Month   Day   Year
❑ Rifle ❑ Handgun ❑ Muzzleloader ❑ Bow ❑ Crossbow ❑ Picked Up

Place Taken _____
Country   State or Province
Locality _____

Guide _____ Hunting Co. _____

I. Length of Main Beam		L _____ /8		R _____ /8
II. Length of Typical Tines	T-1	L _____ /8		R _____ /8
(Use back of form for additional tines)	T-2	L _____ /8		R _____ /8
	T-3	L _____ /8		R _____ /8
	T-4	L _____ /8		R _____ /8
	T-5	L _____ /8		R _____ /8
	T-6	L _____ /8		R _____ /8
	T-7	L _____ /8		R _____ /8
	Subtotal	L _____ /8		R _____ /8
III. Circumference of Main Beam	C-1	L _____ /8		R _____ /8
	C-2	L _____ /8		R _____ /8
	C-3	L _____ /8		R _____ /8
	C-4	L _____ /8		R _____ /8
	Subtotal	L _____ /8		R _____ /8
IV. Inside Span of Main Beams				_____ /8
V. Total Score				_____ /8

Supplemental Information

Length of non-typical tines, if any. (Not to be included in total score)	NT-1	L _____ /8	R _____ /8
	NT-2	L _____ /8	R _____ /8
	NT-3	L _____ /8	R _____ /8
	NT-4	L _____ /8	R _____ /8

Number of Typical Points (All typical tines plus beam tip)	L _____	R _____
Number of Non-typical Points (All non-typical tines)	L _____	R _____
Total Number of Points (All tines plus beam tip)	L _____	R _____

Official Measurer _____

Measurer No. _____ Email _____

Day Measured _____
Month   Day   Year

Signature of Measurer _____

For Office Use Only

Date Received: _____

COPYRIGHT © SAFARI CLUB INTERNATIONAL   6/07

Safari Club International Score Sheets

Non-Typical

SAFARI CLUB INTERNATIONAL

SCI
FIRST FOR HUNTERS

Method 17-NT Entry Form

For white-tailed deer with non-typical antlers. *In this method all tines will count in the score regardless of whether they are typical or non-typical.*

Hunter _____
How you want your name to appear in the Record Book

Membership No. _____ e-mail _____

Address _____

City ___ State ___ Zip ___ Country

Ph. (___) ___ (___) ___ (___) ___
Home   Business   Fax

I certify that, to the best of my knowledge, I took this animal without violating the wildlife laws or ethical hunting practices of the country or province in which I hunted. I also certify that, to the best of my knowledge, the laws of my country have not been violated by my taking or importing this animal.

Free-ranging ☐ Yes ☐ No

Signature _____
The acceptance or denial of all entries are at the discretion of Safari Club International, its Board and committees. Entries are subject to review by the Trophy Records Committee of SCI at any time. All photos and entries subitted to SCI become SCI's property.

Submit to: Safari Club International
4800 W. Gates Pass Rd., Tucson, AZ 85745 USA.
☐ **$35** Record Book processing fee
☐ **$55** Medallion Award processing fee *(Walnut plaque)* includes shipping & handling
☐ **$80** Record Book & Medallion Award processing fee includes shipping & handling

To enter Record Book and/or Medallion:
1) Add the appropriate entry processing fees together as necessary. *(Medallion fee includes shipping & handling.)*
2) All entries must be complete, signed by hunter and accompanied by fees and a photograph of the trophy.
3) Please clearly label back of photo with name of hunter, name and score of animal, and date taken.
 ☐ For simple horns and unbranched antlers: include 1 photo
 ☐ For animals with branched antlers: include enough photos so that all tines can be clearly seen.

Checks on U.S. banks only. Credit cards preferred. Entry fees are valid for 12 months from date of form located in lower right hand corner.
We Accept: ☐ MC ☐ Visa ☐ AMX ☐ Discover ☐ Diners Club

_____
Card Number ___ Expiration Date

Animal _____

Remeasurement? ☐ Yes ☐ No Former Score _____ Record No. _____

Date Taken _____
Month   Day   Year

☐ Rifle ☐ Handgun ☐ Muzzleloader ☐ Bow ☐ Crossbow ☐ Picked Up

Place Taken _____
Country   State or Province

Locality _____

Guide _____ Hunting Co. _____

I. Length of Main Beam		L ___ /8		R ___ /8	

II. Length of Typical Tines	T-1	L ___ /8	R ___ /8
	T-2	L ___ /8	R ___ /8
(Use back of form for additional tines)	T-3	L ___ /8	R ___ /8
	T-4	L ___ /8	R ___ /8
	T-5	L ___ /8	R ___ /8
	T-6	L ___ /8	R ___ /8
	Subtotal	L ___ /8	R ___ /8

III. Length of Non-typical Tines	NT-1	L ___ /8	R ___ /8
	NT-2	L ___ /8	R ___ /8
(Use back of form for additional tines)	NT-3	L ___ /8	R ___ /8
	NT-4	L ___ /8	R ___ /8
	NT-5	L ___ /8	R ___ /8
	NT-6	L ___ /8	R ___ /8
	NT-7	L ___ /8	R ___ /8
	NT-8	L ___ /8	R ___ /8
	NT-9	L ___ /8	R ___ /8
	NT-10	L ___ /8	R ___ /8
	NT-11	L ___ /8	R ___ /8
	NT-12	L ___ /8	R ___ /8
	NT-13	L ___ /8	R ___ /8
	NT-14	L ___ /8	R ___ /8
	Subtotal	L ___ /8	R ___ /8

IV. Circumference of Main Beam	C-1	L ___ /8	R ___ /8
	C-2	L ___ /8	R ___ /8
	C-3	L ___ /8	R ___ /8
	C-4	L ___ /8	R ___ /8
	Subtotal	L ___ /8	R ___ /8

V. Inside Span of Main Beams ___ /8

VI. Total Score ___ /8

Supplemental Information

Total Number of Points L ___ R ___
(All tines plus beam tip)

Official Measurer _____

Measurer No. _____ Email _____

Day Measured _____
Month   Day   Year

Signature of Measurer _____
COPYRIGHT © SAFARI CLUB INTERNATIONAL   5/08

Minimum Scores For White-Tailed Deer

White-tailed Deer
Minimum Scores to Enter Record Book

Boone & Crockett Club

- Typical - 170
- Non-typical - 195

Pope & Young Club

- Typical - 125
- Non-typical - 155

  (Note: Boone & Crockett scoring system)

Longhunter Society

- Typical - 130
- Non-typical - 160

  (Note: Boone & Crockett scoring system)

Safari Club International		Gun	Bow
M103	Anticosti White-tailed Deer (Non typical) Anticosti Island	60	54
M102	Anticosti White-tailed Deer (typical) Anticosti Island	60	54
M14	Central American White-tailed Deer (typical)	30	27
M113	Columbia White-tailed Deer (non-typical)	80	0
M112	Columbia White-tailed Deer (typical)	70	45
M11	Coues White-tailed Deer (non-typical)	98	90
M10	Coues White-tailed Deer (typical)	81	72
M68	Mexican White-tailed Deer (non-typical)	70	65
M62	Mexican White-tailed Deer (typical)	60	54
M100	Mid-Western White-tailed Deer (non-typical)	135	125
M98	Mid-Western White-tailed Deer (typical)	125	115
M52	Northeastern White-tailed Deer (non-typical)	148	133
M51	Northeastern White-tailed Deer (typical)	125	112
M50	Northwestern White-tailed Deer (non-typical)	150	135
M49	Northwestern White-tailed Deer (typical)	125	101
M54	Southeastern White-tailed Deer (non-typical)	120	110
M53	Southeastern White-tailed Deer (typical)	110	100
M07	Texas White-tailed Deer (non-typical)	138	120
M06	Texas White-tailed Deer (typical)	125	112

Cuts for Capping Deer

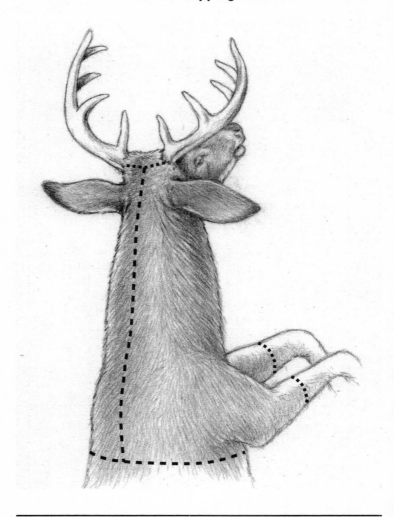

Butcher Cuts

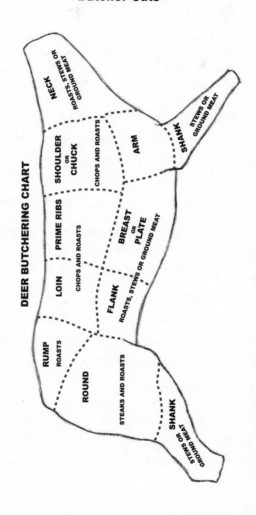

DEER BUTCHERING CHART

NECK — ROASTS, STEWS OR GROUND MEAT

SHANK — STEWS OR GROUND MEAT

SHOULDER OR CHUCK — CHOPS AND ROASTS

ARM

PRIME RIBS — CHOPS AND ROASTS

BREAST OR PLATE — ROASTS, STEWS OR GROUND MEAT

LOIN

FLANK

RUMP — ROASTS

ROUND — STEAKS AND ROASTS

SHANK — STEWS OR GROUND MEAT

Photographing the Trophy Buck

- Take the time to select a good natural location to take photos of you posing with your trophy. Avoid back of pickup, hanging from a tree, porch of cabin or concrete driveway locations.

- Select a site with even light. Avoid bright light.

- Think about the background for the photo. You do not want a lot of limbs and branches in the background that will blend in with the antlers.

- Take the photos before the deer is field dressed if possible.

- Clean up the deer. Use water, baby wipes, etc. to clean all blood off the part of the deer that will appear in the photos, including nose, mouth, antlers, neck and body.

- Cut the deer tongue off.

- Clean up the hunter that is going to appear in the photos. Look neat, no blood, and smile. Clean all blood off hunter, especially hands if he has just field dressed the deer.

- Purchase a set of glass deer eyes from your taxidermist and keep them in your day pack with your camera. When you are ready to photograph a trophy, moisten the glass eyes and insert them over the deer eyes. It makes a big difference in the appearance of the dead animal.

- Make sure the gun to be used in the photo is unloaded, is photographed pointing in a safe direction and is shown with the bolt open or at least with the safety on safe.

- Since most hunters wear a hat with a bream, have them push the cap or hat back, shoot photos using fill flash to lighten up the hunters face.

- Use a tripod whenever possible.

- Shoot lots of photos from different angles.

- Have the hunter in the photo hold the antlers away from him. Do not let the hand cover up the antlers. Always be aware of the antlers blending in with the background. A hill top location with the sky as a background can make the antlers show up. Use flash fill for this setting.

- Shoot many photos from a low position, the photographer lying on the ground shooting up.

- Shoot close up and shoot some vertical shots.

- If using a zoom lens, shoot many photos in the 70 – 90mm range.

- If you must wait several hours before being able to photograph the deer, field dress the deer, cut out the tongue, and clean all blood off the deer. Take it to a walk-in cooler, or secure location if kept outside in temperatures below 40 degrees, and fold its legs under the carcass. Next tie the antlers up so the head is held erect. Let rigor mortis set in with the deer in this life-like laying position. The next day the deer can be carried to the photography location and, after the glass eyes are placed inside the eyes, be posed for photos with ease.

- Always pack a point and shoot camera with you on your hunts. Know how to use it.

SECTION 3

FOOD PLOTS

Two Basic Types of Food Plot Crops

Perennial means long term plantings with very minimal maintenance. Some of these include covers, legumes, grasses, herbs, and lespedeza. Perennials may need occasional reseeding every few years depending on species, weather, climate factors and site conditions and condition of the plants. Some species are short term perennials (couple of years) before they start thinning out and other species will still be alive unchanged after many decades of life.

Annual means seasonal plantings that last one growing season or possibly up to a year with or without fertilizers, ground preparations and some crop rotations for success and maintenance. Annual plantings can be any of the following: legumes, grain grasses, millets, sorghums and the list goes on according to your location. Annuals must be replanted each year.

Steps to Locating and Planting a Food Plot

Site selection

1. For deer, plan on establishing a 2 to 4 acre food plot per 40 acres of hunting land.

2. Locate food plots adjacent to cover.

3. Use soil maps to help choose food plot locations, avoid wet soils, deep sand and heavy clays. Avoid areas that may erode or flood easily.

4. Select locations that get lots of sunlight. Avoid food plots with trees in the plot.

5. Consider existing open areas such old fields, utility rights-of-ways, log landings, fire lanes, unused logging roads or old home sites.

6. Never select a location near a public road or property line to avoid poaching. Locate food plots at least 100 yards inside property boundaries.

Planting

1. Walk the selected food plot site and remove rocks, limbs, trees, saplings, and roots, anything that might cause problems when breaking the ground or planting.

2. If there is a heavy grass, weed or sapling infestation spray with an approved broad-spectrum herbicide. Perennial weeds need to be sprayed when young and growing.

3. Mow the food plot with a pull behind mower to make breaking ground easier.

4. Lime the food plot according to a soil test at least four months before planting.

5. At the recommended planting time for the food plot seed, use a 30 HP or more tractor pulling a heavy duty tandem disk to break up the food plot and to establish a smooth, fine seedbed. Break the ground when it is reasonably dry. Break it at least 4-inches deep. Two or three passes with a disk properly adjusted will result in a good seedbed.

6. Level the seedbed by pulling a short-tooth harrow behind a four-wheel-drive ATV of at least 400CC or behind a tractor.

7. Using a tractor or ATV mounted cyclone spreader, fertilize the plot according to a soil test. Clean spreader after applying fertilizer.

8. Lightly disk food plot to cover fertilizer.

9. Prepare the seed bed by running a cultipacker over the food plot.

10. Using a tractor or ATV mounted spreader that is adjusted for the seed to be sown, sow seed at a depth and rate according to recommendations. Remember, the seed planting depth is critical to you getting a crop.

11. After sowing, cultipack the food plot again to make good seed-to-soil contact for maximum germination.

Understanding pH and Food Plot Crops

The acidity or alkalinity of any soil is expressed in terms of pH. This knowledge of a soil is vital to food plot production and the fertilization of other foods growing in a deer habitat. A pH of 7.0 is neutral, while a soil pH below or above this measurement is acid or alkaline. Most deer forage crops best at pH values between 5.8 and 6.5. Adjusting soil pH with lime within this range maximizes growth and increases yield, fertilizer efficiency, palatability of crops and herbicide effectiveness. When a soil pH becomes too low for plants to use fertilizer it is necessary to apply lime to raise the pH to the desired level.

The best way to determine the pH of a soil is to get a soil test of the soil. The analysis of this soil sample will tell you how much lime, if any, needs to be applied to the food plot. If lime is needed the soil analysis will tell you just how much lime is needed. It should be applied about four months before the crop is planted. Lime is not water soluble and should be incorporated into the soil. Soil test should be done about every two years for food plots growing perennials and every year for annuals.

If lime is not applied properly to a food plot that has a low pH an inferior crop will be the result. Lime is inexpensive and getting a soil test and following the recommendations for lime and fertilizer is one easy way to have a food plot crop that will attract and hold deer.

Relative Neutralizing Values of Some Common Liming Materials

Liming Materials	Neutralizing Values
Dolomitic limestone	95 to 108
Calcitic limestone	85 to 100
Hydrated lime	120 to 135
Basic slag	50 to 85

Tons Per Acre of Ground Limestone Required to Raise Soil pH Above pH 6.0

Original pH	Sand soil	Loam soil	Clay soil
- 4.5	2.0	3.0	4.0
4.5 -4.9	1.5	2.0	3.0
5.0 – 5.4	1.0	1.5	2.0
5.5 – 5.9	0.5	1.0	1.0

Procedure for Taking Soil Samples of a Food Plot

To have a healthy wildlife food plot take a soil test. Proper collection of samples is extremely important. The results of this test will tell you how to fertilize and lime the ground for proper balance of nutrients and optimum soil pH level. Time and money are saved when you apply only the fertilizer needed. Over fertilization may cause harm to plant materials and waste your or your hunting club's money.

- Go to your local county agents office (Cooperative Extension Service) and get a soil test kit. It will consist of soil sample bags or boxes, information sheets, and shipping box. Do-it-yourself soil test kits may be purchased from garden supply stores also.

- Get the tools you will need to take the samples – a clean bucket and a clean garden trowel, spade, or soil probe.

- Following the information given in the soil test kit directions, go to 20 or more sites in each food plot to take samples. One pint of soil is needed for analysis.

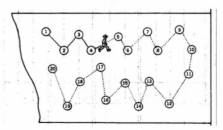

- At each sample site in the food plot, scrape off any plant material from the soil surface. Push the trowel into the soil 3–4inches deep.

- Discard the soil and cut an inch slice from the back of the hole. Place a slice in the bucket. Do this at each sample site.

- When all the samples in the food plot are collected, thoroughly mix the slices. Air dry the samples overnight on a flat surface lined with clean white paper. Pour the sample into the sample bag or box.

- Fill out the bag or box with the required information. Be sure to give each food plot an identification number or name and keep a record so the recommendation you receive from the soil lab can be associated with the food plot from which the sample came.

- Send bag to the state testing lab listed in the kit instructions. A small fee is usually charged.

- Your soil test results provide different nitrogen (N), phosphorous (P), potassium (K), and lime (pH) recommendations for particular plant varieties. Follow the recommendations to the letter. Wildlife knows the difference between a cheap hamburger and prime steak. The food plot planted following the recommendations of a current soil test is "prime steak."

Planting Guide for Deer

Spring Food Plot Crops for Deer
All States

Species	Planting months (after danger of frost)	Planting rate/ac (broadcast)	Annual/ perennial
American jointvetch	May-June	15 lb/ac	Annual
Buckwheat	May-June	40 lb/ac	Annual
Cowpeas	June	2 bu/ac	Annual
Grain sorghum	May	30 lb/ac	Annual
Iron clay peas	May	50 lb/ac	Annual
Kobe lespedeza	March	30 lb/ac	Annual
Lablab	May	45 lb/ac	Annual
Soybean	May	60 lb/ac	Annual

Fall Food Plot Crops For Deer
Northern States

Species	Planting months *(after danger of frost)*	Planting rate/ac *(broadcast)*	Annual/ perennial
Alfalfa	Aug. & Sept.	20 lbs/ac	perennial
Alsike Clover	Aug & Sept	12 lbs/ac	perennial
Birdsfoot trefoil	Aug. & Sept.	5 lbs/ac	perennial
Ladino clover	Aug. & Sept.	5 lb/ac	perennial
Red clover	Aug & Sept	14 lb/ac	annual
Sweetclover	Aug & Sept	14 lb/ac	biennial
Timothy	Aug & Sept	8 lbs/ac	perennial
Turnips	Aug & Sept	4 lbs/ac	annual
Wheat	Aug & Sept	100 lbs/ac	annual

Fall Food Plot Crops For Deer
Southern States

Species	Planting months (after danger of frost)	Planting rate/ac (broadcast)	Annual/ perennial
Arrowleaf clover	Sept & Oct	10 lbs/ac	annual
Austrian winter peas	Sept	30 lbs/ac	annual
Crimson clover	Sept & Oct	20 lbs/ac	annual
Hairy vetch	Sept & Oct	20 lbs/ac	annual
Ladino clover	Sept.	5 lbs/ac	perennial
Turnips	Sept.	4 lbs/ac	annual
Winter Wheat	Sept.	100 lbs/ac	annual

Seeds–Know What You are Buying

Read the Seed Tag

When buying seeds for a food plot you want to get the best seeds available without bringing in weed seeds with them. There are seed dealers that sell "bargain basement" seeds, that is, seeds from an unknown source, seeds from spilled seeds on the floor called "sweepings," seeds infested with weed seeds, and seed mixes of unknown amounts of the various seeds in the mix. These seeds are cheap but give less than desired results and often introduce problems in the form of invasive weeds.

To avoid disappointment and to have the best food plots possible, buy seeds that are bagged with a certified seed tag attached, usually sewn in the top of the bag. These are required in many states. Learn to read the tag. It offers a lot of information about the seed in the bag.

The sample tag below reveals how much of each seed is in the bag. For instance there are 29.75 % of field peas, Austrian Winter Peas variety, in the bag. Test show an 80 % germination rate. The seed came from Montana. The test date of the seed is given and the net weight of the bag is given. There is no noxious weed seed in the bag. The percentage of the other seeds in the mix is given. In short, you know what you are getting and what you can expect with good farming practices.

The name of the seed mix is given, Buckmaster Feeding Frenzy mixture, the name of the shipper and the lot number. You have a place to go and a good reference if there is a problem with the seed.

Avoid seed that do not have a certified seed tag. Know what you are buying.

Lot Number: 72SPI – BMFF14	Name: BUCKMASTER'S FEEDING FRENZY MIXTURE				
Pure Seed	Variety	Kind	Germ. Hard Seed	Total	Origin
29.75%	AUSTRIAN WINTER	FIELD PEAS	80%	80%	MT
10.00%	COKER 227	OATS	80%	80%	GA
14.70%	WINTERGRAZER 70	RYE	80%	80%	NC
14.70%	1529	WHEAT	80%	80%	AR
9.60%	DIXIE	CRIMSON CLOVER	80%	80%	OR
1.95%	DWARF ESSEX	RAPESEED	80%	80%	ID
.95%	PURPLETOP	WHITE GLOBE TURNIP	80%	90%	OR
0.95%	MEDIUM	RED CLOVER	80%	80%	OR

INERT: 0.95%   COATING MATERIAL: 5.50%
OTHER CROP: 0.10%
WEED SEED: 0.05%   TEST DATE: 9 – 08
NOXIOUS WEED SEED: (PER POUND)   NET WEIGHT: 25 LB
NONE

Shipper Name: PENNINGTON SEED INC
Address: Madison, GA 30650 AMS# 628

NOTICE TO CONSUMER
Arbitration/Conciliation/Mediation required by several states. Under the seed laws of several states, arbitration, mediation or conciliation is required as a prerequisite to maintaining a legal action based upon the failure of seed, to which this notice is attached, to produce as represented. The consumer shall file a complaint (sworn, by for FL, IN, MS, SC, TX, WA, signed only CA, GA, ID, ND, SD) along with the requested filing fee (where applicable) with the Commissioner/Director/Secretary of Agriculture, Seed Commissioner (IN), or Chief Agricultural Officer purchased. A copy of the complaint shall be sent to the seller by certified or registered mail or as otherwise provided by state statute.

This seed is treated with MALATHION 5EC and APEX EXP. 6-09 at the rate recommended by the manufacturer. DO NOT USE FOR FOOD, FEED, OR OIL PURPOSES!!

Inoculants for Food Plot Legumes

Legume Group	Bacterium	Inoculate Code
Alfalfa group		
Alfalfa Sweetclover	Rhizobium meliloti	A
Clover group		
Alisike Ball Ladino white White Dutch	Rhizobiium trifolii	B
Arrowleaf	Rhizobium trifolii	O
Subterranean	Rhizobium trifolii	WR
Crimson Berseem	Rhizobium trifolii	R
Cowpea Group		
Cowpea Alyce clover American jointvetch Lablab Lespedeza	Bradyrhizobium spp.	EL

Pea & Vetch Group		
Austrian winter pea Sweet pea Field pea Hairy vetch Common vetch	Rhizobium viceae	C
Other		
Birdsfoot trefoil	Mesorhizobium loti	K
Soybean	Bradyrhizobium japonicum	S

Food Plot Crop Profile

Cool-Season Legume

Common name: alfalfa

Scientific name: *Medicago sativa*

Varieties: Alfagraze, Americagraze,

Annual or perennial: perennial

Range: all of U. S. except deep south

Use: food plot crop

Soil types: well drained loams

pH Range: 6.5 – 7.0

Planting date: August – September

Seeding rate (pounds per acre): broadcast 16, drill 12

Planting method: broadcast or drill

Seed depth: ¼ inch

Fertilizer recommendation: 500 pounds of 0-10-20 when planting

Maintenance: mow in summer, watch for disease, and avoid planting in wet areas

Season used: spring, summer, fall

Cool-Season Legume

Common name: alsike clover

Scientific name: *Trifolium hybridum*

Varieties: Aurora, Dawn, Tetra

Annual or perennial: perennial

Range: northeastern U.S. and southeast Canada

Use: food plots in damp areas

Soil types: wet, heavy soils

pH Range: 6.0 – 7.5

Planting date: Sept. – Oct.

Seeding rate (pounds per acre): 10 when planting alone, 6 when mixed with a grass, timothy, cereal rye, winter wheat, oats.

Planting method: broadcast

Seed depth: ¼ inch

Fertilizer recommendation: 300 lbs. per acre 8-24-24 upon planting, then 200 pounds of 0-20-30 in August.

Maintenance: mow twice during the summer

Season used: spring, summer, fall

Warm-Season Legume

Common name: Alyce clover

Scientific name: *Alysicarpus vaginalis*

Annual or perennial: annual

Range: eastern U.S and southeast Canada

Use: food plot crop

Soil types: moderate to well drained soils

pH Range: 6.0 – 7.0

Planting date: May - June

Seeding rate (pounds per acre): 15 – 20 alone or 10 in mix

Planting method: broadcast or drill

Seed depth: ¼ inch

Fertilizer recommendation: 300 pounds of 8-24-24

Maintenance: keep weed free, plant with American jointvetch

Season used: summer, fall

Warm-Season Legume

Common name: American Jointvetch

Scientific name: *Aeschynomene americana*

Varieties: Glenn, Lee

Annual or perennial: annual

Range: southeast U.S.

Use: shade tolerant food plot crop or planted in fire breaks

Soil types: wet, low fertile soils

pH Range: 5.5 – 6.0

Planting date: April – June

Seeding rate (pounds per acre): 20

Planting method: broadcast

Seed depth: ¼ – ½ inch

Fertilizer recommendation: 300 pounds of 0-20-20

Maintenance: Seed may be difficult to find

Season used: summer, fall

Cool-Season Legume

Common name: arrowleaf clover

Scientific name: Trifolium vesiculosum

Varieties: Yachi, Apache, Amclo

Annual or perennial: annual

Range: southern U.S.

Use: high protein food plot crop usually planted with small grains

Soil types: any, except deep sand

pH Range: 5.0 – 6.5

Planting date: August – September

Seeding rate (pounds per acre): 15 if planted alone, 7 if no-till, or 5 if planted in mixture

Planting method: broadcast or no-till

Seed depth: ¼ – ½ inch

Fertilizer recommendation: 300 pounds of 0-20-20.

Maintenance: best planted as a mix with oats, rye grain or winter wheat

Season used: winter, spring, summer

Cool-Season Legume

Common name: Austrian winter pea

Scientific name: *Pisum sativum*

Varieties: Sioux, Granger

Annual or perennial: annual

Range: lower 2/3's of U. S.

Use: winter food plot crop

Soil types: well drained loam and sandy loam soils

pH Range: 6.0 – 7.5

Planting date: late August – October

Seeding rate (pounds per acre): 40 if broadcast, 30 drilled, or 20 in a mix

Planting method: broadcast or drill

Seed depth: ½ - 1 inch

Fertilizer recommendation: 300 pounds 0-20-20

Maintenance: can be overgrazed easily so mix with winter wheat, white clover, arrowleaf clover, or crimson clover.

Season used: fall, winter, spring

Cool-Season Legume

Common name: Ball clover

Scientific name: Trifolium nigrescens

Varieties: Segrest, Common

Annual or perennial: annual

Range: southern U.S.

Use: late season food plot crop

Soil types: loam and clay soils. Tolerates poor drainage

pH Range: 5.0 – 8.0

Planting date: September – October

Seeding rate (pounds per acre): 3

Planting method: broadcast

Fertilizer recommendation: 300 pounds of 8-24-24

Maintenance: Tolerates heavy grazing

Season used: late winter and spring

Cool-Season Legume

Common name: Berseem clover

Scientific name: *Trifolium alexandrinum*

Varieties: Bigbee

Annual or perennial: annual

Range: eastern U.S to Great Lakes

Use: late season food plot crop

Soil types: widely adapted except deep sand

pH Range: 6.5 – 7.5

Planting date: September – October

Seeding rate (pounds per acre): 20 broadcast or 10 drilled

Planting method: broadcast or drill

Fertilizer recommendation: 300 pounds 8-24-24, include boron

Maintenance: plant with small grain to prevent overgrazing

Season used: winter, spring

Cool-Season Legume

Common name: Birdsfoot trefoil

Scientific name: *Lotus cornicalatus*

Varieties: Empire, Dawn, Viking, Fergus

Annual or perennial: perennial

Range: northeast and northcentral U. S. and Canada

Use: fall and winter food plot crop

Soil types: fertile, well drained

pH Range: 6.0 – 7.0

Planting date: August - September

Seeding rate (pounds per acre): 10 broadcast or 5 drilled

Planting method: broadcast or drill

Seed depth: ¼ inch

Fertilizer recommendation: 300 pounds of 0-20-30

Maintenance: weed control a must, lightly disk in April

Season used: spring, summer, fall

Warm & Cool-Season Forb

Common name: Buckwheat

Scientific name: *Fagopyrum esculentum*

Varieties: Common Gray, Japanese, Manor, Silverhull

Annual or perennial: annual

Range: much of U. S. and southern Canada

Use: warm season food plot crop

Soil types: all but wet soils

pH Range: 6.0 – 7.0

Planting date: April – June

Seeding rate (pounds per acre): 60 broadcast, 45 drill

Seed depth: 1 ½ inches

Planting method: broadcast or drill

Fertilizer recommendation: 300 pounds of 5-10-15

Notes: may take deer a season or two to discover, then heavy use.

Season used: summer, early fall

Warm-Season Legume

Common name: Burgundy Bean

Scientific name: *Macroptilium bracteatum*

Varieties: Juanita, Cadarga

Annual or perennial: annual

Range: central and southern U. S.

Use: food plot crop

Soil types: sandy to heavy clays

pH Range: 5.0 – 6.0

Planting date: April – June

Seeding rate (pounds per acre): 5 - 8

Planting method: broadcast

Seed depth: ½ – 1 inch

Fertilizer recommendation: 100 pounds of 0-46-0

Maintenance: may be planted with corn or Egyptian wheat

Season used: summer, fall

Cold Season Brassica

Common name: Canola

Scientific name: *Brassica napus & rapa*

Annual or perennial: annual

Range: most of U. S. and southern Canada

Use: cool season food plot crop

Soil types: well drained soils

pH Range: 5.5 – 7.0

Planting date: August – September

Seeding rate (pounds per acre): 8 broadcast or 5 drilled

Planting method: broadcast or drill

Seed depth: ¼ inch

Fertilizer recommendation: 200 pounds of 19-19-19 with 150 pounds of 46-0-0

Notes: rotate every two years, may be overgrazed if planted too late

Season used: fall, winter

Warm & Cool-Season Forb

Common name: Chicory

Scientific name: *Chicorium intybus*

Varieties: Puna, Good Hunt, Choice

Annual or perennial: perennial

Range: much of U. S. and southern Canada

Use: cool season food plot crop

Soil types: all but wet soils

pH Range: 6.5 – 7.0

Planting date: August – September

Seeding rate (pounds per acre): 5 broadcast, 5 drill

Seed depth: ¼ to ½ inch

Planting method: broadcast or drill

Fertilizer recommendation: 300 pounds of 19-19-19

Notes: best planted with legume and grass mix

Season used: fall, winter

Warm-Season Grain

Common name: Corn

Scientific name: *Zea mays*

Varieties: select a feed corn variety suited to your area

Annual or perennial: annual

Range: much of the U. S. and southern Canada

Use: food plot crop

Soil types: fertile, well drained

pH Range: 6.0 – 6.8

Planting date: March – June

Seeding rate (pounds per acre): row planting 5 to 10

Planting method: row planting

Seed depth: 1 – 2 inches

Fertilizer recommendation: 300 pounds of 19-19-19 and 150 pounds of 34-0-0 after one month.

Maintenance: Plant in fields 5 acres or larger, keep weed free, protect from other pest species.

Season used: fall, winter

Warm-Season Legume

Common name: Cowpeas

Scientific name: *Vigna unguiculata*

Varieties: Iron and Clay, Tory, Catjang, Black Eye, Wilcox

Annual or perennial: annual

Range: all U. S. and southern Canada

Use: food plot crop

Soil types: well drained, fertile

pH Range: 6.0 – 7.5

Planting date: April – June

Seeding rate (pounds per acre): broadcast 70, drilled 50

Planting method: broadcast or drill

Seed depth: ½ – 1 inch

Fertilizer recommendation: 200 pounds 19-19-19

Notes: can be overgrazed by deer

Season used: summer, fall

Cool-Season Legume

Common name: Crimson clover

Scientific name: *Trifolium incarnatum*

Varieties: Dixie, Chief, Common, Tibbee

Annual or perennial: annual

Range: eastern U.S. to Wisconsin and Maryland

Use: food plot crop. Mixes well with cool season grasses such as winter wheat

Soil types: most soils except sandy soils

pH Range: 5.7 – 6.4

Planting date: August – October

Seeding rate (pounds per acre): 20 pounds when planted alone and 12 pounds when planted with grasses.

Planting method: broadcast or drill

Seed depth: ¼ inch

Fertilizer recommendation: 300 pounds of 8-24-24

Maintenance: proper inoculation is a must to get a good stand

Season used: fall, winter, spring

Cool-Season Legume

Common name: Durana clover

Scientific name: *Trifolium repens*

Varieties: Durana

Annual or perennial: perennial

Range: All U. S.

Use: food plot crop best mixed with annual grains such as winter wheat or oats.

Soil types: wide variety of soils

pH Range: 5.4 – 7.4

Planting date: August – October

Seeding rate (pounds per acre): 5

Planting method: broadcast or drill

Seed depth: ¼ inch

Fertilizer recommendation: 300 pounds of 19-19-19

Maintenance: Mow in summer and fertilize in September with 300 pounds of 0-20-30.

Season used: fall, winter, spring

Warm-Season Grains & Grasses

Common name: Grain Sorghum

Scientific name: *Sorghum bicolor*

Varieties: Cooper's Wildlife Sorghum

Annual or perennial: annual

Range: all U. S. and southern Canada

Use: food plot crop

Soil types: well drained, fertile soils

pH Range: 6.0-7.5

Planting date: April – June

Seeding rate (pounds per acre): 10 broadcast, 5 drilled

Planting method: broadcast or drill

Seed depth: ½ – 1 inch

Fertilizer recommendation: 400 pounds 19-19-19

Maintenance: ideal to plant with Quail Haven soybeans

Season used: fall, winter, spring

Cold Season Brassica

Common name: Kale

Scientific name: *Brassica oleracea*

Varieties: Siberian, Premier, Vates, Redbor

Annual or perennial: annual

Range: most of U. S. and southern Canada

Use: cool season food plot crop

Soil types: well drained loam soil

pH Range: 5.5 – 6.5

Planting date: June – July

Seeding rate (pounds per acre): 5 broadcast

Planting method: broadcast

Seed depth: ¼ inch

Fertilizer recommendation: 200 pounds of 19-19-19 with 150 pounds of 46-0-0

Notes: Rotate every two years, may be overgrazed if planted too late

Season used: fall, winter

Cold Season Brassica

Common name: Kale

Scientific name: *Brassica oleracea*

Varieties: Siberian, Premier, Vates, Redbor

Annual or perennial: annual

Range: most of U. S. and southern Canada

Use: cool season food plot crop

Soil types: well drained loam soil

pH Range: 5.5 – 6.5

Planting date: June – July

Seeding rate (pounds per acre): 5 broadcast

Planting method: broadcast

Seed depth: ¼ inch

Fertilizer recommendation: 200 pounds of 19-19-19 with 150 pounds of 46-0-0

Notes: Rotate every two years, may be overgrazed if planted too late

Season used: fall, winter

Warm-Season Legume

Common name: Kobe (Common) lespedeza

Scientific name: *Kummerowia striata*

Varieties: Marion

Annual or perennial: annual

Range: eastern U. S.

Use: firebreaks, summer food plot crop, erosion control

Soil types: all soils

pH Range: 6.0 – 6.5

Planting date: March – June

Seeding rate (pounds per acre): broadcast 30, drill 20

Planting method: broadcast or drill

Seed depth: ¼ – ½ inch

Fertilizer recommendation: 300 pounds of 0-20-20

Notes: good mid to late summer food source for deer

Season used: summer, fall

Warm-Season Legume

Common name: Korean Lespedeza

Scientific name: *Kummerowia stipulacea*

Varieties:

Annual or perennial: annual

Range: eastern U. S.

Use: food plot crop, firebreaks, log landings, erosion control

Soil types: all soils

pH Range: 6.0-6.5

Planting date: April – June

Seeding rate (pounds per acre): broadcast 25, drill 15

Planting method: broadcast or drill

Seed depth: ¼ – ½ inch

Fertilizer recommendation: 300 pounds of 0-20-20

Notes: not a top choice food for deer

Season used: summer, fall

Cool-Season Legume

Common name: Kura clover

Scientific name: *Trifolium ambiguum*

Varieties: Rhizo, Cossack, Endura

Annual or perennial: perennial

Range: central and northeast U.S.

Use: food plot crop in the snow belt states

Soil types: wide variety of soils

pH Range: 6.0 – 7.4

Planting date: August – October

Seeding rate (pounds per acre): 10 pounds when planted alone and 8 pounds when planted with grasses.

Planting method: broadcast or drill

Seed depth: ¼ – ½ inch

Fertilizer recommendation: 300 pounds of 8-24-24

Maintenance: plant with birdsfoot trefoil, winter wheat, timothy.

Season used: winter, spring, summer

Warm-Season Legume

Common name: Lablab

Scientific name: *Lablab purpureus*

Annual or perennial: annual

Range: much of U. S.

Use: food plot crop

Soil types: well drained soils

pH Range: 6.0 – 7.0

Planting date: March – June

Seeding rate (pounds per acre): 20

Planting method: broadcast

Seed depth: ½ to 1 ½ inch

Fertilizer recommendation: 300 pounds of 0-20-20

Notes: easily overgrazed

Season used: summer early fall

Cool-Season Legume

Common name: Ladino clover

Scientific name: *Trifolium repens*

Varieties: Osceola, California, Regal, Patriot

Annual or perennial: perennial

Range: All U. S.

Use: food plot crop best mixed with annual grains such as winter wheat or oats.

Soil types: wide variety of soils

pH Range: 6.0 – 7.4

Planting date: August – October

Seeding rate (pounds per acre): 5 pounds mixed with 50 pounds of winter wheat

Planting method: broadcast

Seed depth: ¼ inch

Fertilizer recommendation: 300 pounds of 19-19-19

Maintenance: Mow in summer and protect from weeds and grasses.

Season used: fall, winter, spring, summer

Cool-Season Grain

Common name: Oats

Scientific name: *Avena sativa*

Varieties: Buck Forage, Arkansas 604, Blaze, Chapman, Chaps

Annual or perennial: annual

Range: all U. S. and southern Canada

Use: food plot crop usually a part of a mix

Soil types: clay loam to sandy loams

pH Range: 6.0 – 7.0

Planting date: August – October

Seeding rate (pounds per acre): 3 bushels if broadcast, 2 bushels if drilled

Planting method: broadcast or drill

Seed depth: 1 – 1 ½ inch

Fertilizer recommendation: 400 pounds of 6-12-12, top dress 50 pounds of nitrogen

Maintenance: sensitive to cold, mix with legumes for best food plot

Season used: fall, spring

Cold Season Brassica

Common name: rapeseed

Scientific name: *Brassica napus*

Annual or perennial: annual

Range: most of U. S. and southern Canada

Use: cool season food plot crop

Soil types: well drained loam soil

pH Range: 5.5 – 7.0

Planting date: July – September

Seeding rate (pounds per acre): 8 broadcast, 4 drilled

Planting method: broadcast or drill

Seed depth: 1/8 – ¼ inch

Fertilizer recommendation: 300 pounds of 19-19-19 with 100 pounds of 34-0-0

Notes: Rotate every two years

Season used: fall, winter

Cool-Season Legume

Common name: Red clover

Scientific name: *Trifolium pratense*

Varieties: Redman, Kenland, Bulldog, Cherokee

Annual or perennial: perennial

Range: eastern U. S.

Use: food plot crop best mixed with winter wheat, rye, oats

Soil types: sandy loam to clay

pH Range: 6.0 – 7.0

Planting date: August – October

Seeding rate (pounds per acre): broadcast 15, drill 10

Planting method: broadcast or drill

Seed depth: ¼ inch

Fertilizer recommendation: 300 pounds of 19-19-19

Maintenance: Mow in summer and fertilize in September with 100 pounds of 0-46-0.

Season used: fall, winter, spring, summer

Cool-Season Legume

Common name: Rose clover

Scientific name: *Trifolium hirtum*

Varieties: Monte Frio, Hykon, Kondinin

Annual or perennial: annual

Range: western U. S. and in some dry areas of the east

Use: food plot crop usually mixed with other clovers

Soil types: well drained

pH Range: 6.0 – 7.0

Planting date: August – September

Seeding rate (pounds per acre): 8 broadcast, 5 drilled

Planting method: broadcast or drill

Fertilizer recommendation: 300 pounds 0f 0-20-20

Maintenance: can be overgrazed easily so mix with other clovers

Season used: winter and early spring

Cool-Season Grain

Common name: rye

Scientific name: *Secale cereale*

Varieties: Wintergrazer 70, Winter King, Wheeler, Maton

Annual or perennial: annual

Range: all U. S. and southern Canada

Use: food plot crop usually mixed with legumes

Soil types: all but deep sandy soil

pH Range: 6.0 – 7.0

Planting date: August – October

Seeding rate (pounds per acre): broadcast alone 100, half if mixed or drilled

Planting method: broascast or drill

Seed depth: 1 – 1 ½ inch

Fertilizer recommendation: 300 pounds 19-19-19

Maintenance: best when planted with legumes

Season used: fall, winter, spring

Cool-Season Grains & Grasses

Common name: ryegrass

Scientific name: *Lolium spp.*

Varieties: Gulf, Marshall, Italian

Annual or perennial: annual and perennial

Range: all U. S. and southern Canada

Use: remote, small food plots

Soil types: low and fertile uplands

pH Range: 6.0 – 7.0

Planting date: August – October

Seeding rate (pounds per acre): 40 alone, 15 in a mix

Planting method: broadcast

Seed depth: 1/8 inch

Fertilizer recommendation: 400 pounds 13-13-13

Maintenance: This is an aggressive plant that should be only used in remote food plots. Mix with legumes.

Season used: fall, winter, spring, summer

Warm & Cool-Season Forb

Common name: Small Burnet

Scientific name: *Sanguisorba minor*

Varieties: Delar

Annual or perennial: cool-season perennial

Range: much of U. S. and southern Canada

Use: cool season food plot crop

Soil types: well drained soils

pH Range: 6.0 – 7.5

Planting date: August – September

Seeding rate (pounds per acre): 5 broadcast, 5 drill

Seed depth: ½ inch

Planting method: broadcast or drill

Fertilizer recommendation: 300 pounds of 19-19-19

Notes: best planted with legume and grass mix, is slow to establish on poor soil.

Season used: fall, winter, spring, summer

Warm-Season Legume

Common name: soybeans

Scientific name: *Glycine max*

Varieties: Laredo, Quail Haven, Tyrone

Annual or perennial: annual

Range: much of U.S. and southern Canada

Use: food plot crop

Soil types: fertile, well drained

pH Range: 5.5 – 6.5

Planting date: April – June

Seeding rate (pounds per acre): broadcast 80, drill 50

Planting method: broadcast or drill

Seed depth: ½ – 1 inch

Fertilizer recommendation: 300 pounds of 0-20-20

Notes: grow running soybeans with sunflowers, corn, or Egyptian wheat

Season used: summer, fall

Cool-Season Legume

Common name: subterranean clover

Scientific name: *Trifolium subterrean*

Varieties: Mt. Baker, Tallarook, Nangeela

Annual or perennial: annual

Range: southeast and west U. S.

Use: food plots in shade

Soil types: well drained soils

pH Range: 6.0 – 7.0

Planting date: late summer and fall

Seeding rate (pounds per acre): 15 broadcast, 10 drilled

Planting method: broadcast and drill

Seed depth: 1/4 – ½ inch

Fertilizer recommendation: 300 pounds of 8-24-24

Maintenance: Plant as a mixture with wheat and white clover

Season used: late fall and winter

Warm & Cool-Season Forbs

Common name: sugar beet

Scientific name: *Beta vulgaris*

Annual or perennial: cool-season perennial

Range: west and mid west U. S. and south west Canada

Use: cool season food plot crop

Soil types: medium to heavy loam soils

pH Range: 6.0 – 7.5

Planting date: spring and fall

Seeding rate (pounds per acre): 8

Planting method: broadcast

Seed depth: ½ to ¾ inches

Fertilizer recommendation: 300 pounds of 19-19-19

Notes: best planted with legume and grass mix, deer like top and bulb

Season used: fall, winter, spring, summer

Warm-Season Legume

Common name: Sweetclover

Scientific name: *Melilotus spp.*

Annual or perennial: perennial

Range: all U. S. except Gulf Coast and southern Canada

Use: food plot crop

Soil types: clay or loam soils

pH Range: 6.5 – 7.5

Planting date: spring or fall

Seeding rate (pounds per acre): 10-15

Planting method: broadcast

Seed depth: ¼ inch

Fertilizer recommendation: 300 pounds of 0-20-30

Notes: a good year-round clover

Season used: spring, summer, fall

Cool-Season Grains & Grasses

Common name: timothy grass

Scientific name: *Phleum pratense*

Varieties: Bart, Barliza, Climax

Annual or perennial: perennial

Range: northern and central U. S. and southern Canada

Use: fire breaks, old road beds, and food plots when planted with legumes

Soil types: moist, fertile, heavy soils

pH Range: 6.0 – 7.0

Planting date: August – October

Seeding rate (pounds per acre): 5 when planted in a mix

Planting method: broadcast

Seed depth: 1 – 1 ½ inch

Fertilizer recommendation: 300 pounds of 19-19-19

Maintenance: Plant with legumes such as ladino clover, mow twice each summer

Season used: fall, winter, spring, summer

Cool-Season Grains & Grasses

Common name: triticale

Scientific name: *Triticosecale spp.*

Varieties: Nutriseed 2-2-4, Tritigold-22, Begal 82, Trical 102

Annual or perennial: annual

Range: most of U. S. and southern Canada

Use: food plot crop mixed with legumes

Soil types: fertile, well drained soils

pH Range: 6.0 – 7.0

Planting date: August – October

Seeding rate (pounds per acre): 85 if broadcast alone, 50 if drilled or in a mix

Planting method: broadcast or drill

Seed depth: 1 – 1 ½ inch

Fertilizer recommendation: 400 pounds of 13-13-13

Maintenance: Select varieties suited for your area

Season used: fall, winter, spring

Cold Season Brassica

Common name: turnips

Scientific name: *Brassica rapa*

Varieties: Purple Top, Royal Crown, Bankant, All Top, Sirius

Annual or perennial: annual

Range: most of U. S. and southern Canada

Use: cool season food plot crop

Soil types: well drained clay to loam soils

pH Range: 6.0 – 6.5

Planting date: August – September

Seeding rate (pounds per acre): 4 broadcast, 2 drilled

Planting method: broadcast or drill

Seed depth: ¼ inch

Fertilizer recommendation: 400 pounds of 19-19-19, top dress with 100 pounds of 34-0-0 about 60 days later

Notes: Rotate every two years, both tops and bulb eaten by deer

Season used: fall, winter

Cool-Season Grain

Common name: Wheat

Scientific name: *Triticum aestivum*

Varieties: winter varieties proven in your area

Annual or perennial: annual

Range: all U. S. and southern Canada

Use: food plot crop

Soil types: heavy, well drained, medium to high fertility

pH Range: 6.0 – 7.0

Planting date: September – October

Seeding rate (pounds per acre): when broadcasting alone 2 bushels, half for mix or drill

Planting method: broadcast or drill

Seed depth: 1 – 1 ½ inch

Fertilizer recommendation: 300 pounds of 19-19-19

Maintenance: Purchase clean, certified seed

Season used: fall, winter, spring

Cool-Season Legume

Common name: White Dutch

Scientific name: *Trifolium repens*

Varieties: New Zealand

Annual or perennial: perennial

Range: eastern U. S.

Use: food plot drop

Soil types: widely adapted

pH Range: 6.0 – 7.0

Planting date: fall

Seeding rate (pounds per acre): 4

Planting method: broadcast or drill

Fertilizer recommendation: 300 pounds of 8-24-24

Maintenance: control for weeds

Season used: fall, winter, spring

Custom Food Plot Seed Mixes You Can Mix Yourself

Cool Season Annual Mixes Per Acre

Southern U.S.

Mix 1

2 bushels wheat
15 pounds crimson clover

Mix 2

1 bushel wheat
1 bushel grain rye
1 bushel oats
5 pounds crimson clover

Mix 3

10 pounds crimson clover
10 pounds arrowleaf clover
30 pounds grain rye
30 pounds wheat

Mix 4

2 pounds chicory
5 pounds white clover
7 pounds red clover
15 pounds Austrian winter pea
25 pounds wheat
25 pounds grain rye

Mix 5

10 pounds crimson clover
10 pounds Berseem clover
20 pounds Austrian winter pea
30 pounds oats

Mix 6

15 pounds crimson clover
2 pounds white clover

10 pounds ryegrass
60 pounds wheat
20 pounds reseeding vetch

Mix 7 - late winter

10 pounds arrowleaf clover
10 pounds red clover
50 pounds oats

Mix 8

30 pounds oats
5 pounds red clover
5 pounds arrowleaf clover

Mix 9

50 pounds oats
1 pound chicory
5 pounds white clover
20 pounds grain rye

Mix 10

30 pounds wheat
50 pounds grain rye
5 pounds Durana clover
7 pounds red clover
2 pounds chicory

Mix 11

2 pounds rape
1 pound chicory
5 pounds red clover
30 pounds wheat

Northern U.S.

Mix 1

2 bushels grain rye
5 pounds ladino clover

Mix 2 - brassicas

2 pounds rape
2 pounds kale
2 pounds turnips

Mix 3

10 pounds arrowleaf
10 pounds red clover
50 pounds oats

Mix 4

7 pounds red clover
5 pounds white clover
50 pounds wheat

Mix 5

20 pounds Austrian winter pea
50 pounds wheat
5 pounds red clover
5 pounds ladino clover

Mix 6

15 pounds hairy vetch
50 pounds oats

Mix 7

30 pounds oats
5 pounds red clover
3 pounds white clover

Mix 8

50 pounds grain rye
5 pounds birdsfoot trifoil
5 pounds red clover
5 pounds white clover
20 pounds Austrian winter peas

Mix 9

25 pounds trical
25 pounds oats
5 pounds Durana clover
7 pounds red clover

Mix 10

50 pounds wheat
5 pounds red clover

5 pounds white clover
1 pound chicory
20 pounds Austrian winter peas
3 pounds birdsfoot trefoil

Warm Season Annual Mixes Per Acre

Southern U.S.

Mix 1

10 pounds Alyce clover
10 pounds American jointvetch

Mix 2

7 pounds grain sorghum
5 pounds burgundy bean

Mix 3 – early fall

20 pounds cowpeas
20 pounds buckwheat
50 pounds wheat
10 pounds arrowleaf clover

Mix 4

10 pounds Egyptian wheat
5 pounds lablab

5 pounds grain sorghum

*(Note: This food plot mix will
attract squirrels in the fall)*

Mix 5

7 pounds corn
5 pounds grain sorghum
25 pounds soybeans

Mix 6

7 pounds grain sorghum
15 pounds American
  jointvetch
25 pounds soybeans

Mix 7

20 pounds buckwheat
5 pounds tall grain sorghum
25 pounds soybeans

Northern U.S.

Mix 1

10 pounds corn
5 pounds burgundy bean

Mix 2

25 pounds cowpeas
5 pounds grain sorghum
15 pounds Alyce clover

Mix 3

10 pounds corn
5 pounds lablab

Mix 4

20 pounds Quail Haven
    soybeans
15 pounds tall grain sorghum

Mix 5

15 pounds ryegrass
5 pounds ladino clover
7 pounds red clover

Cool Season Perennial Mixes Per Acre

Southern U.S.

Mix 1

10 pounds ladino clover
10 pounds red clover
10 pounds ryegrass
30 pounds grain rye
30 pounds wheat

Mix 2

5 pounds ladino clover
7 pounds red clover
50 pounds wheat

Mix 3

5 pounds Durana
7 pounds red clover
50 pounds wheat

Mix 4

10 pounds birdsfoot trefoil
5 pounds timothy grass

Mix 5

50 pounds wheat
5 pounds ladino clover
2 pounds chicory

Northern U. S.

Mix 1

50 pounds wheat
3 pounds white clover
5 red clover
3 pounds small burnet
3 pounds birdsfoot trefoil

Mix 2

20 pounds timothy grass
5 pounds lidano clover
5 pounds red clover

Mix 3

5 pound birdsfoot trefoil
5 pounds timothy

Mix 4

15 pounds alfalfa
5 pounds ladino clover

Mix 5

5 pounds lidano
7 pounds red clover
20 pounds timothy grass

Mix 6

10 pounds Kura clover
1 pound timothy grass
3 pounds trefoil

Mix 7

6 pounds alsiki clover
50 pounds grain rye
5 pounds birdsfoot trefoil

Warm Season Perennial Food Plot Mix Per Acre

Mix 1 – all states

6 pounds sweetclover
4 pounds grain sorghum

Food Plot Mixes for Erosion Control, Woods Road, or Firebreak

Mix 1

25 pounds common lespedeza
8 pounds timothy grass

Mix 2

5 pounds timothy
15 pounds ryegrass
5 pounds ladino clover
10 pounds red clover

DEER FOOD PLOT RECORD

Name of plot: _____

Size: _____

Location: Lat- _____ Lon- _____

Soil test date: _____ Amount of Lime: _____

Application Date: _____ Crop last planted: _____

Planting rate: _____ Depth: _____

Date planted: _____ Planting method: _____

Seed brand name: _____

Local seed source: _____ Price: _____

Fertilizer data on last crop

Analysis: _____ Rate: _____ Date: _____

Weed control method: _____

Rain after planting

Date: _____ Amount: _____

Date: _____ Amount: _____

Date: _____ Amount: _____

Target species	☐ deer	☐ wild turkey	☐ quail
(circle)	☐ pheasant	☐ rabbits	☐ other _____

Results of last crop	☐ poor	☐ fair	☐ average	☐ above average
(circle):	☐ outstanding			

Crop to be planted this year: _____

Planting rate: _____ Depth: _____

Date to plant: _____ Planting method: _____

Seed brand name: _____

Local seed source: _____ Price: _____

Fertilizer data

Analysis: _____ Rate: _____ Date to apply: _____

Weed control method: _____

Rain after planting

Date: _____ Amount: _____

Date: _____ Amount: _____

Date: _____ Amount: _____

Target species	☐ deer	☐ wild turkey	☐ quail
(circle)	☐ pheasant	☐ rabbit	☐ other _____

Making a Salt or Mineral Lick

Making a man-made salt lick is easy. One of the most natural-looking salt licks is an old stump, especially one you would like to have removed. Here is how to make a stump lick:

The Stump Lick

1. Using a posthole digger, dig deep holes under the stump between the roots

2. Pour 25 pounds of the granular salt or mineral mix in the holes.

3. Cover with dirt.

4. Save a little mix to pour on the top of the stump so deer can find it quicker.

Another salt lick is what is called the natural-looking lick. Here is how to make it:

The Natural Looking Lick

1. Dig a hole about 12 inches deep and at least 36inches in diameter, preferably in a well drained clay soil.

2. Remove the soil and fill the hole with 25 pounds of granular salt or mineral mix.

3. Save some of the mixture to place on top.

4. Place the soil on top of the mix and mix it up a little.

5. Finally, sprinkle the remaining mix on top of the loose soil.

Note: Be sure to check local laws as in some states hunting near salt or mineral licks is considered hunting over bait.

Deer Exclusion Cage

One of the best ways to evaluate the amount of use deer are making of a food plot crop is to construct an exclusion cage, sometimes called a utilization cage or barrier, on each food plot. This prevents deer and other animals from eating on a small area inside the cage. By observing how much forage grows inside the cage, you can see how much forage is being produced and, by comparison, how much the deer are eating.

To make an exclusion cage follow these simple instructions:

1. Obtain a roll of 2"X4" welded wire fence that is 4feet high.

2. Cut a 10-foot length of the fence.

3. Be sure to cut the fence so that the cut is made half way between the 2" horizontal wires. This will leave a 2" wire tab.

4. Make a circle with the 10-foot section of fence and fasten with the wire tabs.

5. Sit the circular cage upright in a food plot just after it is planted and stake down to prevent deer from knocking it over. Use three stakes.

6. Be sure to remove the cage or mark it with bright orange tape before mowing or breaking the plot.

When food plot growers erect an exclusion cage on a newly planted food plot, many who think their food plots are getting little use are surprised at how much forage deer actually eat.

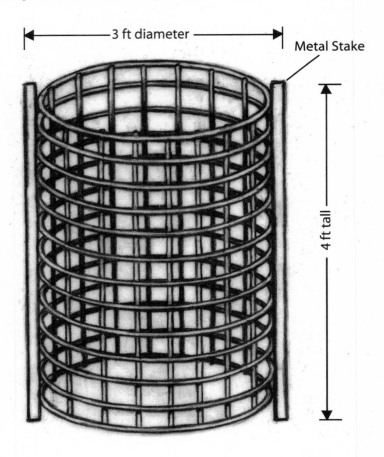

3 ft diameter

Metal Stake

4 ft tall

Deer-Resistant Plants

Annuals

Ageratum houstonianum	Ageratum
Antirrhinum majus	Snapdragon
Brugmansia sp. (Datura)	Angel's Trumpet
Calendula sp.	Pot Marigold
Catharanthus rosea	Annual Vinca
Centaurea cineraria	Dusty Miller
Cleome sp.	Spider Flower
Euphorbia marginata	Snow-on-the-Mountain
Helichrysum	Strawflower
Heliotropium arborescens	Heliotrope
Lobularia maritima	Sweet Alyssum
Matricaria sp. False	Camomile
Myosotis sylvatica	Forget-Me-Not
Nicotiana sp.	Flowering Tobacco
Papaver sp.	Poppy
Pimpinalla anisum	Anise
Rosmarinus officinalis	Rosemary

Biennials

Digitalis purpurea	Common Foxglove

Bulbs

Allium sp.	Ornamental Onion
Colchicum sp.	Autumn Crocus
Endymion sp.	Bluebell
Eranthus hyemalis	Winter Aconite
Fritilaria imperialis	Crown Imperial, Fritilia
Galanthus nivalis	Snowdrops
Narcissus sp.	Daffodil
Scilla siberica Siberian	Squill

Ferns

Athyrium goeringianum (nipponicum)	Japanese Painted Fern
Cyrtomium falcatum	Holly Fern
Dennstaedtia punctilobula	Hayscented Fern
Dryopteris marginalis	Wood Fern
Matteuccia struthiopteris	Ostrich Fern
Onoclea sensibilis	Sensitive Fern
Osmunda cinnamomea	Cinnamon Fern
Osmunda regalis	Royal Fern
Polystichum arcostichoides	Christmas Fern
Thelyptens noveboracensis	New York Fern

Groundcovers

Aegopodium podagaria	Bishop's Weed
Ajuga reptans	Bugleweed

Arctostaphylos uva-ursi	Bearberry
Convallaria majalis	Lily of the Valley
Epimediurn sp.	Barrenwort
Galium odoratum (Asperula odorata)	Sweet Woodruff
Lamium sp. Spotted	Deadnettle
Pachysandra procumbens	Allegheny Spurge
Pachysandra terminalis	Pachysandra

Ornamental Grasses

Acorus sp.	Japanese Sweet Flag
Andropogon sp.	Big Bluestem
Arrhenatherum elatius	Varigated Oat Grass
Arundo donax	Giant Reed
Calamagrostis sp.	Feather Reed Grass
Carex sp. Japanese	Sedge
Chasmanthium latifolium	Northern Sea Oats
Cortaderia selloana Pampus	Grass
Eragrostus curvula	Weeping Love Grass
Erianthus ravennae	Ravenna Grass
Fargesia sp.	Clump Bamboo
Festuca glauca	Blue Fescue
Hakonechloa macra	Hakonechloa
Helictotrichon sempervirens	Blue Oat Grass
Imperata cylindrica	Japanese Blood Grass
Juncus Effusus	Hard Rush
Koeleria glauca	Large Blue June Grass
Leymus arenarius glaucous	Lyme Grass

Miscanthus floridulis	Giant Japanese Silver Grass
Miscanthus sinensis	Japanese Silver Grass
Molinia caerulea	Purple Moor Grass
Molinia caerulea 'Variegata'	Variegated Purple Moor Grass
Panicum virgatum	Switch Grass
Pennisetum alopecuroides	Fountain Grass
Pennisetum orientale	Oriental Fountain Grass
Phyllostachys aurea	Golden Bamboo
Schizachyrium scoparium	Little Bluestem
Sorghastrum nutans	Indian Grass

Perennials

Aconitum sp.	Monkshood
Agastache sp.	Anise Hyssop
Allium sp.	Ornamental Onion
Arabis caucasica	Rock-Cress
Arisaema triphylum	Jack-in-the-pulpit
Armoracia rusticana	Horseradish
Artemisia dracunculus	Tarragon
Artemisia sp.	Silver Mound
Asarum canadense	Wild Ginger
Asarum europaeum	European Ginger
Aubretia deltoidea	Purple Rock-Cress
Aurinia saxatilis	Basket of Gold
Baptisia australis	False Indigo

Bruneria macrophylla	Siberian Bugloss
Cactaceae sp.	Cactus
Coreopsis verticillata	Threadleaf Coreopsis
Corydalis sp.	Corydalis
Dicentra eximia	Fringed Bleeding Heart
Dicentra spectabilis	Bleeding Heart
Echinops ritro	Small Globe Thistle
Euphorbia sp.	(except Spurge 'Chameleon')
Helleborus sp.	Lenten or Christmas Rose
Hesperis matronalis	Dame's Rocket
Hyssopus officinalis	Hyssop
Iris sp. (may eat buds)	Iris
Lavandula sp.	Lavendar
Ligularia dentata	Bigleaf Goldenray
Ligularia	Rocket Ligularia
Limonium latifolium	Statice
Linaria vulgaris	Butter & Eggs
Lychnis coronaria	Rose Campion
Majorana	Marjoram
Marrubium vulgare	Horehound
Melissa officinalis	Lemon Balm
Mentha sp.	Mint
Myosotis sp.	Forget-Me-Not
Nepeta sp.	Catmint
Oreganum sp.	Oregano

Paeonia sp. (may eat buds)	Peony
Perovskio atriplicifolia	Russian Sage
Phlomis sp.	Greek Jerusalem Sage
Podophyllum	May Apple
Potentilla sp.	Potentilla, Cinquefoil
Pulmonaria sp.	Lungwort
Ranunculus sp.	Buttercup
Rodgersia sp.	Rodgers Flower
Ruta sp.	Rue
Salvia officinalis	Garden Sage
Santolina chamaecyparissus	Lavender-Cotton
Stachys byzantina	Lamb's Ear
Tanacetum vulgare	Common Tansy
Teucrium Chamaedrys	Germander
Thalictrum sp.	Meadow Rue
Thymus sp.	Thyme
Yucca filimentosa	Yucca

Shrubs

Aralia spinosa	Devil's Walking Stick
Berberis sp.	Barberry
Buddleia sp.	Butterfly Bush
Buxus sempervirens	Common Boxwood
Calliuna sp.	Heather
Caryopteris clandonensis	Blue Mist Shrub
Cephalotaxus harringtonia	Japanese Plum Yew
Cytisus sp.	Broom

Daphne sp.	Daphne
Elaeagnus angustifolia	Russian Olive
Erica sp.	Heath
Ilex x 'John T. Morris'	John T. Morris Holly
Ilex x 'Lydia Morris'	Lydia Morris Holly
Juniperus horizontalis	'Prince of Wales Juniper of Wales'
Juniperus scopulorum	Moonglow Juniper
Leucothoe fontanesiana	Drooping Leucothoe
Mahonia aquifolium	Oregon Grape Holly
Mahonia bealei	Leatherleaf Mahonia
Microbiota decussata	Russian Cypress
Myrica pensylvanica	Bayberry
Pieris floribunda	Mountain Pieris
Pieris japonica	Japanese Pieris, Andromeda
Potentilla fruticosa	Bush Cinquefoil
Rhus aromatica	Fragrant Sumac
Sambucus racemosa	Red Elderberry
Sarcoccoca hookeriana	Sweet Box
Skimmia japonica	Japanese Skimmia
Viburnum dentatum	Arrowwood Viburnum

Trees

Aesculus parviflora	Bottlebrush Buckeye
Albizia julibrissin	Mimosa
Asimina triloba	Pawpaw

Betula nigra	River Birch
Betula papyrifera	Paper Birch
Cercidiphyllum japonicum	Katsura Tree
Ilex opaca	American Holly
Piceaglauca	'Conica' Dwarf Alberta Spruce
Pinus resinosa	Red Pine
Pinus rigida	Pitch Pine
Pinus thunbergiana	Japanese Black Pine

SECTION 4

MAST & BROWSE PLANTS

Some Common Mast & Browse Plants Preferred by White-Tailed Deer

SPRING

- American beautyberry
- Blackberry
- Blueberry
- Common persimmon
- Crabapple
- Flowering dogwood
- Greenbrier
- Hawthorn
- Japanese honeysuckle
- Oak
- Plumb

- Poison ivy & oak
- Polkweed
- Red maple
- Red mulberry
- Sassafras
- Virginia creeper
- Wild cherry
- Wild grape
- Willow
- Yellow popular

SUMMER

- American beautyberry
- Apple
- Aspen
- Blackberry
- Blueberry
- Elderberry
- Flowering dogwood
- Fringetree

- Greenbrier
- Japanese honeysuckle
- Jewelweed
- Pear
- Plumb
- Poison ivy & oak
- Polkweed
- Red mulberry

- Sassafras
- Strawberry bush
- Striped maple
- Sumac
- Virginia creeper

- Wild cherry
- Wild grape
- Wild rose
- Yellow popular

FALL

- American beautyberry
- American beech
- Blueberry
- Common persimmon
- Flowering dogwood
- Greenbrier
- Honey locust
- Japanese honeysuckle

- Oak
- Pecan
- Plum
- Red raspberry
- Sassafras
- Strawberry bush
- Sugar maple
- Sumac

WINTER

- American beech
- Aspen
- Blueberry
- Greenbrier
- Japanese honeysuckle
- Mushrooms
- Northern white cedar
- Oak

- Red maple
- Striped maple
- Sumac
- Yellow popular

How to Fertilize Mast-Producing Trees

Method #1. Granular Fertilizer

- Fertilizing a selected mast producing tree is more than a matter of scattering a handful of fertilizer at its base. There are two methods of fertilizing your selected trees. The first is the use of 13-13-13 granular fertilizer.

- This should be applied in early spring. Apply it at a rate of 2 pounds per 1000 square feet of crown. A mature white oak with a crown measuring 80 x 80 feet, or 6400 square feet, would require about 13 pounds of fertilizer.

- You want to apply the fertilizer from the edge of the drip line, that is the outer edge of the furthermost tips of branches from the tree trunk, to within three feet of the trunk of the tree.

- If there is a lot of leaves and limbs on the ground in the fertilized area, you will want to take a rake with you to rake them away so that the fertilizer will come in contact with the soil quickly.

Method #2. Fertilizer Sticks

- A second method is to purchase a box of fruit or shade tree fertilizer spikes at a nursery or garden supply store and follow the instructions on the box. They are more expensive than granular fertilizer but are easy to carry into the woods for use.

Results Take Time.

While this is a good way to increase the mast production of a selected tree, do not expect to see bushels of fruit appear on the tree the next fall. It is usually the third year with all the other things going right, such as no late spring frost, that you can see a significant increase in the fruit crop. Like most habitat management, it takes time. This, of course, is a long term project that requires fertilization every year.

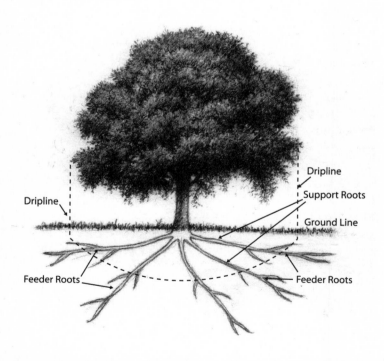

Planting Bareroot Seedlings

Most state forestry agencies offer both pine and hardwood tree, as well as shrub, bareroot seedlings at a reasonable price. The seedlings are grown in a nursery bed until ready to be transplanted and then they are lifted out without any soil around the roots and shipped to the landowner. They are usually shipped with moss or gel around the roots to keep them moist. Bareroot seedlings are less expensive than balled plants and much faster and easier to plant. When planted correctly they can help improve the deer habitat on property. Here is how to plant bareroot seedlings:

SPACING FOR PINES

For pine 6'X7' spacing is generally recommended and requires 1000 seedlings per acre. For creating a bedding area a spacing of 5'X5' (1700 seedlings per acre) is good.

For creating a corridor for deer a spacing of 6'X8' (900 seedlings per acre) is ideal.

SPACING FOR HARDWOODS

For hardwood trees such as oaks plant 40'X40' to allow for large crowns when the trees mature.

SPACING FOR SHRUBS

Follow instructions given by your state forester.

PLANTING

1. Insert bar 8" in soil and work a hole.

2. Place tree at correct depth.

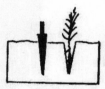

3. Insert bar 3" to 4" behind seedling.

4. Pull back to close hole at bottom.

5. Push forward to close hole at top.

6. Close second hole and firm soil with heel.

- Use a dibble to loosen the soil to a depth of a few inches deeper than the length of the roots.

- Plant seedlings to the same depth they were planted in the nursery. There will be a color change on the stem of the seedling at this point.

- Be sure the roots are pointing straight down and not bent into a J shape.

- Insert the dibble about 4-inches behind the seedling and pull back to close the hole. Push forward to close hole on top.

- Close second hole and firm soil with heel.

- Keep weed competition controlled the first two to three years.

- Use a tree shelter on hardwoods.

- Fertilizer will help bareroot hardwood or shrub seedlings become established.

Use Tree Shelters When Planting Hardwood Tree Seedlings

ADVANTAGES

- Protects seedlings from wildlife browsing and girdling

- Protects seedlings from damage from mowers and weed trimmers

- Help locate seedlings

- Simplify herbicide applications

- Improve survival

- Improved growth due to greenhouse effect

APPLICATION

- Tree shelters are long, tubular devices made of plastic, that are placed around hardwood tree seedlings for the first 3 – 5 years after planting.

- Tree shelters come in a variety of heights. Select the right height for your seedlings.

- Hardwood seedlings usually require a 48-inch tree shelter due to rapid growth.

- In areas where deer browsing is a problem the 72-inch shelter is better.

- Shorter tree shelters are available for protection from rabbits and small animals.

- Keep tree shelter around the seedling until it has grown well out the top, usually 3 to 5 years.

- Tree shelters are available from many garden stores, forestry supply stores or www.nwtf.com

Oaks Used by Deer

White oaks – acorns mature in 1 year, leaves have rounded tips on most species, bark gray in color, acorn meat white and usually sweet. Acorns preferred by deer over red oak acorns.

- **Eastern White Oak** – Quercus alba

- **Sawtooth Oak** – Quercus acutissma

- **Bur Oak** – Quercus macrocarpa

- **Overcup Oak** – Quercus lyrata

- **Post Oak** – Quercus stellata

- **Swamp Chestnut Oak** – Quercus prinus

- **Chestnut Oak** – Quercus montana

- **Swamp White Oak** – Quercus bicolor

- **Chinkapin Oak** – Quercus muehlenbergi

- **Oregon White Oak** – Quercus garryana

- **California White Oak** – Quercus lobata

- **English Oak** – Quercus robur

- **Durand Oak** – Quercus sinuata

- **Bluff oak** – Quercus austrina

- **Chapman Oak** – Quercus chapmanii

- **Basket Oak** – Quercus michauxii

- **Virginia Live Oak** – Quercus virginiana

- **Oglethorpe Oak** – Quercus oglethropensis

Red (black) oaks – Acorns require 2 years to mature, leaves usually have pointed tips, bark dark, acorn meat usually yellow and bitter.

- **Northern Red Oak** – Quercus rubra

- **Black Oak** – Quercus velutina

- **Shumard Oak** – Quercus shumardii

- **Southern Red Oak** – Quercus falcata

- **Swamp Red Oak, Cherrybark Oak** – Quercus falcata var.

- **Scarlet Oak** – Quercus coccinea

- **Pin Oak** – Quercus palustris

- **Northern Pin Oak, Jack Oak** – Quercus ellipsoidalis

- **Nuttall Oak** – Quercus texana

- **Blackjack Oak** – Quercus marilandica

- **Turkey Oak** – Quercus laevis

- **Buckley Oak** – Quercus buckleyi

- **Bear Oak** – Quercus ilicifolia

- **Georgia Oak** – Quercus georgiana

- **Arkansas Oak** – Quercus arkansana

- **Water Oak** – Quercus nigra

- **Shingle Oak** – Quercus imbricaria

- **Willow Oak** – Quercus phellos

- **Bluejack Oak, Sand Oak** – Quercus incana

- **Myrtle Oak** – Quercus myrtifolia

- **Sand Live Oak** – Quercus geminata

- **Laurel Oak** – Quercus laurifolia

Prescribed Burning Plan

One of the best deer habitat improvement tools in a pine forest
is the use of a controlled fire, called prescribed burning. This
intentional use of fire, usually in the late winter or early spring, does
several positive things:

- Burns natural litter from the forest floor allowing sunlight to
  hit the mineral soil.

- It scarifies seeds so they can sprout.

- It releases nutrients that can offer a quick production of
  grasses, legumes, forbs, and other plant materials that deer
  favor.

Prescribed burning for wildlife management is a precise science that
requires a lot of knowledge, skill, and planning. It is best to get your
local state forestry department involved if you think burning is what
your hunting property needs.

Assuming your pine trees are old enough to withstand a prescribed
burn and the land can be burned in several small units, here is an
example from Alabama of some of the things you will be required to
put into your burn plan before you can request a burn permit. Since
each state has different rules and regulations for prescribed burning
you will want to check with your local forester for your state's
requirements for a plan.

Minimum Standards for Prescribed Burn Plan

As Required under the Alabama Prescribed Burn Act

1. Personal information to include:

    a. Name of property owner

    b. Owner's mailing address

    c. Owner's phone number

    d. Same information on individual preparing the plan and/or executing the burn

    e. Prescribed burn manager certification number

2. Description of area to be burned:

    a. County

    b. Section, township, range

    c. Acres to be burned

    d. type and size of overstory

    e. Type and size of understory

    f. Fuel type and amount

    g. Topography

3. **Purpose of burn:**

4. **Pre-burn information to include:**

   a. Needed manpower and equipment

   b. Firing techniques to be used

   c. List of areas around site that could be adversely impacted by smoke from burn

   d. Special precautions taken

5. **Range of desired weather information to include:**

   a. Surface wind speed and direction

   b. Minimum and maximum relative humidity

   c. Maximum temperature

   d. Transport wind speed and direction

   e. minimum mixing height

   f. Dispersion index

6. **Starting time and completion of ignition**

7. **Sketch of area to be burned**

8. **Signature of Burn Manager, dated and notarized or witnessed**

9. **Burn Permit Number**

Make a Deer Corridor

Deer corridors are strips of heavy cover that connect deer bedding areas to deer feeding areas. They are natural funnels for older age class deer due to the fact they offer safe cover when traveling during daylight hours. Examples of naturally occurring corridors may include a wide, thickly vegetated fence row running between a plantation of young planted pines and a soy bean field, or a streamside management zone (SMZ) which is a wooded strip purposefully left after a timber harvest that runs along a stream and connects tracts of woodlands, or brushy ditch bank that runs between agricultural fields. Excellent corridors can be poorly drained areas that run between agricultural fields and lowlands.

Any strip of high growing, thick cover that gives a buck a sense of security when he is traveling during daylight hours can become a corridor; thus property with lots of corridors will generally have more daytime buck movement due to the buck feeling safe to move about in these areas.

If your property lacks corridors, you can create a system of corridors within a few years. Each corridor can become a great place to hunt.

- Start by planning your corridor system. Take a topo or aerial photo of your property and mark all known or suspected deer bedding areas. For mature bucks, this is usually the thickest areas. Swamps, wetlands, young planted pines and thick brushy areas are often choice bedding areas. Any thick area seldom hunted may be a bedding area.

- Next, mark deer feeding areas such as food plots, agricultural crops that offer highly desired food, patches of Japanese honeysuckle, Smilax, etc., or groves of mast producing trees. Connect the bedding areas to the food sources by following creeks, ditches, fence rows, or any natural depression running between the two. These are your potential corridor sites.

- With the corridor sites identified, the next step is to do whatever it takes to get the area to become grownup in thick trees, brush, and high grass. Give the bucks a strip, at least 10 yards wide and head high, of vegetated cover to travel in and feel safe. A small creek bank, in many areas, will become thick quickly with alder, gum trees, high grass and vines if it is not mowed or sprayed with herbicide. An un-mowed strip on either side of a ditch, gulley or fencerow will usually do the same.

- An annual application of 13-13-13 fertilizer at the rate of 300 pounds per acre broadcast throughout the corridor will help speed up the growth process.

- If you want to plant your selected strip in fast growing cover crops, consult your county agricultural agent to ascertain what works best in your area. Consider planted strips in autumn olive, blackberry, Japanese honeysuckle, switch grass and pines alone fencerows and ditches to create a corridor. Every now and then, plant a female persimmon, plum and crab apple to offer some soft mast in the corridor.

- If your property is open and flat not having a depression connecting bedding areas to food sources, you can plant a 10-yard wide strip of pines or cedars connecting the two areas. Within about three years, you will have a corridor that will get better each year.

Hunting corridors can be most productive for mature bucks but a word of caution is advised. Since most corridors are narrow, too much hunting pressure will cause the bucks to quit using the corridor during daylight hours. Develop as many corridors as you can on a tract of land; and after hunting a day or two in one corridor, change to another corridor giving each a non-hunting break of five or six days before hunting it again.

Restore Old Apple Trees

Many old farms and abandoned acreage had an orchard that contained a few apples. Often these old apple trees are still alive and may be bearing a little fruit each year. If so, they can be improved to produce more fruit and if they are not bearing fruit, with a little work they can be brought into production. Do this and you have a "food plot" in the middle of a prime buck area.

Here is a three-step way you can manage abandoned apple, pear or crabapple trees to bring them back into production for deer food.

Step-one – Tree selection

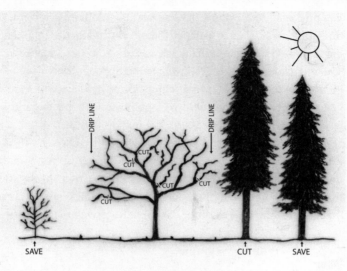

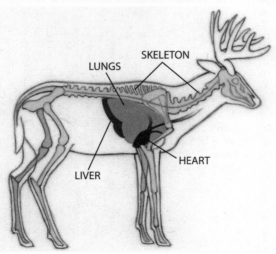

Examine each of the apple trees around the old farmstead. You may find apple trees in other parts of the old yard as they were often grown in several areas of many farmsteads. Select and mark with surveyors tape the healthiest trees. Remember apples require cross-pollination to bear fruit, so there must be an apple tree of another variety nearby. Also, they will cross-pollinate with a crabapple. Leave as many apple trees as you can for this reason.

Apple trees require lots of direct sunlight to produce fruit and they don't do well when there is a lot of competition from shrubs and trees growing under and near the tree. Remove all shrubs and trees that are growing next to, under or over shadowing the apple trees.

Step-two – Pruning, year one

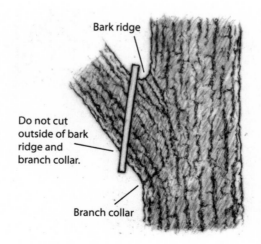

Bark ridge

Do not cut outside of bark ridge and branch collar.

Branch collar

Apples are produced on young fruiting wood and old unmanaged apple trees have lots of limbs and branches that are not fruit producers. Pruning will be necessary to reduce the amount of old wood, encourage the growth of new wood and get sunlight into the tree. It's well worth the effort as apple trees that have been managed for four or five years will produce three to four times the fruit of an unmanaged tree.

Always, plan on doing your annual pruning in the early spring, after the last frost, but before the tree blooms.

Start your pruning by removing all the dead branches and limbs from the tree. Using a pruning saw or pruning shears cut the dead limbs as close to the living tissue as possible.

Next, in the tree's canopy remove no more than one-third of the limbs to reduce the tree's height and to let more sunlight into the tree.

Fertilize the tree with 3 pounds of 6-24-24 fertilizer in a band spread around the drip line. Do this each year.

Step-three – Annual pruning

Open up thick clusters of small branches by pruning out those which are rubbing against one another, growing into one another, or have died. Never remove more than one-third of the live growth of the tree.

SECTION 5

HUNTING LEASE MANAGEMENT

LAND MEASUREMENTS

Basic Measurements

1 foot = 12 inches

1 yard = 3 feet

1 meter = 3.28 feet

1 rod = 16 ½ feet

1 furlong = 660 feet

1 chain = 66 feet

1 hectare = 2.471 acres

1 mile = 5280 feet

1 mile = 320 rods

1 sq. mile = 640 acres

1 sq. mile = 27,878,400 sq. feet

1 mile = 1760 yards

1 mile = 4840 sq. yards

1 mile = 43,560 sq. feet.

1 quarter section = 160 acres

1 section = 640 acres or 1 sq. mile

1 township 36 sq. miles

1 township = 6 miles sq.

1 cubic yard =27 cubic feet

1 cord of wood = 4X4X8 ft. or 128 cu. Ft.

1 cubic foot = 1728 cubic inches

1 bushel = 2150.42 cu. Inches

1 gallon = 231 cu. inches

1 cubic foot of water = 62.5 pounds

1 gallon of water = 8.33 pounds
1 gallon of gasoline = 6.0 pounds
1 gallon of fuel oil = 7.3 pounds

One Acre Measurements

1 acre = 43,560 sq. ft.
1 acre = 4,840 sq. yards.
1 acre = 160 sq. rods
1 acre = 6,272,640 sq. inches
1 acre = 1.1834 sq. arpents
1 acre = 160 perches
1 acre = 160 poles
1 acre = .4047 hectare
1 acre = 4047 sq. meters
1 acre square = 5645.376 sq. varas
1 acre = 165 ft. X 264 ft.
1 acre = 198 ft. X 220 ft.
1 acre = 66 feet X 660 feet
1 acre = 220 feet X 198 feet
1 sq. acre = 208.71 ft. X 208.71 ft.
An American football field is 1.32 acres

Arpent measurements vary by locality:

1 arpent (in LA, MS, AL, FL) = .84625 of an acre

1 arpent Square (in LA, MS, AL, FL) = 191.994 feet or 2.909 chains on each side

1 arpent (AR and MO) = .8507 of an acre

1 arpent Square (AR and MO) = 192.5 feet or 2.91667 chains on each side

1 caballeria (Texas-Spanish) = 108 acres

1 centimeter = .3937 inches
1 centimeter = .032808 feet

1 chain = 66 feet
1 chain = 4 rods
1 chain = 4 perches
1 chain = 4 poles
1 chain = 100 links
1 chain = 20.1168 meters

1 foot = 12 inches
1 foot = .36 varas
1 furlong = 660 feet
1 furlong = 40 rods

1 foot = 0.3048006 meter
1 hectare = 10,000 square meters
1 hectare = 2.471 acres

1 inch = .0254 meter

1 kilometer = 3280.83 feet
1 kilometer = .62 mile

1 knot = 6080.2 feet

1 labor (Texas-Spanish)= 1,000,000 square varas
1 labor = 177.136 acres

1 league (Texas-Spanish) = 25,000,000 square varas
1 league = 4428.4 acres

1 link = 7.92 inches
1 link = .66 feet
1 link = .2017 meter

1 meter = 3.280833 feet
1 meter = 39.37 inches

1 meter Square = 10.764 square feet
1 mile = 5,280 feet
1 mile = 8 furlongs
1 mile = 320 rods

1 mile = 80 chains
1 mile = 1.60935 kilometers
1 mile = 320 perches
1 mile = 320 poles
1 mile = 8000 links
1 mile = 1,609.2655 meters

1 mile Square = a regular section of land
1 mile Square = 27,878,400 square feet
1 mile Square = 640 acres
1 mile Square = 259 hectares
1 mile Square = 2.59 square hectares

1 perch = 25 links
1 perch = 1 pole
1 perch = 1 rod
1 perch = 16.5 feet

1 pole = 16.5 feet
1 pole = 1 perch
1 pole = 1 Rod

1 rod = 1 pole
1 rod = 1 perch
1 rod = 16.5 feet

1 section = 1 mile long, by 1 mile wide
1 section = 640 acres

1 sitio (Texas-Spanish) = 1 league

1 township = 6 miles long, by 6 miles wide
1 township = 36 sections
1 township = 36 square miles

Vara Measurements differ by locality:

1 vara (Texas-Spanish) = 33 1/3 inches
1 vara (Southern Colorado) = 32.993 inches
1 vara (Florida) = 33.372 inches

1 yard = 36 inches
1 yard = 3 feet

1 yard Square = 9 square feet

Pond Measurements

Surface Measurements

If the pond is rectangular or square, use the following formula:

Surface area, in acres =
length, in feet X width, in feet

43,560 sq ft per acre

Example: (Figure A)

$$\frac{80 \text{ feet} \times 140 \text{ feet}}{43,560 \text{ sq ft per acre}} \times \begin{array}{c} .2571 \text{ A, or} \\ \text{approximately} \\ 1/4 \text{ acre} \end{array}$$

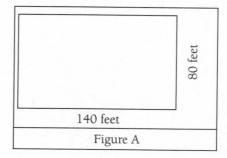

140 feet

80 feet

Figure A

If the pond is circular or nearly so, use this formula to determine surface area:

$$\text{Surface area, in acres} = \frac{(\text{total feet of shoreline}) \text{ squared}}{547,390}$$

Example: (Figure B)

$$\frac{(520 \text{ feet}) \times (520 \text{ feet})}{547,390} = \begin{array}{c} 0.4939 \text{ acre,} \\ \text{or approximately} \\ 1/2 \text{ acre} \end{array}$$

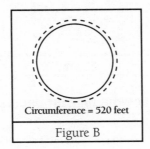

Circumference = 520 feet

Figure B

Many ponds are irregularly-shaped, which makes the area measurements more difficult. In this case, approximate the pond shape as either a square, rectangle or circle by measuring boundary lines that most nearly represent the actual shoreline.

Example: This pond shape can be approximated as a rectangle (Figure C).

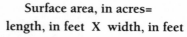

Surface area, in acres=
length, in feet X width, in feet
_____

43,560

$$= \frac{250 \text{ X } 120}{43,560} = 0.6887 \text{ acre}$$

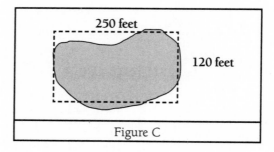

Figure C

Volume Measurements

Calculating the total volume of water in the pond is a two-step process:

Step 1: Determine average depth of the pond by taking uniformly-spaced soundings over the entire pond surface. This can be done from a boat, or during the winter when ice covers the entire surface. The measurements can be taken with a long pole, chain, or weighted rope marked off in feet. At least 15 measurements should be taken.

Add the measurements and divide by the number of measurements taken.

Example: Average depth =

$$\frac{2 + 3 + 5 + 8 + 9 + 1 + 4 + 6 + 9 + 0 + 1 + 2 + 3 + 3 + 8}{15}$$

$$= \frac{64}{15} = 4.27 \text{ feet}$$

Step 2: Once you have determined average depth and surface area, acre-feet are determined by multiplying the two measurements:

Volume, in acre-feet = Surface area, in acres X Average depth, in feet

Example: A 1.5-acre pond has an average depth of 4.27 feet.

Acre-feet = 1.5 acres X 4.27 feet = 6.405 acre-feet

Subdividing One Section of Land

20 chains = 80 rods	20 chains = 80 rods	40 chains = 160 rods				
W½ N W¼	E½ N W ¾	NE ¼				
80 acres	80 acres	160 acres				
1320 feet	1320 feet	2640 feet				
NW ¼ SW ¼ 40 acres	NE ¼ SW ¼ 40 acres	N½ NW¼ SE¼ 20 acres S½ NW¼ SE¼ 20 acres	W½ NE¼ SE ¼ 20 acres 10 chains	E½ NE¼ SE ¼ 20 acres 10 chains		
SW¼ SW¼ 40 acres = 80 rods	SE¼ SW¼ 40 acres = 440 yards	NW¼ SW¼ SE¼ 10 acres	NE¼ SW¼ SE¼ 10 acres	5 Acres		5 acs 20 rods
				5 acres 1 furlong	5 acs 5 chains	
		SW¼ SW¼ SE¼ 10 acres / 660 feet	SE¼ SW¼ SE¼ 10 acres/ 660 feet	2½ acs	2½ acs	10 acres equals 80 lots of 30' X 125'
				330 ft	330 ft	

SAMPLE LAND LEASE AGREEMENT

This sample is for information only and not a substitute for legal counsel since statutes pertaining to leasing varies from state to state.

This lease is entered into by and between
_____, hereinafter referred to as "Lessor"
and _____ hereinafter referred to as
"Lessee". By doing so, each agrees to the following provisions:

#1

Lessor does hereby lease, for the term and amount as per provisions #2 and #3, and subject to the reservations and conditions hereinafter set forth, the exclusive right to hunt on the following described tract of land located in _____County, _____State, and described as follows:

(LEGAL DESCRIPTION)

_____

_____

_____

_____

_____

_____

_____

_____

_____

_____

_____

_____

_____

_____

_____

_____

_____

_____

_____

_____

_____

_____

_____

_____

_____

_____

_____

#2

This lease shall be for a term of _____ years, commencing _____ (date) and terminating _____ (date) _____ unless sooner terminated pursuant to provisions of this agreement hereinafter set forth. Either the Lessor or the Lessee may cancel this agreement by giving written notice of its intent to do so ninety (90) days prior to the date that payment for the next year is due. In which event, Lessee shall be relieved of the obligation to pay further lease payments under the terms hereof and shall deliver possession of the premises.

#3

The consideration for which this lease is granted is an annual cash payment to be paid as follows, to-wit:

$_____ on execution hereof;

$_____on_____(date)_____;

$_____on_____(date)_____.

#4

Lessee agrees that it will not transfer, assign, or sublease in whole or in part this lease.

#5

Lessee agrees that all property of every kind, that may be on the premises during the continuance of this lease, whether same is property of Lessor or Lessee, shall be there at the sole risk of Lessee. Lessor shall not be liable to Lessee or to any other person for any injury, loss, or damage regardless of the nature thereof to any person or property on the leased premises. Lessee agrees to indemnify and hold harmless Lessor against any and all liability whatsoever for damages to any person or thing because of personal injury or property damage arising out of or resulting from Lessee's use and enjoyment of the privileges herein granted, whether said personal injury or property damage should result from accident, use of firearms, or otherwise occurring on the leased premises during or connected with any hunting, or any other activity organized or conducted by Lessee, its members, guests, servants or employees. In this connection, it is agreed that one of the terms and conditions under which the above premises is leased is that the Lessee assumes responsibility for the conditions of the premises and for any occurrences which happen thereon, including use of roads or other facilities constructed or maintained by Lessor.

Lessee shall, at Lessee's own expense, carry insurance for the duration of the lease as follows:

Comprehensive General Liability with minimum limits of $500,000 per person and $1,000,000 per occurrence for bodily injury and $150,000 for property damage.

A certificate indicating this insurance is in effect and a statement that the insurance carrier will not cancel without giving the Lessor 30 days notice must be filed with Lessor and shall be subject to Lessor's approval.

#6

Lessee will report all game harvested to the Lessor in order that long-term wildlife management programs may be carried out on the property.

#7

Lessee may camp or erect any type structure on this tract only after written approval of Lessor is obtained.

#8

Lessee agrees to take good care of the property and will be responsible for any damage to fields, farm equipment, livestock, fences, trees, roads, or structures.

#9

Lessee agrees to exercise extreme care in order that wild fires are avoided and to aid in the prevention and suppression of any fires encountered on the tract. All forest or grass fires will be reported to the county forest ranger promptly.

#10

The Lessee will abide by all county, state, and federal laws regarding hunting and fishing. Lessee shall be responsible for the conduct of Lessee's club members or guests. Any violation of the laws shall be considered just cause for immediate cancellation of this lease by Lessor, and no perorations of the lease payment previously paid shall be made.

#11

Lessee acknowledges that Lessor owns this tract of land primarily for the growing of agricultural crops and/or forest and Lessee shall not interfere with Lessor's forest management or farming operation. Lessor reserves the right in its sole discretion at any time to perform farming or forestry operations upon any or all portions of this tract. At any time there are forest management or farming workers on this tract, there will be a 300-yard "no hunting" zone in effect around the work area.

#12

Lessee agrees that it shall limit the total number of hunters on the tract at one time to one hunter per acres. All hunters must have on their person written permission to hunt signed by the Lessee.

#13

Lessee agrees that no nails, spikes, or metal objects will be screwed or driven into any trees on the premises for any purpose whatsoever, except that trees along property line may be used for boundary posting purposes, provided aluminum nails are used.

All hunting stands shall be portable and shall not be permanently affixed to or built in trees.

#14

Lessor reserves and shall have the right of ingress and egress into, over, and across the said lands during the term of this lease at any time and for any reason it may deem necessary or desirable. Lessor further reserves the right to build or to grant rights of way over, on, or under the leased premises for purpose which Lessor deems necessary.

#15

Lessee shall not construct any roads, food plots, or other improvements, or make alterations on said lands without prior written consent of Lessor.

#16

Lessor reserves the right to deny access to the leased premises to any person or persons for any of the following reasons: carelessness with guns, violations of game and fish laws, trespassing on property of adjoining landowners, acts which could reasonably be expected to strain relations with adjoining landowners, acts which hinder forestry or farming operations on Lessor or its grantees, or any other activities which to the ordinary person would be considered unsafe, objectionable, offensive, or to cause embarrassment to Lessor or be detrimental to the Lessor's interest. Failure of Lessee to expel or deny access to the premises to any person or persons after being notified to do so by Lessor may result in the termination of this lease at discretion of Lessor.

#17

Modifications of this lease shall be made in writing and signed copies of same will be attached to the original lease.

#18

Special Provisions: _____

_____

_____

_____

_____

_____

_____

_____

_____

_____

_____

_____

_____

_____

_____

Thus done and signed on this_____ day of
_____, 20____in the presence of the undersigned
witnesses.

WITNESSES: LESSOR:

_____   _____

_____   _____

WITNESSES: LESSEE:

_____   _____

_____   _____

SAMPLE

Release of Liability and Acknowledgement
of Dangers, Risks, and Hazards Of Hunting on
Name and address of Property

This is my acknowledgment that this document is sufficient
warning that natural and man-made dangerous conditions, risks,
and hazards do exist on this property. My presence and activities on
the premises expose me and my property to dangerous conditions,
risks, and hazards, including but not limited to the following:
elevated hunting stands, whether or not erected by the landowners;
shooting activities; poisonous snakes, insects, and spiders; use of
all-terrain vehicles and tractors; use of target throwing equipment;
hazardous and dangerous driving and walking conditions; animals
both wild and domesticated that may be potentially dangerous;
deep and/or swift water; persons with firearms both on or off the
premises; and the use of vehicles. I hereby state that I expressly
assume all such dangers, risks, and hazards.

In consideration for the rights to enter the premises, I hereby release
and agree to protect, indemnify, and hold harmless the landowners
and their respective agents, employees, employers, and assigns
from and against any and all claims, demands, causes of action, and
damages, including attorneys' fees, resulting from any accident,
incident, or occurrence arising out of, incidental to, or in any way
resulting from the use of the premises and improvements thereon,
whether or not caused by the landowners' negligence or gross

negligence. This release applies during the time that I am permitted on the premises. I hereby further covenant and agree that heirs, my successors, assigns, and I will not make any claim or institute any suit or action at law or in equity against the landowners or their respective heirs, agents, representatives, employees, successors, or assigns.

As used in this release, the terms *I, my person,* and *myself* include minors in my care while on the premises.

Dated and signed this_____ day
of_____,20_____

_____

(Signature)

_____

(Printed Name)

_____

Address:

Sample Deer Cooperative Agreement

1. _____   _____

    Landowner's name   _Date_

    _____   _____

    Address   _Telephone Number_

    _____   _____

    City   _State_   _Zip Code_

2. I am the owner or authorized agent of tract or tracts of land located on county/state road

    _____ containing _____ acres,

    _____ containing _____ acres,

    _____ containing _____ acres.

3. I agree to cooperate with the goals and bylaws of the Cross Creek Deer Management Co-op.

4. This agreement does not give any unauthorized person the right to trespass on above listed property.

5. I am in no way obligated to the Cross Creek Management Co-op. I agree with the management practices recommended and will require all hunting on my property to follow the agreed upon deer management plan.

6. This agreement is valid for the life of the co-op unless revoked in writing.

7. Annual membership dues are $5.00 which will be used for postage, advertisement, and educational programs.

_____

_____

Signature of Landowner/Agent

Sample Hunt Club Bylaws

Article I

The name of this organization shall be:

_____ .

Article II: PURPOSE

1. To abide by all requirements of the landowner;

2. To abide by all federal and state game laws and seasons;

3. To establish, foster, and promote an organization that provides an equitable, enjoyable, and harmonious outdoor environment for all club members; and

4. To participate in and promote a quality deer management program and management of all other wildlife species.

Article III: GOVERNING BODY

1. Directors

A. The affairs and business of this club shall be conducted by the board of directors. The board of directors will consist of at least five (5) directors who will each serve for a period of year(s), or until such time as a successor in office has been duly elected and qualified to succeed him.

B. The officers of the club (President, VicePresident, Secretary and Treasurer) shall be elected annually.

C. The board of directors shall be elected by majority vote of the membership present at a called meeting. If an elected board member is unable to complete his term, the club shall elect another director to complete the rest of the term.

D. The board of directors is authorized to act on behalf of the club in all matters of club business, including (but not limited to) the following:

   1) Propose rules and rule changes for the club. Any rule or rule change must be approved by 2/3 (67%) vote of club membership present at a called meeting.

   2) Discipline any member, including dropping that member from the club.

3) Make any decision/restriction necessary regarding the deer management program on the club.

4) Assign committees, call work days, etc. so that all members participate in the working needs of the club.

5) Set annual dues and assessments as required for lease payment and annual operation of the club.

E. The duties of the officers shall be as follows:

1) **President** – presides over all board and club meetings and functions.

2) **Vice President** – preside over all board and club meetings and functions in the absence of the President. Assume the position of the President should the elected President be unable to complete his term.

3) **Secretary** – record minutes for all board and club meetings. Handle all correspondence between club and landowner.

4) **Treasurer** – handle all income, payments and expenditures on behalf of the club.

Article IV: MEMBERSHIP

1. Membership of Club is limited to a maximum of 25 members.

2. A member may participate and/or vote in any called meeting by being present at the meeting or by submitting a written and signed proxy before the meeting. A quorum for purposes of voting at a called meeting will be set at 51% of the total membership or represented by proxy.

3. A member is responsible for his guest(s) and their actions.

4. All members and their guests must register at the camp, the purpose of their visit to the club, and all game harvested on club property in the log book at camp. All required deer data must be recorded for all deer harvested on the club.

5. The club reserves the right to expel, by a majority vote of 2/3 (67%) of the members present at a called meeting, any member for good cause or who does not conform to the stated purpose of the club. All club members must be notified in writing at least 10 days prior to a meeting called for this purpose. Any member expelled by he club forfeits all dues and is not due any compensation from the club.

6. A prospective membership list will be maintained by the Board of Directors for the purpose of evaluating prospective new

members and filling vacancies with the club. All prospective new members must complete an Application for Membership.

7. A prospective new member must be approved by a majority vote of 2/3 (67%) of the membership present at a called meeting. If approved, a prospective new member will be admitted on a probationary basis for a period of one (1) year. Upon completion of the probationary year, he will be evaluated to full membership status or be dismissed from the club.

Article V: CARE OF PROPERTY

1. Each member will show the utmost courtesy and respect for the lease landowner and adjoining landowners' property. Gates must be kept closed at all times.

Article VI: GUESTS

1. A guest is defined as any non-club member brought onto club property by a member.

2. During non-hunting seasons, there are no guest restrictions.

3. All guests must be accompanied by a member while on club property. All guests 15 years of age and younger must be within view of the member while hunting any game.

Article VII: FINANCES

1. The board of directors shall be authorized to make payment from club treasury all expenses necessary to operate the club. Any individual expense that exceeds $250.00 must be approved by 2/3 (67%) of club membership.

2. All checks written for Hunting Club must be signed by two (2) directors.

3. As of September 1 of each year, dues must be fully paid in order to maintain club membership.

Article VIII: AMENDMENTS

Any proposed change in bylaws must be approved by a majority vote of 3/4 (75%) of club members present at a called meeting.

Article IX: CLUB PRIDE

Hunting Club is more than a place to hunt – it is a fellowship of responsible sportsmen who belong to a special club. It is a privilege and an honor to be in the Club; each member should be cognizant and proud of this fact, and should do their fair share to make the club a better place for all.

Article X: RULES AND REGULATIONS

1. Rules and Regulations for Club and Amendments to these rules and regulations must be approved by 2/3 (67%) vote of the membership present at a called meeting.

2. Consumption of alcoholic beverages at any time of the day eliminates that member for the remainder of that day's hunt. Consumption of alcoholic beverages after 12:01 a.m. disqualifies any member from that day's hunt.

3. No firearm will be allowed in the camp house with a shell in the chamber or the magazine. No firearm will be allowed in the camp yard with a shell in the chamber. A muzzleloader must have the percussion cap removed from the nipple.

4. No trespassing on any adjacent landowner/club. If tracking a wounded deer, notify a board member (if present) or another member before crossing the property/club line.

5. All permanent deer stands will be marked on the stand map. Stands being hunted must be so indicated on the stand map.

6. Main roads (all vehicles, ATV roads, foot travel only roads, and parking areas will be designated on the club. No vehicle is to be used on any non-designated road except in an emergency or during workdays. ATV vehicles may be used on foot travel only roads to set up stands and/or retrieve deer.

7. A member should not knowingly go by a stand occupied by
    another member between daylight and 9:00 a.m. and between
    3:30 p.m. and dark, except any stand located adjacent to an all
    vehicle main road.

8. Tree stands will not be fastened to trees with any metal device,
    including, but not limited to, nails, screws, and wire, but may
    be tied to trees with rope. Chains and binders may be used
    to secure tree stands on a temporary basis, but these must be
    removed from the tree immediately after the hunting season.

Deer Observation Form

Date	Total Observation Time	Deer Sighted				Location/ Behavior/ comments
		# Antlered Bucks	# Does	# Fawns	# unknown sex/age	

Topographical (TOPO) Map Symbols

BATHYMETRIC FEATURES

Area exposed at mean low tide; sounding datum line***	
Channel***	
Sunken rock***	

BOUNDARIES

National	
State or territorial	
County or equivalent	
Civil township or equivalent	
Incorporated city or equivalent	
Federally administered park, reservation, or monument (external)	
Federally administered park, reservation, or monument (internal)	
State forest, park, reservation, or monument and large county park	
Forest Service administrative area*	
Forest Service ranger district*	
National Forest System land status, Forest Service lands*	
National Forest System land status, non-Forest Service lands*	
Small park (county or city)	

BUILDINGS AND RELATED FEATURES

Building	
School; house of worship	
Athletic field	
Built-up area	
Forest headquarters*	
Ranger district office*	
Guard station or work center*	
Racetrack or raceway	
Airport, paved landing strip, runway, taxiway, or apron	
Unpaved landing strip	
Well (other than water), windmill or wind generator	
Tanks	
Covered reservoir	
Gaging station	
Located or landmark object (feature as labeled)	
Boat ramp or boat access*	
Roadside park or rest area	
Picnic area	
Campground	
Winter recreation area*	
Cemetery	

COASTAL FEATURES

Foreshore flat	
Coral or rock reef	
Rock, bare or awash; dangerous to navigation	
Group of rocks, bare or awash	
Exposed wreck	
Depth curve; sounding	
Breakwater, pier, jetty, or wharf	
Seawall	
Oil or gas well; platform	

CONTOURS

Topographic

Index	
Approximate or indefinite	
Intermediate	
Approximate or indefinite	
Supplementary	
Depression	
Cut	
Fill	
Continental divide	

Bathymetric

Index***	
Intermediate***	
Index primary***	
Primary***	
Supplementary***	

CONTROL DATA AND MONUMENTS

Principal point**	
U.S. mineral or location monument	
River mileage marker	

Boundary monument

Third-order or better elevation, with tablet	
Third-order or better elevation, recoverable mark, no tablet	
With number and elevation	

Horizontal control

Third-order or better, permanent mark	
With third-order or better elevation	
With checked spot elevation	
Coincident with found section corner	
Unmonumented**	

CONTROL DATA AND MONUMENTS – *continued*

Vertical control

Third-order or better elevation, with tablet	BM $\times$ 5280
Third-order or better elevation, recoverable mark, no tablet	$\times$ 528
Bench mark coincident with found section corner	BM + 5280
Spot elevation	$\times$ 7523

GLACIERS AND PERMANENT SNOWFIELDS

Contours and limits	
Formlines	
Glacial advance	
Glacial retreat	

LAND SURVEYS

Public land survey system

Range or Township line	
Location approximate	
Location doubtful	
Protracted	
Protracted (AK 1:63,360-scale)	
Range or Township labels	R1E T2N R3W 14S
Section line	
Location approximate	
Location doubtful	
Protracted	
Protracted (AK 1:63,360-scale)	
Section numbers	1 - 36 1 - 36
Found section corner	+
Found closing corner	+
Witness corner	WC +
Meander corner	MC
Weak corner*	+

Other land surveys

Range or Township line	
Section line	
Land grant, mining claim, donation land claim, or tract	
Land grant, homestead, mineral, or other special survey monument	
Fence or field lines	

MARINE SHORELINES

Shoreline	
Apparent (edge of vegetation)***	
Indefinite or unsurveyed	

MINES AND CAVES

Quarry or open pit mine	$\times$
Gravel, sand, clay, or borrow pit	$\times$
Mine tunnel or cave entrance	
Mine shaft	
Prospect	X
Tailings	(Tailings)
Mine dump	
Former disposal site or mine	

PROJECTION AND GRIDS

Neatline	39°15' 90°37'30"
Graticule tick	55'
Graticule intersection	
Datum shift tick	

State plane coordinate systems

Primary zone tick	640 000 FEET
Secondary zone tick	247 500 METERS
Tertiary zone tick	260 000 METERS
Quaternary zone tick	98 500 METERS
Quintary zone tick	320 000 FEET

Universal transverse mercator grid

UTM grid (full grid)	273
UTM grid ticks*	269

RAILROADS AND RELATED FEATURES

Standard guage railroad, single track	
Standard guage railroad, multiple track	
Narrow guage railroad, single track	
Narrow guage railroad, multiple track	
Railroad siding	
Railroad in highway	
Railroad in road	
Railroad in light duty road*	
Railroad underpass; overpass	
Railroad bridge; drawbridge	
Railroad tunnel	
Railroad yard	
Railroad turntable; roundhouse	

RIVERS, LAKES, AND CANALS

Perennial stream	
Perennial river	
Intermittent stream	
Intermittent river	
Disappearing stream	
Falls, small	
Falls, large	
Rapids, small	
Rapids, large	
Masonry dam	
Dam with lock	
Dam carrying road	

RIVERS, LAKES, AND CANALS – continued

Perennial lake/pond	
Intermittent lake/pond	
Dry lake/pond	
Narrow wash	
Wide wash	
Canal, flume, or aqueduct with lock	
Elevated aqueduct, flume, or conduit	
Aqueduct tunnel	
Water well, geyser, fumarole, or mud pot	
Spring or seep	

ROADS AND RELATED FEATURES
Please note: Roads on Provisional-edition maps are not classified as primary, secondary, or light duty. These roads are all classified as improved roads and are symbolized the same as light duty roads.

Primary highway	
Secondary highway	
Light duty road	
Light duty road, paved*	
Light duty road, gravel*	
Light duty road, dirt*	
Light duty road, unspecified*	
Unimproved road	
Unimproved road*	
4WD road	
4WD road*	
Trail	
Highway or road with median strip	
Highway or road under construction	Under Const
Highway or road underpass; overpass	
Highway or road bridge; drawbridge	
Highway or road tunnel	
Road block, berm, or barrier*	
Gate on road*	
Trailhead*	

SUBMERGED AREAS AND BOGS

Marsh or swamp	
Submerged marsh or swamp	
Wooded marsh or swamp	
Submerged wooded marsh or swamp	
Land subject to inundation	Max Pool 431

SURFACE FEATURES

Levee	Levee
Sand or mud	Sand
Disturbed surface	
Gravel beach or glacial moraine	Gravel
Tailings pond	Tailings

TRANSMISSION LINES AND PIPELINES

Power transmission line; pole; tower	
Telephone line	Telephone
Aboveground pipeline	
Underground pipeline	Pipeline

VEGETATION

Woodland	
Shrubland	
Orchard	
Vineyard	
Mangrove	Mangrove

* USGS-USDA Forest Service Single-Edition Quadrangle maps only.
In August 1993, the U.S. Geological Survey and the U.S. Department of Agriculture's Forest Service signed an Interagency Agreement to begin a single-edition joint mapping program. This agreement established the coordination for producing and maintaining single-edition primary series topographic maps for quadrangles containing National Forest System lands. The joint mapping program eliminates duplication of effort by the agencies and results in a more frequent revision cycle for quadrangles containing National Forests. Maps are revised on the basis of jointly developed standards and contain normal features mapped by the USGS, as well as additional features required for efficient management of National Forest System lands. Single-edition maps look slightly different but meet the content, accuracy, and quality criteria of other USGS products.

** Provisional-Edition maps only.
Provisional-edition maps were established to expedite completion of the remaining large-scale topographic quadrangles of the conterminous United States. They contain essentially the same level of information as the standard series maps. This series can be easily recognized by the title "Provisional Edition" in the lower right-hand corner.

*** Topographic Bathymetric maps only.

Weather Map Symbols

CLOUD COVERAGE

○	clear	◕	5/8
①	1/10	◗	broken
◔	scattered	◗	9/10
◑	3/8	●	overcast
◑	1/2	⊗	sky obscured

FRONTS

cold
warm
stationary
occluded
dry line

WIND SPEED

◎ calm
―――― 1-2 knots (1-2 mph)
3-7 knots (3-8 mph)
8-12 knots (9-14 mph)
13-17 knots (15-20 mph)

18-22 knots (21-25 mph)
23-27 knots (26-31 mph)
48-52 knots (55-60 mph)
73-77 knots (84-89 mph)
103-107 knots (119-123 mph)

SELECTED WEATHER SYMBOLS

● rain
▽ rain shower
thunderstorm
drizzle
blowing snow
H high air pressure

★ snow
▽ snow shower
freezing rain
freezing drizzle
↔ ice crystals
L low air pressure

= fog
∞ haze
smoke
dust or sand
△ hail

CLOUD TYPES

scattered cirrus
dense cirrus
cirrostratus
heavy cirrostratus
cirrus & cirrostratus
altostratus

stratocumulus
fair weather cumulus
developing cumulus
cumulonimbus
cirrocumulus
stratus

SECTION 6

FIREARMS

White Tail Deer Ballistic Tables

Ballistics tables are provided in the following pages from the following manufacturers:

- Federal Premium Ammunition
- Remington
- Winchester Ammunition

All information is used with kind permission of the manufacturers. Consult their websites for additional information on their products.

Federal Premium Ammunition
www.federalpremium.com

Remington
www.remington.com

Winchester Ammunition
www.winchester.com

Federal Ballistics Charts

PREMIUM VITAL SHOK RIFLE BALLISTICS

243 Win. (6.16x51mm)

Bullet Style	Sierra GameKing BTHP						
Bullet Weight	85 grains.						
Velocity (fps)	Muzzle	100	200	300	400	500	-
	3300	2980	2680	2410	2140	1900	-
Energy (ft-lb)	Muzzle	100	200	300	400	500	-
	2055	1675	1360	1090	870	680	-
Short-Range Trajectory (yds)	50	100	200	300	-	-	-
	-0.3	zero	-2.4	-9.7	-	-	-
Long-Range Trajectory (yds)	50	100	200	300	400	500	-
	0.3	1.2	zero	-6.0	-18.2	-37.7	-

243 Win. (6.16x51mm)

Bullet Style	Barnes Triple-Shock X-Bullet						
Bullet Weight	85 grains.						
Velocity (fps)	Muzzle	100	200	300	400	500	-
	3200	2900	2630	2370	2120	1890	-
Energy (ft-lb)	Muzzle	100	200	300	400	500	-
	1935	1590	1305	1055	850	675	-
Short-Range Trajectory (yds)	50	100	200	300	-	-	-
	-0.3	zero	-2.7	-10.3	-	-	-
Long-Range Trajectory (yds)	50	100	200	300	400	500	-
	0.4	1.3	zero	-6.3	-19.0	-39.2	-

243 Win. (6.16x51mm)

Bullet Style	Nosler Ballistic Tip						
Bullet Weight	95 grains.						
Velocity (fps)	Muzzle	100	200	300	400	500	-
	3025	2770	2540	2310	2100	1890	-
Energy (ft-lb)	Muzzle	100	200	300	400	500	-
	1930	1625	1355	1125	925	755	-
Short-Range Trajectory (yds)	50	100	200	300	-	-	-
	-0.2	zero	-3.0	-11.5	-	-	-
Long-Range Trajectory (yds)	50	100	200	300	400	500	-
	0.5	1.5	zero	-6.9	-20.4	-41.6	-

243 Win. (6.16x51mm)

Bullet Style	Nosler Partition*						
Bullet Weight	100 grains.						
Velocity (fps)	Muzzle	100	200	300	400	500	-
	2850	2610	2390	2170	1970	1780	-
Energy (ft-lb)	Muzzle	100	200	300	400	500	-
	1805	1515	1265	1045	860	700	-
Short-Range Trajectory (yds)	50	100	200	300	-	-	-
	-0.2	zero	-3.6	-13.4	-	-	-
Long-Range Trajectory (yds)	50	100	200	300	400	500	-
	0.7	1.8	zero	-8.0	-23.3	-47.6	-

243 Win. (6.16x51mm)

Bullet Style	Sierra GameKing BTSP						
Bullet Weight	100 grains.						
Velocity (fps)	Muzzle	100	200	300	400	500	-
	2960	2740	2530	2330	2150	1960	-
Energy (ft-lb)	Muzzle	100	200	300	400	500	-
	1945	1670	1425	1210	1020	855	-
Short-Range Trajectory (yds)	50	100	200	300	-	-	-
	-0.2	zero	-3.1	-11.7	-	-	-
Long-Range Trajectory (yds)	50	100	200	300	400	500	-
	0.6	1.6	zero	-7.0	-20.4	-41.3	-

6mm Rem.

Bullet Style	Barnes Triple Shock X-Bullet						
Bullet Weight	85 grains.						
Velocity (fps)	Muzzle	100	200	300	400	500	-
	3350	3040	2760	2490	2240	2000	-
Energy (ft-lb)	Muzzle	100	200	300	400	500	-
	2120	1750	1435	1170	945	755	-
Short-Range Trajectory (yds)	50	100	200	300	-	-	-
	-0.3	zero	-2.3	-9.1	-	-	-
Long-Range Trajectory (yds)	50	100	200	300	400	500	-
	0.2	1.1	zero	-5.7	-17.0	-35.3	-

6mm Rem.

Bullet Style	Nosler Partition*						
Bullet Weight	100 grains.						
Velocity (fps)	Muzzle	100	200	300	400	500	-
	3100	2850	2610	2380	2170	1970	-
Energy (ft-lb)	Muzzle	100	200	300	400	500	-
	2135	1800	1515	1260	1045	860	-
Short-Range Trajectory (yds)	50	100	200	300	-	-	-
	-0.3	zero	-2.8	-10.7	-	-	-
Long-Range Trajectory (yds)	50	100	200	300	400	500	-
	0.4	1.4	zero	-6.5	-19.2	-39.2	-

257 Roberts +P

Bullet Style	Nosler Partition						
Bullet Weight	120 grains.						
Velocity (fps)	Muzzle	100	200	300	400	500	-
	2800	2570	2350	2140	1940	1760	-
Energy (ft-lb)	Muzzle	100	200	300	400	500	-
	2090	1760	1470	1220	1005	820	-
Short-Range Trajectory (yds)	50	100	200	300	-	-	-
	-0.1	zero	-3.8	-13.9	-	-	-
Long-Range Trajectory (yds)	50	100	200	300	400	500	-
	0.8	1.9	zero	-8.3	-24.0	-49.2	-

25-06 Rem.

Bullet Style	Barnes Triple-Shock X-Bullet						
Bullet Weight	100 grains.						
Velocity (fps)	Muzzle	100	200	300	400	500	-
	3210	2970	2750	2540	2330	2140	-
Energy (ft-lb)	Muzzle	100	200	300	400	500	-
	2290	1965	1680	1430	1205	1015	-
Short-Range Trajectory (yds)	50	100	200	300	-	-	-
	-0.3	zero	-2.4	-9.5	-	-	-
Long-Range Trajectory (yds)	50	100	200	300	400	500	-
	0.3	1.2	zero	-5.8	-17.0	-34.8	-

25-06 Rem.

Bullet Style	Nosler Ballistic Tip						
Bullet Weight	100 grains.						
Velocity (fps)	Muzzle	100	200	300	400	500	-
	3220	2970	2730	2500	2290	2080	-
Energy (ft-lb)	Muzzle	100	200	300	400	500	-
	2300	1955	1655	1390	1160	965	-
Short-Range Trajectory (yds)	50	100	200	300	-	-	-
	-0.3	zero	-2.5	-9.6	-	-	-
Long-Range Trajectory (yds)	50	100	200	300	400	500	-
	0.3	1.2	zero	-5.9	-17.3	-35.5	-

25-06 Rem.

Bullet Style	Nosler Partition						
Bullet Weight	115 grains.						
Velocity (fps)	Muzzle	100	200	300	400	500	-
	3030	2790	2550	2330	2120	1930	-
Energy (ft-lb)	Muzzle	100	200	300	400	500	-
	2345	1980	1665	1390	1150	945	-
Short-Range Trajectory (yds)	50	100	200	300	-	-	-
	-0.2	zero	-3.0	-11.3	-	-	-
Long-Range Trajectory (yds)	50	100	200	300	400	500	-
	0.5	1.5	zero	-6.8	-20.1	-40.9	-

25-06 Rem.

Bullet Style	Sierra GameKing BTSP						
Bullet Weight	117 grains.						
Velocity (fps)	Muzzle	100	200	300	400	500	-
	3030	2800	2580	2370	2170	1980	-
Energy (ft-lb)	Muzzle	100	200	300	400	500	-
	2385	2035	1725	1455	1220	1015	-
Short-Range Trajectory (yds)	50	100	200	300	-	-	-
	-0.2	zero	-3.0	-11.1	-	-	-
Long-Range Trajectory (yds)	50	100	200	300	400	500	-
	0.5	1.5	zero	-6.7	-19.7	-40.0	-

260 Rem.

Bullet Style	Barnes Triple-Shock X-Bullet						
Bullet Weight	120 grains.						
Velocity (fps)	Muzzle	100	200	300	400	500	-
	2930	2690	2450	2240	2030	1830	-
Energy (ft-lb)	Muzzle	100	200	300	400	500	-
	2285	1920	1605	1330	1095	890	-
Short-Range Trajectory (yds)	50	100	200	300	-	-	-
	-0.2	zero	-3.3	-12.4	-	-	-
Long-Range Trajectory (yds)	50	100	200	300	400	500	-
	0.6	1.7	zero	-7.5	-21.9	-44.7	-

260 Rem.

Bullet Style	Nosler Ballistic Tip						
Bullet Weight	120 grains.						
Velocity (fps)	Muzzle	100	200	300	400	500	-
	2950	2730	2510	2310	2110	1930	-
Energy (ft-lb)	Muzzle	100	200	300	400	500	-
	2320	1980	1680	1420	1190	990	-
Short-Range Trajectory (yds)	50	100	200	300	-	-	-
	-0.2	zero	-3.2	-11.9	-	-	-
Long-Range Trajectory (yds)	50	100	200	300	400	500	-
	0.6	1.6	zero	-7.1	-20.8	-42.1	-

260 Rem.

Bullet Style	Sierra GameKing BTSP						
Bullet Weight	140 grains.						
Velocity (fps)	Muzzle	100	200	300	400	500	-
	2700	2490	2280	2090	1910	1730	-
Energy (ft-lb)	Muzzle	100	200	300	400	500	-
	2265	1920	1620	1360	1130	935	-
Short-Range Trajectory (yds)	50	100	200	300	-	-	-
	-0.1	zero	-4.1	-15.0	-	-	-
Long-Range Trajectory (yds)	50	100	200	300	400	500	-
	0.9	2.1	zero	-8.8	-25.3	-51.9	-

270 Win.

Bullet Style	Barnes Tipped Triple-Shock X-Bullet						
Bullet Weight	110 grains.						
Velocity (fps)	Muzzle	100	200	300	400	500	-
	3400	3130	2870	2620	2390	2180	-
Energy (ft-lb)	Muzzle	100	200	300	400	500	-
	2825	2385	2010	1680	1400	1155	-
Short-Range Trajectory (yds)	50	100	200	300	-	-	-
	-0.3	zero	-2.1	-8.4	-	-	-
Long-Range Trajectory (yds)	50	100	200	300	400	500	-
	0.2	1.0	zero	-5.3	-15.6	-32.1	-

270 Win.

Bullet Style	Trophy Bonded Tip						
Bullet Weight	130 grains.						
Velocity (fps)	Muzzle	100	200	300	400	500	-
	3060	2840	2630	2430	2240	2060	-
Energy (ft-lb)	Muzzle	100	200	300	400	500	-
	2705	2330	2000	1710	1455	1230	-
Short-Range Trajectory (yds)	50	100	200	300	-	-	-
	-0.3	zero	-2.8	-10.6	-	-	-
Long-Range Trajectory (yds)	50	100	200	300	400	500	-
	0.5	1.4	zero	-6.4	-18.7	-38.0	-

270 Win.

Bullet Style	Sierra GameKing BTSP						
Bullet Weight	130 grains.						
Velocity (fps)	Muzzle	100	200	300	400	500	-
	3060	2840	2630	2430	2240	2060	-
Energy (ft-lb)	Muzzle	100	200	300	400	500	-
	2705	2325	1995	1705	1445	1220	-
Short-Range Trajectory (yds)	50	100	200	300	-	-	-
	-0.3	zero	-2.8	-10.7	-	-	-
Long-Range Trajectory (yds)	50	100	200	300	400	500	-
	0.5	1.4	zero	-6.4	-18.8	-38.1	-

270 Win.

Bullet Style	Nosler Ballistic Tip						
Bullet Weight	130 grains.						
Velocity (fps)	Muzzle	100	200	300	400	500	-
	3060	2840	2630	2420	2230	2050	-
Energy (ft-lb)	Muzzle	100	200	300	400	500	-
	2705	2325	1990	1695	1435	1210	-
Short-Range Trajectory (yds)	50	100	200	300	-	-	-
	-0.3	zero	-2.9	-10.7	-	-	-
Long-Range Trajectory (yds)	50	100	200	300	400	500	-
	0.5	1.4	zero	-6.4	-18.8	-38.2	-

270 Win.

Bullet Style	Barnes Triple-Shock X-Bullet						
Bullet Weight	130 grains.						
Velocity (fps)	Muzzle	100	200	300	400	500	-
	3060	2840	2630	2420	2230	2040	-
Energy (ft-lb)	Muzzle	100	200	300	400	500	-
	2705	2325	1990	1695	1435	1205	-
Short-Range Trajectory (yds)	50	100	200	300	-	-	-
	-0.3	zero	-2.9	-10.7	-	-	-
Long-Range Trajectory (yds)	50	100	200	300	400	500	-
	0.5	1.4	zero	-6.4	-18.8	-38.3	-

270 Win.

Bullet Style	Nosler Partition						
Bullet Weight	130 grains.						
Velocity (fps)	Muzzle	100	200	300	400	500	-
	3060	2830	2610	2400	2200	2010	-
Energy (ft-lb)	Muzzle	100	200	300	400	500	-
	2705	2310	1965	1665	1400	1170	-
Short-Range Trajectory (yds)	50	100	200	300	-	-	-
	-0.2	zero	-2.9	-10.8	-	-	-
Long-Range Trajectory (yds)	50	100	200	300	400	500	-
	0.5	1.4	zero	-6.5	-19.1	-38.8	-

270 Win.

Bullet Style	Trophy Bonded Tip						
Bullet Weight	130 grains.						
Velocity (fps)	Muzzle	100	200	300	400	500	-
	3200	2970	2760	2560	2360	2170	-
Energy (ft-lb)	Muzzle	100	200	300	400	500	-
	2955	2555	2200	1885	1610	1365	-
Short-Range Trajectory (yds)	50	100	200	300	-	-	-
	-0.3	zero	-2.4	-9.5	-	-	-
Long-Range Trajectory (yds)	50	100	200	300	400	500	-
	0.3	1.2	zero	-5.8	-16.9	-34.3	-

270 Win.

Bullet Style	Nosler AccuBond						
Bullet Weight	140 grains.						
Velocity (fps)	Muzzle	100	200	300	400	500	-
	2950	2760	2580	2400	2240	2080	-
Energy (ft-lb)	Muzzle	100	200	300	400	500	-
	2705	2370	2065	1795	1555	1340	-
Short-Range Trajectory (yds)	50	100	200	300	-	-	-
	-0.2	zero	-3.1	-11.3	-	-	-
Long-Range Trajectory (yds)	50	100	200	300	400	500	-
	0.6	1.5	zero	-6.7	-19.5	-39.3	-

270 Win.

Bullet Style	Trophy Bonded Tip						
Bullet Weight	150 grains.						
Velocity (fps)	Muzzle	100	200	300	400	500	-
	2830	2640	2450	2270	2100	1940	-
Energy (ft-lb)	Muzzle	100	200	300	400	500	-
	2665	2315	1995	1715	1465	1245	-
Short-Range Trajectory (yds)	50	100	200	300	-	-	-
	-0.2	zero	-3.5	-12.8	-	-	-
Long-Range Trajectory (yds)	50	100	200	300	400	500	-
	0.7	1.7	zero	-7.6	-22.0	-44.0	-

270 Win.

Bullet Style	Sierra GameKing BTSP						
Bullet Weight	150 grains.						
Velocity (fps)	Muzzle	100	200	300	400	500	-
	2830	2640	2460	2280	2110	1950	-
Energy (ft-lb)	Muzzle	100	200	300	400	500	-
	2665	2320	2010	1735	1485	1270	-
Short-Range Trajectory (yds)	50	100	200	300	-	-	-
	-0.2	zero	-3.5	-12.7	-	-	-
Long-Range Trajectory (yds)	50	100	200	300	400	500	-
	0.7	1.7	zero	-7.5	-21.8	-43.7	-

270 Win.

Bullet Style	Nosler Partition						
Bullet Weight	150 grains.						
Velocity (fps)	Muzzle	100	200	300	400	500	-
	2830	2630	2450	2270	2090	1930	-
Energy (ft-lb)	Muzzle	100	200	300	400	500	-
	2665	2310	1990	1710	1460	1240	-
Short-Range Trajectory (yds)	50	100	200	300	-	-	-
	-0.2	zero	-3.5	-12.8	-	-	-
Long-Range Trajectory (yds)	50	100	200	300	400	500	-
	0.7	1.7	zero	-7.6	-22.0	-44.1	-

270 Win. Short Magnum

Bullet Style	Barnes Tipped Triple-Shock X-Bullet						
Bullet Weight	110 grains.						
Velocity (fps)	Muzzle	100	200	300	400	500	-
	3500	3220	2960	2710	2470	2250	-
Energy (ft-lb)	Muzzle	100	200	300	400	500	-
	2990	2530	2135	1790	1495	1235	-
Short-Range Trajectory (yds)	50	100	200	300	-	-	-
	-0.4	zero	-1.9	-7.7	-	-	-
Long-Range Trajectory (yds)	50	100	200	300	400	500	-
	0.1	0.9	zero	-4.9	-14.6	-30.0	-

270 Win. Short Magnum

Bullet Style	Trophy Bonded Tip						
Bullet Weight	130 grains.						
Velocity (fps)	Muzzle	100	200	300	400	500	-
	3280	3050	2830	2620	2430	2240	-
Energy (ft-lb)	Muzzle	100	200	300	400	500	-
	3105	2685	2315	1990	1700	1445	-
Short-Range Trajectory (yds)	50	100	200	300	-	-	-
	-0.3	zero	-2.2	-8.8	-	-	-
Long-Range Trajectory (yds)	50	100	200	300	400	500	-
	0.2	1.1	zero	-5.5	-16.0	-32.4	-

270 Win. Short Magnum

Bullet Style	Nosler Ballistic Tip						
Bullet Weight	130 grains.						
Velocity (fps)	Muzzle	100	200	300	400	500	-
	3300	3070	2840	2630	2430	2240	-
Energy (ft-lb)	Muzzle	100	200	300	400	500	-
	3145	2710	2335	2000	1705	1445	-
Short-Range Trajectory (yds)	50	100	200	300	-	-	-
	-0.3	zero	-2.2	-8.7	-	-	-
Long-Range Trajectory (yds)	50	100	200	300	400	500	-
	0.2	1.1	zero	-5.4	-15.8	-32.2	-

270 Win. Short Magnum

Bullet Style	Barnes Triple-Shock X-Bullet						
Bullet Weight	130 grains.						
Velocity (fps)	Muzzle	100	200	300	400	500	-
	3280	3050	2820	2610	2410	2220	-
Energy (ft-lb)	Muzzle	100	200	300	400	500	-
	3105	2675	2300	1970	1675	1420	-
Short-Range Trajectory (yds)	50	100	200	300	-	-	-
	-0.3	zero	-2.2	-8.9	-	-	-
Long-Range Trajectory (yds)	50	100	200	300	400	500	-
	0.2	1.1	zero	-5.5	-16.1	-32.7	-

270 Win. Short Magnum

Bullet Style	Nosler AccuBond						
Bullet Weight	140 grains.						
Velocity (fps)	Muzzle	100	200	300	400	500	-
	3200	3000	2810	2620	2450	2280	-
Energy (ft-lb)	Muzzle	100	200	300	400	500	-
	3185	2795	2450	2140	1860	1615	-
Short-Range Trajectory (yds)	50	100	200	300	-	-	-
	-0.3	zero	-2.4	-9.2	-	-	-
Long-Range Trajectory (yds)	50	100	200	300	400	500	-
	0.3	1.2	zero	-5.6	-16.2	-32.7	-

270 Win. Short Magnum

Bullet Style	Trophy Bonded Tip						
Bullet Weight	150 grains.						
Velocity (fps)	Muzzle	100	200	300	400	500	-
	3100	2890	2700	2510	2330	2150	-
Energy (ft-lb)	Muzzle	100	200	300	400	500	-
	3200	2790	2420	2095	1800	1540	-
Short-Range Trajectory (yds)	50	100	200	300	-	-	-
	-0.3	zero	-2.7	-10.1	-	-	-
Long-Range Trajectory (yds)	50	100	200	300	400	500	-
	0.4	1.3	zero	-6.1	-17.7	-35.9	-

270 Win. Short Magnum

Bullet Style	Nosler Partition						
Bullet Weight	150 grains.						
Velocity (fps)	Muzzle	100	200	300	400	500	-
	3100	2890	2690	2500	2320	2150	-
Energy (ft-lb)	Muzzle	100	200	300	400	500	-
	3200	2785	2415	2085	1790	1530	-
Short-Range Trajectory (yds)	50	100	200	300	-	-	-
	-0.3	zero	-2.7	-10.1	-	-	-
Long-Range Trajectory (yds)	50	100	200	300	400	500	-
	0.4	1.3	zero	-6.1	-17.8	-36.0	-

270 Weatherby Magnum

Bullet Style	Trophy Bonded Tip						
Bullet Weight	130 grains.						
Velocity (fps)	Muzzle	100	200	300	400	500	-
	3200	2970	2760	2560	2360	2170	-
Energy (ft-lb)	Muzzle	100	200	300	400	500	-
	2955	2555	2200	1885	1610	1365	-
Short-Range Trajectory (yds)	50	100	200	300	-	-	-
	-0.3	zero	-2.4	-9.5	-	-	-
Long-Range Trajectory (yds)	50	100	200	300	400	500	-
	0.3	1.2	zero	-5.8	-16.9	-34.3	-

270 Weatherby Magnum

Bullet Style	Barnes Triple-Shock X-Bullet						
Bullet Weight	130 grains.						
Velocity (fps)	Muzzle	100	200	300	400	500	-
	3200	2970	2750	2540	2340	2150	-
Energy (ft-lb)	Muzzle	100	200	300	400	500	-
	2955	2545	2185	1865	1585	1340	-
Short-Range Trajectory (yds)	50	100	200	300	-	-	-
	-0.3	zero	-2.4	-9.5	-	-	-
Long-Range Trajectory (yds)	50	100	200	300	400	500	-
	0.3	1.2	zero	-5.8	-17.0	-34.6	-

7-30 Waters

Bullet Style	Sierra GameKing BTSP FN						
Bullet Weight	120 grains.						
Velocity (fps)	Muzzle	100	200	300	400	500	-
	2700	2300	1930	1600	1330	1130	-
Energy (ft-lb)	Muzzle	100	200	300	400	500	-
	1940	1405	990	685	470	340	-
Short-Range Trajectory (yds)	50	100	200	300	-	-	-
	-0.1	zero	-5.1	-19.9	-	-	-
Long-Range Trajectory (yds)	50	100	200	300	400	500	-
	1.2	2.6	zero	-12.2	-38.1	-84.5	-

7mm Mauser (7x57mm Mauser)

Bullet Style	Nosler Partition						
Bullet Weight	140 grains.						
Velocity (fps)	Muzzle	100	200	300	400	500	-
	2660	2460	2260	2080	1900	1740	-
Energy (ft-lb)	Muzzle	100	200	300	400	500	-
	2200	1875	1595	1345	1125	940	-
Short-Range Trajectory (yds)	50	100	200	300	-	-	-
	-0.1	zero	-4.3	-15.4	-	-	-
Long-Range Trajectory (yds)	50	100	200	300	400	500	-
	1.0	2.1	zero	-9.0	-25.8	-52.6	-

7mm-08 Rem.

Bullet Style	Trophy Bonded Tip						
Bullet Weight	140 grains.						
Velocity (fps)	Muzzle	100	200	300	400	500	-
	2800	2590	2390	2200	2010	1840	-
Energy (ft-lb)	Muzzle	100	200	300	400	500	-
	2435	2085	1770	1500	1260	1050	-
Short-Range Trajectory (yds)	50	100	200	300	-	-	-
	-0.1	zero	-3.7	-13.5	-	-	-
Long-Range Trajectory (yds)	50	100	200	300	400	500	-
	0.8	1.8	zero	-8.0	-23.2	-46.8	-

7mm-08 Rem.

Bullet Style	Nosler Partition						
Bullet Weight	140 grains.						
Velocity (fps)	Muzzle	100	200	300	400	500	-
	2800	2590	2390	2200	2020	1850	-
Energy (ft-lb)	Muzzle	100	200	300	400	500	-
	2435	2090	1780	1505	1270	1060	-
Short-Range Trajectory (yds)	50	100	200	300	-	-	-
	-0.1	zero	-3.6	-13.5	-	-	-
Long-Range Trajectory (yds)	50	100	200	300	400	500	-
	0.8	1.8	zero	-8.0	-23.1	-46.6	-

7mm-08 Rem.

Bullet Style	Nosler Ballistic Tip						
Bullet Weight	140 grains.						
Velocity (fps)	Muzzle	100	200	300	400	500	-
	2800	2610	2430	2260	2090	1940	-
Energy (ft-lb)	Muzzle	100	200	300	400	500	-
	2435	2120	1840	1585	1365	1165	-
Short-Range Trajectory (yds)	50	100	200	300	-	-	-
	-0.2	zero	-3.6	-13.1	-	-	-
Long-Range Trajectory (yds)	50	100	200	300	400	500	-
	0.7	1.8	zero	-7.7	-22.3	-44.5	-

7mm-08 Rem.

Bullet Style	Barnes Triple-Shock X-Bullet						
Bullet Weight	140 grains.						
Velocity (fps)	Muzzle	100	200	300	400	500	-
	2820	2590	2370	2160	1960	1780	-
Energy (ft-lb)	Muzzle	100	200	300	400	500	-
	2470	2085	1745	1450	1200	980	-
Short-Range Trajectory (yds)	50	100	200	300	-	-	-
	-0.2	zero	-3.7	-13.6	-	-	-
Long-Range Trajectory (yds)	50	100	200	300	400	500	-
	0.8	1.8	zero	-8.1	-23.6	-48.1	-

280 Rem.

Bullet Style	Trophy Bonded Tip						
Bullet Weight	140 grains.						
Velocity (fps)	Muzzle	100	200	300	400	500	-
	2950	2730	2520	2330	2140	1960	-
Energy (ft-lb)	Muzzle	100	200	300	400	500	-
	2705	2320	1980	1680	1420	1190	-
Short-Range Trajectory (yds)	50	100	200	300	-	-	-
	-0.2	zero	-3.2	-11.8	-	-	-
Long-Range Trajectory (yds)	50	100	200	300	400	500	-
	0.6	1.6	zero	-7.0	-20.6	-41.5	-

280 Rem.

Bullet Style	Nosler Ballistic Tip						
Bullet Weight	140 grains.						
Velocity (fps)	Muzzle	100	200	300	400	500	-
	2990	2790	2610	2430	2260	2090	-
Energy (ft-lb)	Muzzle	100	200	300	400	500	-
	2780	2425	2115	1830	1580	1355	-
Short-Range Trajectory (yds)	50	100	200	300	-	-	-
	-0.2	zero	-3.0	-11.0	-	-	-
Long-Range Trajectory (yds)	50	100	200	300	400	500	-
	0.5	1.5	zero	-6.5	-19.1	-38.5	-

280 Rem.

Bullet Style	Barnes Triple-Shock X-Bullet						
Bullet Weight	140 grains.						
Velocity (fps)	Muzzle	100	200	300	400	500	-
	2960	2720	2500	2280	2080	1880	-
Energy (ft-lb)	Muzzle	100	200	300	400	500	-
	2725	2305	1935	1620	1340	1105	-
Short-Range Trajectory (yds)	50	100	200	300	-	-	-
	-0.2	zero	-3.2	-12.0	-	-	-
Long-Range Trajectory (yds)	50	100	200	300	400	500	-
	0.6	1.6	zero	-7.2	-21.1	-42.8	-

280 Rem.

Bullet Style	Nosler Partition						
Bullet Weight	150 grains.						
Velocity (fps)	Muzzle	100	200	300	400	500	-
	2890	2690	2490	2310	2130	1960	-
Energy (ft-lb)	Muzzle	100	200	300	400	500	-
	2780	2405	2070	1775	1510	1280	-
Short-Range Trajectory (yds)	50	100	200	300	-	-	-
	-0.2	zero	-3.3	-12.2	-	-	-
Long-Range Trajectory (yds)	50	100	200	300	400	500	-
	0.6	1.7	zero	-7.2	-21.1	-42.4	-

280 Rem.

Bullet Style	Trophy Bonded Tip						
Bullet Weight	160 grains.						
Velocity (fps)	Muzzle	100	200	300	400	500	-
	2800	2630	2460	2290	2140	1990	-
Energy (ft-lb)	Muzzle	100	200	300	400	500	-
	2785	2450	2145	1870	1625	1405	-
Short-Range Trajectory (yds)	50	100	200	300	-	-	-
	-0.2	zero	-3.5	-12.8	-	-	-
Long-Range Trajectory (yds)	50	100	200	300	400	500	-
	0.7	1.8	zero	-7.5	-21.8	-43.6	-

7mm Rem. Magnum

Bullet Style	Barnes Tipped Triple-Shock X-Bullet						
Bullet Weight	110 grains.						
Velocity (fps)	Muzzle	100	200	300	400	500	-
	3500	3200	2920	2650	2400	2170	-
Energy (ft-lb)	Muzzle	100	200	300	400	500	-
	2990	2500	2075	1720	1410	1145	-
Short-Range Trajectory (yds)	50	100	200	300	-	-	-
	-0.4	zero	-1.9	-7.9	-	-	-
Long-Range Trajectory (yds)	50	100	200	300	400	500	-
	0.1	0.9	zero	-5.1	-15.0	-31.2	-

7mm Rem. Magnum

Bullet Style	Trophy Bonded Tip						
Bullet Weight	140 grains.						
Velocity (fps)	Muzzle	100	200	300	400	500	-
	3150	2920	2710	2500	2300	2110	-
Energy (ft-lb)	Muzzle	100	200	300	400	500	-
	3085	2655	2275	1940	1645	1390	-
Short-Range Trajectory (yds)	50	100	200	300	-	-	-
	-0.3	zero	-2.6	-10.0	-	-	-
Long-Range Trajectory (yds)	50	100	200	300	400	500	-
	0.4	1.3	zero	-6.1	-17.6	-35.9	-

7mm Rem. Magnum

Bullet Style	Nosler Partition						
Bullet Weight	140 grains.						
Velocity (fps)	Muzzle	100	200	300	400	500	-
	3150	2920	2710	2500	2310	2120	-
Energy (ft-lb)	Muzzle	100	200	300	400	500	-
	3085	2655	2280	1950	1655	1400	-
Short-Range Trajectory (yds)	50	100	200	300	-	-	-
	-0.3	zero	-2.6	-9.9	-	-	-
Long-Range Trajectory (yds)	50	100	200	300	400	500	-
	0.4	1.3	zero	-6.0	-17.6	-35.8	-

7mm Rem. Magnum

Bullet Style	Barnes Triple-Shock X-Bullet						
Bullet Weight	140 grains.						
Velocity (fps)	Muzzle	100	200	300	400	500	-
	3120	2870	2640	2420	2210	2010	-
Energy (ft-lb)	Muzzle	100	200	300	400	500	-
	3025	2565	2165	1815	1515	1250	-
Short-Range Trajectory (yds)	50	100	200	300	-	-	-
	-0.3	zero	-2.7	-10.4	-	-	-
Long-Range Trajectory (yds)	50	100	200	300	400	500	-
	0.4	1.4	zero	-6.3	-18.7	-38.1	-

7mm Rem. Magnum

Bullet Style	Nosler Ballistic Tip						
Bullet Weight	150 grains.						
Velocity (fps)	Muzzle	100	200	300	400	500	-
	3025	2830	2650	2470	2300	2130	-
Energy (ft-lb)	Muzzle	100	200	300	400	500	-
	3045	2670	2335	2030	1760	1515	-
Short-Range Trajectory (yds)	50	100	200	300	-	-	-
	-0.2	zero	-2.9	-10.7	-	-	-
Long-Range Trajectory (yds)	50	100	200	300	400	500	-
	0.5	1.4	zero	-6.4	-18.4	-37.2	-

7mm Rem. Magnum

Bullet Style	Sierra GameKing BTSP						
Bullet Weight	150 grains.						
Velocity (fps)	Muzzle	100	200	300	400	500	-
	3110	2890	2680	2470	2280	2090	-
Energy (ft-lb)	Muzzle	100	200	300	400	500	-
	3220	2775	2385	2035	1730	1460	-
Short-Range Trajectory (yds)	50	100	200	300	-	-	-
	-0.3	zero	-2.7	-10.2	-	-	-
Long-Range Trajectory (yds)	50	100	200	300	400	500	-
	0.4	1.4	zero	-6.2	-18.1	-36.7	-

7mm Rem. Magnum

Bullet Style	Nosler AccuBond						
Bullet Weight	160 grains.						
Velocity (fps)	Muzzle	100	200	300	400	500	-
	2900	2730	2560	2390	2240	2090	-
Energy (ft-lb)	Muzzle	100	200	300	400	500	-
	2990	2635	2320	2035	1775	1545	-
Short-Range Trajectory (yds)	50	100	200	300	-	-	-
	-0.2	zero	-3.2	-11.7	-	-	-
Long-Range Trajectory (yds)	50	100	200	300	400	500	-
	0.6	1.6	zero	-6.9	-19.9	-39.9	-

7mm Rem. Magnum

Bullet Style	Barnes Triple-Shock X-Bullet						
Bullet Weight	160 grains.						
Velocity (fps)	Muzzle	100	200	300	400	500	-
	2940	2760	2580	2410	2240	2090	-
Energy (ft-lb)	Muzzle	100	200	300	400	500	-
	3070	2695	2360	2060	1785	1545	-
Short-Range Trajectory (yds)	50	100	200	300	-	-	-
	-0.2	zero	-3.1	-11.4	-	-	-
Long-Range Trajectory (yds)	50	100	200	300	400	500	-
	0.6	1.6	zero	-6.7	-19.5	-39.3	-

7mm Rem. Magnum

Bullet Style	Trophy Bonded Tip						
Bullet Weight	160 grains.						
Velocity (fps)	Muzzle	100	200	300	400	500	-
	2900	2720	2550	2380	2220	2070	-
Energy (ft-lb)	Muzzle	100	200	300	400	500	-
	2990	2630	2310	2015	1755	1525	-
Short-Range Trajectory (yds)	50	100	200	300	-	-	-
	-0.2	zero	-3.2	-11.7	-	-	-
Long-Range Trajectory (yds)	50	100	200	300	400	500	-
	0.6	1.6	zero	-6.9	-20.0	-40.2	-

7mm Rem. Magnum

Bullet Style	Nosler Partition						
Bullet Weight	160 grains.						
Velocity (fps)	Muzzle	100	200	300	400	500	-
	2950	2750	2560	2380	2210	2040	-
Energy (ft-lb)	Muzzle	100	200	300	400	500	-
	3090	2690	2335	2015	1730	1480	-
Short-Range Trajectory (yds)	50	100	200	300	-	-	-
	-0.2	zero	-3.1	-11.5	-	-	-
Long-Range Trajectory (yds)	50	100	200	300	400	500	-
	0.6	1.6	zero	-6.8	-19.8	-40.0	-

7mm Rem. Magnum

Bullet Style	Sierra GameKing BTSP						
Bullet Weight	165 grains.						
Velocity (fps)	Muzzle	100	200	300	400	500	-
	2950	2750	2550	2360	2180	2010	-
Energy (ft-lb)	Muzzle	100	200	300	400	500	-
	3190	2760	2380	2045	1745	1480	-
Short-Range Trajectory (yds)	50	100	200	300	-	-	-
	-0.2	zero	-3.1	-11.6	-	-	-
Long-Range Trajectory (yds)	50	100	200	300	400	500	-
	0.6	1.6	zero	-6.9	-20.1	-40.5	-

7mm Rem. Magnum

Bullet Style	Trophy Bonded Bear Claw						
Bullet Weight	175 grains.						
Velocity (fps)	Muzzle	100	200	300	400	500	-
	2750	2530	2320	2120	1930	1750	-
Energy (ft-lb)	Muzzle	100	200	300	400	500	-
	2940	2485	2090	1745	1450	1195	-
Short-Range Trajectory (yds)	50	100	200	300	-	-	-
	-0.1	zero	-3.9	-14.4	-	-	-
Long-Range Trajectory (yds)	50	100	200	300	400	500	-
	0.9	2.0	zero	-8.5	-24.6	-50.2	-

7mm Win. Short Magnum

Bullet Style	Trophy Bonded Tip						
Bullet Weight	140 grains.						
Velocity (fps)	Muzzle	100	200	300	400	500	-
	3200	2970	2750	2540	2340	2150	-
Energy (ft-lb)	Muzzle	100	200	300	400	500	-
	3185	2740	2350	2010	1705	1440	-
Short-Range Trajectory (yds)	50	100	200	300	-	-	-
	-0.3	zero	-2.5	-9.5	-	-	-
Long-Range Trajectory (yds)	50	100	200	300	400	500	-
	0.3	1.2	zero	-5.8	-17.0	-34.7	-

7mm Win. Short Magnum

Bullet Style	Nosler Ballistic Tip						
Bullet Weight	140 grains.						
Velocity (fps)	Muzzle	100	200	300	400	500	-
	3310	3100	2900	2700	2520	2340	-
Energy (ft-lb)	Muzzle	100	200	300	400	500	-
	3405	2985	2610	2270	1975	1705	-
Short-Range Trajectory (yds)	50	100	200	300	-	-	-
	-0.3	zero	-2.1	-8.4	-	-	-
Long-Range Trajectory (yds)	50	100	200	300	400	500	-
	0.2	1.1	zero	-5.2	-15.2	-30.6	-

7mm Win. Short Magnum

Bullet Style	Barnes Triple-Shock X-Bullet						
Bullet Weight	160 grains.						
Velocity (fps)	Muzzle	100	200	300	400	500	-
	2990	2800	2620	2450	2290	2130	-
Energy (ft-lb)	Muzzle	100	200	300	400	500	-
	3175	2790	2445	2135	1855	1605	-
Short-Range Trajectory (yds)	50	100	200	300	-	-	-
	-0.2	zero	-3.0	-10.9	-	-	-
Long-Range Trajectory (yds)	50	100	200	300	400	500	-
	0.5	1.5	zero	-6.5	-18.8	-37.8	-

7mm Win. Short Magnum

Bullet Style	Trophy Bonded Tip						
Bullet Weight	160 grains.						
Velocity (fps)	Muzzle	100	200	300	400	500	-
	3000	2820	2640	2470	2310	2150	-
Energy (ft-lb)	Muzzle	100	200	300	400	500	-
	3195	2820	2480	2170	1895	1645	-
Short-Range Trajectory (yds)	50	100	200	300	-	-	-
	-0.2	zero	-2.9	-10.8	-	-	-
Long-Range Trajectory (yds)	50	100	200	300	400	500	-
	0.5	1.5	zero	-6.4	-18.5	-37.2	-

7mm Weatherby Magnum

Bullet Style	Trophy Bonded Tip						
Bullet Weight	160 grains.						
Velocity (fps)	Muzzle	100	200	300	400	500	-
	3100	2910	2730	2560	2390	2240	-
Energy (ft-lb)	Muzzle	100	200	300	400	500	-
	3415	3015	2655	2330	2035	1775	-
Short-Range Trajectory (yds)	50	100	200	300	-	-	-
	-0.3	zero	-2.6	-9.9	-	-	-
Long-Range Trajectory (yds)	50	100	200	300	400	500	-
	0.4	1.3	zero	-6.0	-17.2	-34.6	-

7mm STW

Bullet Style	Trophy Bonded Tip						
Bullet Weight	160 grains.						
Velocity (fps)	Muzzle	100	200	300	400	500	-
	3100	2910	2730	2560	2390	2240	-
Energy (ft-lb)	Muzzle	100	200	300	400	500	-
	3415	3015	2655	2330	2035	1775	-
Short-Range Trajectory (yds)	50	100	200	300	-	-	-
	-0.3	zero	-2.6	-9.9	-	-	-
Long-Range Trajectory (yds)	50	100	200	300	400	500	-
	0.4	1.3	zero	-6.0	-17.2	-34.6	-

30-30 Win.

Bullet Style	Barnes Triple-Shock X-Bullet						
Bullet Weight	150 grains.						
Velocity (fps)	Muzzle	100	200	300	400	500	-
	2220	1800	1450	1180	1020	920	-
Energy (ft-lb)	Muzzle	100	200	300	400	500	-
	1640	1085	695	460	345	280	-
Short-Range Trajectory (yds)	50	100	200	300	-	-	-
	0.3	zero	-9.4	-35.8	-	-	-
Long-Range Trajectory (yds)	50	100	200	300	400	500	-
	2.7	4.7	zero	-21.7	-68.6	-147.8	-

30-30 Win.

Bullet Style	Nosler Partition						
Bullet Weight	170 grains.						
Velocity (fps)	Muzzle	100	200	300	400	500	-
	2200	1890	1620	1380	1190	1060	-
Energy (ft-lb)	Muzzle	100	200	300	400	500	-
	1825	1355	990	720	535	425	-
Short-Range Trajectory (yds)	50	100	200	300	-	-	-
	0.3	zero	-8.4	-30.0	-	-	-
Long-Range Trajectory (yds)	50	100	200	300	400	500	-
	2.4	4.2	zero	-17.4	-53.5	-114.4	-

308 Win. (7.62x51mm)

Bullet Style	Nosler Ballistic Tip						
Bullet Weight	150 grains.						
Velocity (fps)	Muzzle	100	200	300	400	500	-
	2820	2610	2410	2220	2040	1860	-
Energy (ft-lb)	Muzzle	100	200	300	400	500	-
	2650	2270	1935	1640	1380	1155	-
Short-Range Trajectory (yds)	50	100	200	300	-	-	-
	-0.2	zero	-3.6	-13.2	-	-	-
Long-Range Trajectory (yds)	50	100	200	300	400	500	-
	0.7	1.8	zero	-7.8	-22.7	-45.8	-

308 Win. (7.62x51mm)

Bullet Style	Nosler Partition						
Bullet Weight	150 grains.						
Velocity (fps)	Muzzle	100	200	300	400	500	-
	2840	2600	2380	2170	1970	1780	-
Energy (ft-lb)	Muzzle	100	200	300	400	500	-
	2685	2260	1885	1565	1285	1050	-
Short-Range Trajectory (yds)	50	100	200	300	-	-	-
	-0.2	zero	-3.6	-13.4	-	-	-
Long-Range Trajectory (yds)	50	100	200	300	400	500	-
	0.7	1.8	zero	-8.0	-23.4	-47.8	-

308 Win. (7.62x51mm)

Bullet Style	Barnes Triple-Shock X-Bullet						
Bullet Weight	150 grains.						
Velocity (fps)	Muzzle	100	200	300	400	500	-
	2820	2570	2340	2120	1910	1720	-
Energy (ft-lb)	Muzzle	100	200	300	400	500	-
	2650	2205	1825	1495	1215	980	-
Short-Range Trajectory (yds)	50	100	200	300	-	-	-
	-0.2	zero	-3.7	-13.9	-	-	-
Long-Range Trajectory (yds)	50	100	200	300	400	500	-
	0.8	1.9	zero	-8.3	-24.2	-49.9	-

308 Win. (7.62x51mm)

Bullet Style	Barnes Triple-Shock X-Bullet						
Bullet Weight	165 grains.						
Velocity (fps)	Muzzle	100	200	300	400	500	-
	2650	2420	2200	1990	1800	1620	-
Energy (ft-lb)	Muzzle	100	200	300	400	500	-
	2575	2145	1775	1455	1185	960	-
Short-Range Trajectory (yds)	50	100	200	300	-	-	-
	-0.1	zero	-4.5	-16.2	-	-	-
Long-Range Trajectory (yds)	50	100	200	300	400	500	-
	1.0	2.2	zero	-9.5	-27.5	-56.8	-

308 Win. (7.62x51mm)

Bullet Style	Trophy Bonded Tip						
Bullet Weight	165 grains.						
Velocity (fps)	Muzzle	100	200	300	400	500	-
	2880	2680	2480	2290	2110	1940	-
Energy (ft-lb)	Muzzle	100	200	300	400	500	-
	3040	2620	2250	1920	1635	1375	-
Short-Range Trajectory (yds)	50	100	200	300	-	-	-
	-0.2	zero	-3.4	-12.4	-	-	-
Long-Range Trajectory (yds)	50	100	200	300	400	500	-
	0.7	1.7	zero	-7.3	-21.4	-43.0	-

308 Win. (7.62x51mm)

Bullet Style	Trophy Bonded Tip						
Bullet Weight	165 grains.						
Velocity (fps)	Muzzle	100	200	300	400	500	-
	2700	2500	2310	2130	1960	1800	-
Energy (ft-lb)	Muzzle	100	200	300	400	500	-
	2670	2295	1960	1665	1410	1180	-
Short-Range Trajectory (yds)	50	100	200	300	-	-	-
	-0.1	zero	-4.1	-14.7	-	-	-
Long-Range Trajectory (yds)	50	100	200	300	400	500	-
	0.9	2.0	zero	-8.6	-24.7	-49.9	-

308 Win. (7.62x51mm)

Bullet Style	Sierra GameKing BTSP						
Bullet Weight	165 grains.						
Velocity (fps)	Muzzle	100	200	300	400	500	-
	2700	2480	2270	2070	1880	1710	-
Energy (ft-lb)	Muzzle	100	200	300	400	500	-
	2670	2255	1890	1575	1300	1070	-
Short-Range Trajectory (yds)	50	100	200	300	-	-	-
	-0.1	zero	-4.2	-15.1	-	-	-
Long-Range Trajectory (yds)	50	100	200	300	400	500	-
	0.9	2.1	zero	-8.9	-25.6	-52.7	-

308 Win. (7.62x51mm)

Bullet Style	Nosler Partition						
Bullet Weight	180 grains.						
Velocity (fps)	Muzzle	100	200	300	400	500	-
	2570	2390	2210	2050	1890	1730	-
Energy (ft-lb)	Muzzle	100	200	300	400	500	-
	2640	2280	1955	1670	1420	1200	-
Short-Range Trajectory (yds)	50	100	200	300	-	-	-
	-0.1	zero	-4.7	-16.4	-	-	-
Long-Range Trajectory (yds)	50	100	200	300	400	500	-
	1.1	2.3	zero	-9.4	-26.9	-54.7	-

308 Win. (7.62x51mm)

Bullet Style	Trophy Bonded Tip						
Bullet Weight	180 grains.						
Velocity (fps)	Muzzle	100	200	300	400	500	-
	2620	2450	2280	2120	1960	1810	-
Energy (ft-lb)	Muzzle	100	200	300	400	500	-
	2745	2390	2070	1790	1535	1315	-
Short-Range Trajectory (yds)	50	100	200	300	-	-	-
	-0.1	zero	-4.3	-15.4	-	-	-
Long-Range Trajectory (yds)	50	100	200	300	400	500	-
	1.0	2.2	zero	-8.9	-25.5	-51.1	-

308 Win. (7.62x51mm)

Bullet Style	Barnes MRX-Bullet						
Bullet Weight	180 grains.						
Velocity (fps)	Muzzle	100	200	300	400	500	-
	2600	2440	2290	2140	2000	1860	-
Energy (ft-lb)	Muzzle	100	200	300	400	500	-
	2700	2385	2095	1835	1600	1390	-
Short-Range Trajectory (yds)	50	100	200	300	-	-	-
	-0.1	zero	-4.3	-15.4	-	-	-
Long-Range Trajectory (yds)	50	100	200	300	400	500	-
	1.0	2.2	zero	-8.9	-25.2	-50.0	-

30-06 Spring. (7.62x63mm)

Bullet Style	Barnes Tipped Triple-Shock X-Bullet						
Bullet Weight	110 grains.						
Velocity (fps)	Muzzle	100	200	300	400	500	-
	3400	3090	2800	2520	2270	2030	-
Energy (ft-lb)	Muzzle	100	200	300	400	500	-
	2825	2330	1910	1555	1255	1000	-
Short-Range Trajectory (yds)	50	100	200	300	-	-	-
	-0.3	zero	-2.1	-8.8	-	-	-
Long-Range Trajectory (yds)	50	100	200	300	400	500	-
	0.2	1.1	zero	-5.5	-16.5	-34.4	-

30-06 Spring. (7.62x63mm)

Bullet Style	Sierra GameKing BTSP						
Bullet Weight	150 grains.						
Velocity (fps)	Muzzle	100	200	300	400	500	-
	2910	2670	2440	2220	2010	1810	-
Energy (ft-lb)	Muzzle	100	200	300	400	500	-
	2820	2370	1975	1635	1345	1095	-
Short-Range Trajectory (yds)	50	100	200	300	-	-	-
	-0.2	zero	-3.4	-12.7	-	-	-
Long-Range Trajectory (yds)	50	100	200	300	400	500	-
	0.7	1.7	zero	-7.6	-22.3	-45.5	-

30-06 Spring. (7.62x63mm)

Bullet Style	Nosler Ballistic Tip						
Bullet Weight	150 grains.						
Velocity (fps)	Muzzle	100	200	300	400	500	-
	2910	2700	2490	2300	2110	1930	-
Energy (ft-lb)	Muzzle	100	200	300	400	500	-
	2820	2420	2070	1755	1485	1245	-
Short-Range Trajectory (yds)	50	100	200	300	-	-	-
	-0.2	zero	-3.3	-12.2	-	-	-
Long-Range Trajectory (yds)	50	100	200	300	400	500	-
	0.6	1.6	zero	-7.2	-21.1	-42.6	-

30-06 Spring. (7.62x63mm)

Bullet Style	Nosler Ballistic Tip						
Bullet Weight	165 grains.						
Velocity (fps)	Muzzle	100	200	300	400	500	-
	2800	2610	2430	2250	2080	1920	-
Energy (ft-lb)	Muzzle	100	200	300	400	500	-
	2870	2495	2155	1855	1585	1350	-
Short-Range Trajectory (yds)	50	100	200	300	-	-	-
	-0.2	zero	-3.6	-13.1	-	-	-
Long-Range Trajectory (yds)	50	100	200	300	400	500	-
	0.7	1.8	zero	-7.8	-22.4	-44.9	-

30-06 Spring. (7.62x63mm)

Bullet Style	Trophy Bonded Tip						
Bullet Weight	165 grains.						
Velocity (fps)	Muzzle	100	200	300	400	500	-
	2800	2600	2410	2220	2040	1880	-
Energy (ft-lb)	Muzzle	100	200	300	400	500	-
	2870	2475	2120	1805	1530	1290	-
Short-Range Trajectory (yds)	50	100	200	300	-	-	-
	-0.2	zero	-3.6	-13.3	-	-	-
Long-Range Trajectory (yds)	50	100	200	300	400	500	-
	0.8	1.8	zero	-7.9	-22.8	-45.8	-

30-06 Spring. (7.62x63mm)

Bullet Style	Nosler Partition						
Bullet Weight	165 grains.						
Velocity (fps)	Muzzle	100	200	300	400	500	-
	2830	2610	2400	2190	2000	1820	-
Energy (ft-lb)	Muzzle	100	200	300	400	500	-
	2935	2490	2100	1760	1465	1210	-
Short-Range Trajectory (yds)	50	100	200	300	-	-	-
	-0.2	zero	-3.6	-13.3	-	-	-
Long-Range Trajectory (yds)	50	100	200	300	400	500	-
	0.7	1.8	zero	-7.9	-23.0	-46.8	-

30-06 Spring. (7.62x63mm)

Bullet Style	Barnes Triple-Shock X-Bullet						
Bullet Weight	165 grains.						
Velocity (fps)	Muzzle	100	200	300	400	500	-
	2800	2560	2340	2120	1920	1730	-
Energy (ft-lb)	Muzzle	100	200	300	400	500	-
	2870	2405	2000	1650	1350	1095	-
Short-Range Trajectory (yds)	50	100	200	300	-	-	-
	-0.1	zero	-3.8	-14.0	-	-	-
Long-Range Trajectory (yds)	50	100	200	300	400	500	-
	0.8	1.9	zero	-8.4	-24.2	-49.9	-

30-06 Spring. (7.62x63mm)

Bullet Style	Sierra GameKing BTSP						
Bullet Weight	165 grains.						
Velocity (fps)	Muzzle	100	200	300	400	500	-
	2800	2580	2360	2160	1970	1780	-
Energy (ft-lb)	Muzzle	100	200	300	400	500	-
	2870	2430	2045	1710	1415	1165	-
Short-Range Trajectory (yds)	50	100	200	300	-	-	-
	-0.1	zero	-3.7	-13.8	-	-	-
Long-Range Trajectory (yds)	50	100	200	300	400	500	-
	0.8	1.9	zero	-8.2	-23.7	-48.3	-

30-06 Spring. (7.62x63mm)

Bullet Style	Nosler Partition						
Bullet Weight	180 grains.						
Velocity (fps)	Muzzle	100	200	300	400	500	-
	2700	2510	2330	2160	2000	1840	-
Energy (ft-lb)	Muzzle	100	200	300	400	500	-
	2915	2525	2175	1865	1590	1350	-
Short-Range Trajectory (yds)	50	100	200	300	-	-	-
	-0.1	zero	-4.0	-14.5	-	-	-
Long-Range Trajectory (yds)	50	100	200	300	400	500	-
	0.9	2.0	zero	-8.5	-24.4	-48.7	-

30-06 Spring. (7.62x63mm)

Bullet Style	Barnes MRX-Bullet						
Bullet Weight	180 grains.						
Velocity (fps)	Muzzle	100	200	300	400	500	-
	2700	2540	2380	2230	2090	1950	-
Energy (ft-lb)	Muzzle	100	200	300	400	500	-
	2915	2575	2270	1990	1740	1515	-
Short-Range Trajectory (yds)	50	100	200	300	-	-	-
	-0.1	zero	-3.9	-13.9	-	-	-
Long-Range Trajectory (yds)	50	100	200	300	400	500	-
	0.8	1.9	zero	-8.1	-23.3	-46.1	-

30-06 Spring. (7.62x63mm)

Bullet Style	Barnes Triple-Shock X-Bullet						
Bullet Weight	180 grains.						
Velocity (fps)	Muzzle	100	200	300	400	500	-
	2700	2500	2320	2140	1970	1800	-
Energy (ft-lb)	Muzzle	100	200	300	400	500	-
	2915	2505	2145	1825	1545	1295	-
Short-Range Trajectory (yds)	50	100	200	300	-	-	-
	-0.1	zero	-4.0	-14.7	-	-	-
Long-Range Trajectory (yds)	50	100	200	300	400	500	-
	0.9	2.0	zero	-8.6	-24.7	-49.7	-

30-06 Spring. (7.62x63mm)

Bullet Style	Nosler AccuBond						
Bullet Weight	180 grains.						
Velocity (fps)	Muzzle	100	200	300	400	500	-
	2700	2520	2360	2190	2040	1890	-
Energy (ft-lb)	Muzzle	100	200	300	400	500	-
	2915	2545	2215	1920	1660	1425	-
Short-Range Trajectory (yds)	50	100	200	300	-	-	-
	-0.1	zero	-3.9	-14.2	-	-	-
Long-Range Trajectory (yds)	50	100	200	300	400	500	-
	0.9	2.0	zero	-8.3	-23.8	-47.4	-

30-06 Spring. (7.62x63mm)

Bullet Style	Trophy Bonded Tip						
Bullet Weight	180 grains.						
Velocity (fps)	Muzzle	100	200	300	400	500	-
	2880	2700	2520	2350	2180	2020	-
Energy (ft-lb)	Muzzle	100	200	300	400	500	-
	3315	2900	2530	2200	1900	1635	-
Short-Range Trajectory (yds)	50	100	200	300	-	-	-
	-0.2	zero	-3.3	-12.0	-	-	-
Long-Range Trajectory (yds)	50	100	200	300	400	500	-
	0.6	1.6	zero	-7.1	-20.6	-41.4	-

30-06 Spring. (7.62x63mm)

Bullet Style	Trophy Bonded Tip						
Bullet Weight	180 grains.						
Velocity (fps)	Muzzle	100	200	300	400	500	-
	2700	2520	2350	2190	2030	1880	-
Energy (ft-lb)	Muzzle	100	200	300	400	500	-
	2915	2540	2210	1910	1645	1410	-
Short-Range Trajectory (yds)	50	100	200	300	-	-	-
	-0.1	zero	-3.9	-14.3	-	-	-
Long-Range Trajectory (yds)	50	100	200	300	400	500	-
	0.9	2.0	zero	-8.4	-23.9	-47.7	-

300 H&H Magnum

Bullet Style	Nosler Partition						
Bullet Weight	180 grains.						
Velocity (fps)	Muzzle	100	200	300	400	500	-
	2880	2620	2380	2150	1930	1730	-
Energy (ft-lb)	Muzzle	100	200	300	400	500	-
	3315	2750	2260	1845	1490	1190	-
Short-Range Trajectory (yds)	50	100	200	300	-	-	-
	-0.2	zero	-3.5	-13.3	-	-	-
Long-Range Trajectory (yds)	50	100	200	300	400	500	-
	0.7	1.8	zero	-8.0	-23.4	-48.5	-

300 H&H Magnum

Bullet Style	Barnes Triple-Shock X-Bullet						
Bullet Weight	180 grains.						
Velocity (fps)	Muzzle	100	200	300	400	500	-
	2880	2680	2480	2290	2120	1950	-
Energy (ft-lb)	Muzzle	100	200	300	400	500	-
	3315	2860	2460	2105	1790	1510	-
Short-Range Trajectory (yds)	50	100	200	300	-	-	-
	-0.2	zero	-3.4	-12.3	-	-	-
Long-Range Trajectory (yds)	50	100	200	300	400	500	-
	0.7	1.7	zero	-7.3	-21.3	-42.9	-

300 H&H Magnum

Bullet Style	Trophy Bonded Tip						
Bullet Weight	180 grains.						
Velocity (fps)	Muzzle	100	200	300	400	500	-
	2880	2700	2520	2350	2180	2020	-
Energy (ft-lb)	Muzzle	100	200	300	400	500	-
	3315	2900	2530	2200	1900	1635	-
Short-Range Trajectory (yds)	50	100	200	300	-	-	-
	-0.2	zero	-3.3	-12.0	-	-	-
Long-Range Trajectory (yds)	50	100	200	300	400	500	-
	0.6	1.6	zero	-7.1	-20.6	-41.4	-

300 Win. Magnum

Bullet Style	Barnes Tipped Triple-Shock X-Bullet						
Bullet Weight	130 grains.						
Velocity (fps)	Muzzle	100	200	300	400	500	-
	3500	3200	2930	2670	2420	2190	-
Energy (ft-lb)	Muzzle	100	200	300	400	500	-
	3535	2965	2475	2055	1690	1385	-
Short-Range Trajectory (yds)	50	100	200	300	-	-	-
	-0.4	zero	-1.9	-7.9	-	-	-
Long-Range Trajectory (yds)	50	100	200	300	400	500	-
	0.1	0.9	zero	-5.0	-14.9	-30.8	-

300 Win. Magnum

Bullet Style	Trophy Bonded Tip						
Bullet Weight	165 grains.						
Velocity (fps)	Muzzle	100	200	300	400	500	-
	3050	2840	2630	2440	2250	2080	-
Energy (ft-lb)	Muzzle	100	200	300	400	500	-
	3410	2950	2540	2180	1860	1575	-
Short-Range Trajectory (yds)	50	100	200	300	-	-	-
	-0.2	zero	-2.9	-10.7	-	-	-
Long-Range Trajectory (yds)	50	100	200	300	400	500	-
	0.5	1.4	zero	-6.4	-18.7	-37.9	-

300 Win. Magnum

Bullet Style	Barnes Triple-Shock X-Bullet						
Bullet Weight	165 grains.						
Velocity (fps)	Muzzle	100	200	300	400	500	-
	3050	2800	2560	2340	2120	1920	-
Energy (ft-lb)	Muzzle	100	200	300	400	500	-
	3410	2870	2400	1995	1650	1345	-
Short-Range Trajectory (yds)	50	100	200	300	-	-	-
	-0.2	zero	-3.0	-11.2	-	-	-
Long-Range Trajectory (yds)	50	100	200	300	400	500	-
	0.5	1.5	zero	-6.7	-20.0	-40.8	-

300 Win. Magnum

Bullet Style	Nosler Partition						
Bullet Weight	165 grains.						
Velocity (fps)	Muzzle	100	200	300	400	500	-
	3050	2820	2590	2380	2180	1990	-
Energy (ft-lb)	Muzzle	100	200	300	400	500	-
	3410	2905	2465	2080	1740	1450	-
Short-Range Trajectory (yds)	50	100	200	300	-	-	-
	-0.2	zero	-2.9	-10.9	-	-	-
Long-Range Trajectory (yds)	50	100	200	300	400	500	-
	0.5	1.5	zero	-6.6	-19.4	-39.5	-

300 Win. Magnum

Bullet Style	Trophy Bonded Tip						
Bullet Weight	180 grains.						
Velocity (fps)	Muzzle	100	200	300	400	500	-
	2960	2770	2590	2420	2250	2090	-
Energy (ft-lb)	Muzzle	100	200	300	400	500	-
	3500	3070	2680	2335	2025	1745	-
Short-Range Trajectory (yds)	50	100	200	300	-	-	-
	-0.2	zero	-3.1	-11.2	-	-	-
Long-Range Trajectory (yds)	50	100	200	300	400	500	-
	0.5	1.5	zero	-6.6	-19.3	-38.9	-

300 Win. Magnum

Bullet Style	Barnes MRX-Bullet						
Bullet Weight	180 grains.						
Velocity (fps)	Muzzle	100	200	300	400	500	-
	2960	2790	2620	2470	2310	2160	-
Energy (ft-lb)	Muzzle	100	200	300	400	500	-
	3500	3110	2750	2430	2135	1870	-
Short-Range Trajectory (yds)	50	100	200	300	-	-	-
	-0.2	zero	-3.0	-11.0	-	-	-
Long-Range Trajectory (yds)	50	100	200	300	400	500	-
	0.5	1.5	zero	-6.5	-18.7	-37.6	-

300 Win. Magnum

Bullet Style	Barnes Triple-Shock X-Bullet						
Bullet Weight	180 grains.						
Velocity (fps)	Muzzle	100	200	300	400	500	-
	2960	2750	2550	2360	2180	2010	-
Energy (ft-lb)	Muzzle	100	200	300	400	500	-
	3500	3025	2605	2235	1905	1610	-
Short-Range Trajectory (yds)	50	100	200	300	-	-	-
	-0.2	zero	-3.1	-11.5	-	-	-
Long-Range Trajectory (yds)	50	100	200	300	400	500	-
	0.6	1.6	zero	-6.8	-20.0	-40.4	-

300 Win. Magnum

Bullet Style	Nosler Partition						
Bullet Weight	180 grains.						
Velocity (fps)	Muzzle	100	200	300	400	500	-
	2960	2700	2460	2220	2010	1800	-
Energy (ft-lb)	Muzzle	100	200	300	400	500	-
	3500	2915	2410	1980	1605	1295	-
Short-Range Trajectory (yds)	50	100	200	300	-	-	-
	-0.2	zero	-3.3	-12.3	-	-	-
Long-Range Trajectory (yds)	50	100	200	300	400	500	-
	0.6	1.6	zero	-7.4	-21.9	-45.0	-

300 Win. Magnum

Bullet Style	Nosler AccuBond						
Bullet Weight	180 grains.						
Velocity (fps)	Muzzle	100	200	300	400	500	-
	2960	2770	2600	2420	2260	2100	-
Energy (ft-lb)	Muzzle	100	200	300	400	500	-
	3500	3075	2690	2350	2040	1765	-
Short-Range Trajectory (yds)	50	100	200	300	-	-	-
	-0.2	zero	-3.0	-11.2	-	-	-
Long-Range Trajectory (yds)	50	100	200	300	400	500	-
	0.5	1.5	zero	-6.6	-19.2	-38.7	-

300 Win. Magnum

Bullet Style	Trophy Bonded Bear Claw						
Bullet Weight	200 grains.						
Velocity (fps)	Muzzle	100	200	300	400	500	-
	2700	2480	2260	2060	1870	1690	-
Energy (ft-lb)	Muzzle	100	200	300	400	500	-
	3235	2720	2275	1885	1550	1265	-
Short-Range Trajectory (yds)	50	100	200	300	-	-	-
	-0.1	zero	-4.2	-15.2	-	-	-
Long-Range Trajectory (yds)	50	100	200	300	400	500	-
	0.9	2.1	zero	-8.9	-25.9	-53.3	-

300 Win. Short Magnum

Bullet Style	Barnes Tipped Triple-Shock						
Bullet Weight	130 grains.						
Velocity (fps)	Muzzle	100	200	300	400	500	-
	3500	3200	2930	2670	2420	2190	-
Energy (ft-lb)	Muzzle	100	200	300	400	500	-
	3535	2965	2475	2055	1690	1385	-
Short-Range Trajectory (yds)	50	100	200	300	-	-	-
	-0.4	zero	-1.9	-7.9	-	-	-
Long-Range Trajectory (yds)	50	100	200	300	400	500	-
	0.1	0.9	zero	-5.0	-14.9	-30.8	-

300 Win. Short Magnum

Bullet Style	Nosler Ballistic Tip						
Bullet Weight	150 grains.						
Velocity (fps)	Muzzle	100	200	300	400	500	-
	3250	3020	2800	2590	2390	2200	-
Energy (ft-lb)	Muzzle	100	200	300	400	500	-
	3520	3035	2610	2235	1905	1615	-
Short-Range Trajectory (yds)	50	100	200	300	-	-	-
	-0.3	zero	-2.3	-9.1	-	-	-
Long-Range Trajectory (yds)	50	100	200	300	400	500	-
	0.3	1.2	zero	-5.6	-16.3	-33.3	-

300 Win. Short Magnum

Bullet Style	Trophy Bonded Tip						
Bullet Weight	165 grains.						
Velocity (fps)	Muzzle	100	200	300	400	500	-
	3130	2910	2710	2510	2320	2140	-
Energy (ft-lb)	Muzzle	100	200	300	400	500	-
	3590	3110	2680	2305	1970	1675	-
Short-Range Trajectory (yds)	50	100	200	300	-	-	-
	-0.3	zero	-2.6	-10.0	-	-	-
Long-Range Trajectory (yds)	50	100	200	300	400	500	-
	0.4	1.3	zero	-6.0	-17.6	-35.7	-

300 Win. Short Magnum

Bullet Style	Nosler Partition						
Bullet Weight	165 grains.						
Velocity (fps)	Muzzle	100	200	300	400	500	-
	3120	2880	2660	2450	2240	2050	-
Energy (ft-lb)	Muzzle	100	200	300	400	500	-
	3565	3045	2590	2190	1840	1535	-
Short-Range Trajectory (yds)	50	100	200	300	-	-	-
	-0.3	zero	-2.7	-10.3	-	-	-
Long-Range Trajectory (yds)	50	100	200	300	400	500	-
	0.4	1.4	zero	-6.2	-18.3	-37.4	-

300 Win. Short Magnum

Bullet Style	Barnes Triple-Shock X-Bullet						
Bullet Weight	165 grains.						
Velocity (fps)	Muzzle	100	200	300	400	500	-
	3130	2870	2630	2400	2190	1980	-
Energy (ft-lb)	Muzzle	100	200	300	400	500	-
	3590	3025	2540	2115	1750	1435	-
Short-Range Trajectory (yds)	50	100	200	300	-	-	-
	-0.3	zero	-2.7	-10.5	-	-	-
Long-Range Trajectory (yds)	50	100	200	300	400	500	-
	0.4	1.4	zero	-6.3	-18.8	-38.5	-

300 Win. Short Magnum

Bullet Style	Barnes MRX-Bullet						
Bullet Weight	180 grains.						
Velocity (fps)	Muzzle	100	200	300	400	500	-
	2980	2810	2640	2480	2330	2180	-
Energy (ft-lb)	Muzzle	100	200	300	400	500	-
	3550	3150	2790	2465	2170	1900	-
Short-Range Trajectory (yds)	50	100	200	300	-	-	-
	-0.2	zero	-2.9	-10.8	-	-	-
Long-Range Trajectory (yds)	50	100	200	300	400	500	-
	0.5	1.5	zero	-6.4	-18.4	-37.0	-

300 Win. Short Magnum

Bullet Style	Trophy Bonded Tip						
Bullet Weight	180 grains.						
Velocity (fps)	Muzzle	100	200	300	400	500	-
	2960	2770	2590	2420	2250	2090	-
Energy (ft-lb)	Muzzle	100	200	300	400	500	-
	3500	3070	2680	2335	2025	1745	-
Short-Range Trajectory (yds)	50	100	200	300	-	-	-
	-0.2	zero	-3.1	-11.2	-	-	-
Long-Range Trajectory (yds)	50	100	200	300	400	500	-
	0.5	1.5	zero	-6.6	-19.3	-38.9	-

300 Win. Short Magnum

Bullet Style	Barnes Triple-Shock X-Bullet						
Bullet Weight	180 grains.						
Velocity (fps)	Muzzle	100	200	300	400	500	-
	2980	2770	2570	2380	2200	2030	-
Energy (ft-lb)	Muzzle	100	200	300	400	500	-
	3550	3070	2645	2265	1935	1640	-
Short-Range Trajectory (yds)	50	100	200	300	-	-	-
	-0.2	zero	-3.1	-11.3	-	-	-
Long-Range Trajectory (yds)	50	100	200	300	400	500	-
	0.5	1.5	zero	-6.7	-19.7	-39.8	-

300 Win. Short Magnum

Bullet Style	Nosler AccuBond						
Bullet Weight	180 grains.						
Velocity (fps)	Muzzle	100	200	300	400	500	-
	2960	2770	2600	2420	2260	2100	-
Energy (ft-lb)	Muzzle	100	200	300	400	500	-
	3500	3075	2690	2350	2040	1765	-
Short-Range Trajectory (yds)	50	100	200	300	-	-	-
	-0.2	zero	-3.0	-11.2	-	-	-
Long-Range Trajectory (yds)	50	100	200	300	400	500	-
	0.5	1.5	zero	-6.6	-19.2	-38.7	-

300 Win. Short Magnum

Bullet Style	Nosler Partition						
Bullet Weight	180 grains.						
Velocity (fps)	Muzzle	100	200	300	400	500	-
	2980	2780	2590	2410	2230	2060	-
Energy (ft-lb)	Muzzle	100	200	300	400	500	-
	3550	3090	2680	2315	1990	1700	-
Short-Range Trajectory (yds)	50	100	200	300	-	-	-
	-0.2	zero	-3.0	-11.2	-	-	-
Long-Range Trajectory (yds)	50	100	200	300	400	500	-
	0.5	1.5	zero	-6.6	-19.4	-39.1	-

300 Weatherby Magnum

Bullet Style	Nosler Partition						
Bullet Weight	180 grains.						
Velocity (fps)	Muzzle	100	200	300	400	500	-
	3080	2880	2680	2490	2320	2140	-
Energy (ft-lb)	Muzzle	100	200	300	400	500	-
	3790	3305	2870	2485	2140	1835	-
Short-Range Trajectory (yds)	50	100	200	300	-	-	-
	-0.3	zero	-2.7	-10.3	-	-	-
Long-Range Trajectory (yds)	50	100	200	300	400	500	-
	0.4	1.4	zero	-6.2	-17.9	-36.3	-

300 Weatherby Magnum

Bullet Style	Barnes Triple-Shock X-Bullet						
Bullet Weight	180 grains.						
Velocity (fps)	Muzzle	100	200	300	400	500	-
	3110	2900	2690	2500	2310	2130	-
Energy (ft-lb)	Muzzle	100	200	300	400	500	-
	3865	3350	2895	2485	2130	1810	-
Short-Range Trajectory (yds)	50	100	200	300	-	-	-
	-0.3	zero	-2.7	-10.2	-	-	-
Long-Range Trajectory (yds)	50	100	200	300	400	500	-
	0.4	1.3	zero	-6.1	-17.8	-36.2	-

300 Weatherby Magnum

Bullet Style	Trophy Bonded Tip						
Bullet Weight	180 grains.						
Velocity (fps)	Muzzle	100	200	300	400	500	-
	3100	2910	2720	2540	2370	2200	-
Energy (ft-lb)	Muzzle	100	200	300	400	500	-
	3840	3375	2955	2580	2240	1940	-
Short-Range Trajectory (yds)	50	100	200	300	-	-	-
	-0.3	zero	-2.6	-10.0	-	-	-
Long-Range Trajectory (yds)	50	100	200	300	400	500	-
	0.4	1.3	zero	-6.0	-17.4	-35.1	-

300 Rem. Ultra Magnum

Bullet Style	Barnes Triple-Shock X-Bullet						
Bullet Weight	180 grains.						
Velocity (fps)	Muzzle	100	200	300	400	500	-
	3150	2930	2730	2530	2340	2160	-
Energy (ft-lb)	Muzzle	100	200	300	400	500	-
	3965	3440	2970	2555	2190	1865	-
Short-Range Trajectory (yds)	50	100	200	300	-	-	-
	-0.3	zero	-2.6	-9.8	-	-	-
Long-Range Trajectory (yds)	50	100	200	300	400	500	-
	0.4	1.3	zero	-6.0	-17.3	-35.1	-

300 Rem. Ultra Magnum

Bullet Style	Trophy Bonded Tip						
Bullet Weight	180 grains.						
Velocity (fps)	Muzzle	100	200	300	400	500	-
	3200	3000	2810	2630	2450	2280	-
Energy (ft-lb)	Muzzle	100	200	300	400	500	-
	4090	3600	3155	2760	2405	2085	-
Short-Range Trajectory (yds)	50	100	200	300	-	-	-
	-0.3	zero	-2.4	-9.2	-	-	-
Long-Range Trajectory (yds)	50	100	200	300	400	500	-
	0.3	1.2	zero	-5.6	-16.2	-32.6	-

300 Rem. Ultra Magnum

Bullet Style	Nosler Partition						
Bullet Weight	200 grains.						
Velocity (fps)	Muzzle	100	200	300	400	500	-
	3070	2870	2680	2490	2320	2150	-
Energy (ft-lb)	Muzzle	100	200	300	400	500	-
	4185	3655	3180	2760	2380	2045	-
Short-Range Trajectory (yds)	50	100	200	300	-	-	-
	-0.3	zero	-2.8	-10.4	-	-	-
Long-Range Trajectory (yds)	50	100	200	300	400	500	-
	0.4	1.4	zero	-6.2	-18.0	-36.4	-

POWER-SHOK RIFLE BALLISTICS

243 Win. (6.16x51mm)

Bullet Style	Soft Point						
Bullet Weight	80 grains.						
Velocity (fps)	Muzzle	100	200	300	400	500	-
	3330	3050	2790	2540	2310	2090	-
Energy (ft-lb)	Muzzle	100	200	300	400	500	-
	1970	1655	1380	1150	945	775	-
Short-Range Trajectory (yds)	50	100	200	300	-	-	-
	-0.3	zero	-2.2	-9.0	-	-	-
Long-Range Trajectory (yds)	50	100	200	300	400	500	-
	0.2	1.1	zero	-5.6	-16.6	-34.2	-

243 Win. (6.16x51mm)

Bullet Style	Soft Point						
Bullet Weight	100 grains.						
Velocity (fps)	Muzzle	100	200	300	400	500	-
	2960	2700	2450	2210	1990	1780	-
Energy (ft-lb)	Muzzle	100	200	300	400	500	-
	1945	1615	1330	1085	880	705	-
Short-Range Trajectory (yds)	50	100	200	300	-	-	-
	-0.2	zero	-3.3	-12.4	-	-	-
Long-Range Trajectory (yds)	50	100	200	300	400	500	-
	0.6	1.6	zero	-7.5	-22.1	-45.4	-

6mm Rem.

Bullet Style	Soft Point						
Bullet Weight	80 grains.						
Velocity (fps)	Muzzle	100	200	300	400	500	-
	3400	3120	2850	2600	2360	2140	-
Energy (ft-lb)	Muzzle	100	200	300	400	500	-
	2055	1725	1445	1200	995	815	-
Short-Range Trajectory (yds)	50	100	200	300	-	-	-
	-0.3	zero	-2.1	-8.5	-	-	-
Long-Range Trajectory (yds)	50	100	200	300	400	500	-
	0.2	1.0	zero	-5.4	-15.8	-32.6	-

6mm Rem.

Bullet Style	Soft Point						
Bullet Weight	100 grains.						
Velocity (fps)	Muzzle	100	200	300	400	500	-
	3100	2830	2570	2330	2100	1880	-
Energy (ft-lb)	Muzzle	100	200	300	400	500	-
	2135	1775	1470	1205	980	785	-
Short-Range Trajectory (yds)	50	100	200	300	-	-	-
	-0.3	zero	-2.9	-11.0	-	-	-
Long-Range Trajectory (yds)	50	100	200	300	400	500	-
	0.5	1.4	zero	-6.7	-19.9	-40.7	-

25-06 Rem.

Bullet Style	Soft Point						
Bullet Weight	117 grains.						
Velocity (fps)	Muzzle	100	200	300	400	500	-
	3030	2770	2520	2280	2060	1850	-
Energy (ft-lb)	Muzzle	100	200	300	400	500	-
	2385	1990	1650	1355	1105	890	-
Short-Range Trajectory (yds)	50	100	200	300	-	-	-
	-0.2	zero	-3.1	-11.6	-	-	-
Long-Range Trajectory (yds)	50	100	200	300	400	500	-
	0.5	1.5	zero	-7.0	-20.8	-42.5	-

6.5x55mm Swedish

Bullet Style	Soft Point*						
Bullet Weight	140 grains.						
Velocity (fps)	Muzzle	100	200	300	400	500	-
	2650	2450	2260	2080	1900	1740	-
Energy (ft-lb)	Muzzle	100	200	300	400	500	-
	2185	1865	1585	1340	1120	935	-
Short-Range Trajectory (yds)	50	100	200	300	-	-	-
	-0.1	zero	-4.3	-15.5	-	-	-
Long-Range Trajectory (yds)	50	100	200	300	400	500	-
	1.0	2.2	zero	-9.0	-25.9	-52.8	-

270 Win.

Bullet Style	Soft Point						
Bullet Weight	130 grains.						
Velocity (fps)	Muzzle	100	200	300	400	500	-
	3060	2800	2560	2330	2110	1900	-
Energy (ft-lb)	Muzzle	100	200	300	400	500	-
	2705	2265	1890	1565	1285	1045	-
Short-Range Trajectory (yds)	50	100	200	300	-	-	-
	-0.2	zero	-3.0	-11.2	-	-	-
Long-Range Trajectory (yds)	50	100	200	300	400	500	-
	0.5	1.5	zero	-6.7	-20.0	-40.9	-

270 Win.

Bullet Style	Soft Point RN						
Bullet Weight	150 grains.						
Velocity (fps)	Muzzle	100	200	300	400	500	-
	2830	2490	2170	1870	1610	1370	-
Energy (ft-lb)	Muzzle	100	200	300	400	500	-
	2665	2055	1565	1165	860	630	-
Short-Range Trajectory (yds)	50	100	200	300	-	-	-
	-0.1	zero	-4.2	-15.7	-	-	-
Long-Range Trajectory (yds)	50	100	200	300	400	500	-
	0.9	2.1	zero	-9.4	-29.2	-62.6	-

270 Win. Short Magnum

Bullet Style	Soft Point						
Bullet Weight	130 grains.						
Velocity (fps)	Muzzle	100	200	300	400	500	-
	3250	2980	2720	2480	2250	2030	-
Energy (ft-lb)	Muzzle	100	200	300	400	500	-
	3050	2560	2140	1775	1460	1195	-
Short-Range Trajectory (yds)	50	100	200	300	-	-	-
	-0.3	zero	-2.4	-9.6	-	-	-
Long-Range Trajectory (yds)	50	100	200	300	400	500	-
	0.3	1.2	zero	-5.9	-17.5	-36.0	-

7mm Mauser (7x57mm Mauser)

Bullet Style	Soft Point						
Bullet Weight	140 grains.						
Velocity (fps)	Muzzle	100	200	300	400	500	-
	2660	2450	2260	2070	1890	1720	-
Energy (ft-lb)	Muzzle	100	200	300	400	500	-
	2200	1870	1585	1330	1110	920	-
Short-Range Trajectory (yds)	50	100	200	300	-	-	-
	-0.1	zero	-4.3	-15.5	-	-	-
Long-Range Trajectory (yds)	50	100	200	300	400	500	-
	1.0	2.1	zero	-9.0	-25.9	-53.1	-

7mm Mauser (7x57mm Mauser)

Bullet Style	Soft Point RN						
Bullet Weight	175 grains.						
Velocity (fps)	Muzzle	100	200	300	400	500	-
	2390	2090	1810	1560	1350	1180	-
Energy (ft-lb)	Muzzle	100	200	300	400	500	-
	2220	1695	1275	950	705	540	-
Short-Range Trajectory (yds)	50	100	200	300	-	-	-
	0.1	zero	-6.5	-23.7	-	-	-
Long-Range Trajectory (yds)	50	100	200	300	400	500	-
	1.7	3.2	zero	-14.1	-42.4	-90.4	-

7mm-08 Rem.

Bullet Style	Soft Point						
Bullet Weight	150 grains.						
Velocity (fps)	Muzzle	100	200	300	400	500	-
	2650	2440	2240	2040	1860	1690	-
Energy (ft-lb)	Muzzle	100	200	300	400	500	-
	2340	1980	1665	1390	1150	950	-
Short-Range Trajectory (yds)	50	100	200	300	-	-	-
	-0.1	zero	-4.4	-15.7	-	-	-
Long-Range Trajectory (yds)	50	100	200	300	400	500	-
	1.0	2.2	zero	-9.2	-26.5	-54.4	-

280 Rem.

Bullet Style	Soft Point						
Bullet Weight	150 grains.						
Velocity (fps)	Muzzle	100	200	300	400	500	-
	2890	2670	2460	2250	2060	1880	-
Energy (ft-lb)	Muzzle	100	200	300	400	500	-
	2780	2370	2010	1690	1415	1175	-
Short-Range Trajectory (yds)	50	100	200	300	-	-	-
	-0.2	zero	-3.4	-12.6	-	-	-
Long-Range Trajectory (yds)	50	100	200	300	400	500	-
	0.7	1.7	zero	-7.5	-21.9	-44.2	-

7mm Rem. Magnum

Bullet Style	Soft Point						
Bullet Weight	150 grains.						
Velocity (fps)	Muzzle	100	200	300	400	500	-
	3110	2840	2590	2350	2120	1910	-
Energy (ft-lb)	Muzzle	100	200	300	400	500	-
	3220	2685	2230	1835	1495	1210	-
Short-Range Trajectory (yds)	50	100	200	300	-	-	-
	-0.3	zero	-2.8	-10.8	-	-	-
Long-Range Trajectory (yds)	50	100	200	300	400	500	-
	0.4	1.4	zero	-6.6	-19.6	-40.1	-

7mm Rem. Magnum

Bullet Style	Soft Point						
Bullet Weight	175 grains.						
Velocity (fps)	Muzzle	100	200	300	400	500	-
	2860	2650	2440	2250	2060	1880	-
Energy (ft-lb)	Muzzle	100	200	300	400	500	-
	3180	2720	2315	1960	1650	1375	-
Short-Range Trajectory (yds)	50	100	200	300	-	-	-
	-0.2	zero	-3.5	-12.8	-	-	-
Long-Range Trajectory (yds)	50	100	200	300	400	500	-
	0.7	1.7	zero	-7.6	-22.1	-44.6	-

7mm Win. Short Magnum

Bullet Style	Soft Point						
Bullet Weight	150 grains.						
Velocity (fps)	Muzzle	100	200	300	400	500	-
	3100	2830	2580	2340	2110	1900	-
Energy (ft-lb)	Muzzle	100	200	300	400	500	-
	3200	2670	2215	1820	1485	1200	-
Short-Range Trajectory (yds)	50	100	200	300	-	-	-
	-0.3	zero	-2.9	-10.9	-	-	-
Long-Range Trajectory (yds)	50	100	200	300	400	500	-
	0.5	1.4	zero	-6.6	-19.7	-40.4	-

7.62x39mm Soviet

Bullet Style	Soft Point						
Bullet Weight	123 grains.						
Velocity (fps)	Muzzle	100	200	300	400	500	-
	2350	2060	1780	1540	1330	1160	-
Energy (ft-lb)	Muzzle	100	200	300	400	500	-
	1510	1155	870	645	480	370	-
Short-Range Trajectory (yds)	50	100	200	300	-	-	-
	0.2	zero	-6.7	-24.6	-	-	-
Long-Range Trajectory (yds)	50	100	200	300	400	500	-
	1.8	3.4	zero	-14.5	-43.9	-93.3	-

30-30 Win.

Bullet Style	Soft Point FN						
Bullet Weight	150 grains.						
Velocity (fps)	Muzzle	100	200	300	400	500	-
	2390	2020	1690	1400	1180	1040	-
Energy (ft-lb)	Muzzle	100	200	300	400	500	-
	1900	1360	945	650	465	360	-
Short-Range Trajectory (yds)	50	100	200	300	-	-	-
	0.1	zero	-7.2	-26.7	-	-	-
Long-Range Trajectory (yds)	50	100	200	300	400	500	-
	1.9	3.6	zero	-15.9	-50.1	-109.8	-

30-30 Win.

Bullet Style	Soft Point RN						
Bullet Weight	170 grains.						
Velocity (fps)	Muzzle	100	200	300	400	500	-
	2200	1890	1620	1380	1190	1060	-
Energy (ft-lb)	Muzzle	100	200	300	400	500	-
	1825	1355	990	720	535	425	-
Short-Range Trajectory (yds)	50	100	200	300	-	-	-
	0.3	zero	-8.4	-30.0	-	-	-
Long-Range Trajectory (yds)	50	100	200	300	400	500	-
	2.4	4.2	zero	-17.4	-53.5	-114.4	-

300 Savage

Bullet Style	Soft Point						
Bullet Weight	150 grains.						
Velocity (fps)	Muzzle	100	200	300	400	500	-
	2630	2350	2090	1850	1630	1430	-
Energy (ft-lb)	Muzzle	100	200	300	400	500	-
	2305	1845	1460	1140	885	680	-
Short-Range Trajectory (yds)	50	100	200	300	-	-	-
	-0.1	zero	-4.8	-17.5	-	-	-
Long-Range Trajectory (yds)	50	100	200	300	400	500	-
	1.2	2.4	zero	-10.2	-31.1	-64.8	-

300 Savage

Bullet Style	Soft Point						
Bullet Weight	180 grains.						
Velocity (fps)	Muzzle	100	200	300	400	500	-
	2350	2140	1930	1750	1570	1410	-
Energy (ft-lb)	Muzzle	100	200	300	400	500	-
	2205	1825	1495	1215	985	795	-
Short-Range Trajectory (yds)	50	100	200	300	-	-	-
	0.1	zero	-6.1	-21.6	-	-	-
Long-Range Trajectory (yds)	50	100	200	300	400	500	-
	1.6	3.0	zero	-12.5	-36.5	-74.4	-

308 Win. (7.62x51mm)

Bullet Style	Soft Point						
Bullet Weight	150 grains.						
Velocity (fps)	Muzzle	100	200	300	400	500	-
	2820	2530	2260	2010	1770	1560	-
Energy (ft-lb)	Muzzle	100	200	300	400	500	-
	2650	2135	1700	1340	1045	805	-
Short-Range Trajectory (yds)	50	100	200	300	-	-	-
	-0.1	zero	-3.9	-14.7	-	-	-
Long-Range Trajectory (yds)	50	100	200	300	400	500	-
	0.8	2.0	zero	-8.8	-26.3	-55.2	-

308 Win. (7.62x51mm)

Bullet Style	Soft Point						
Bullet Weight	180 grains.						
Velocity (fps)	Muzzle	100	200	300	400	500	-
	2570	2350	2130	1930	1740	1570	-
Energy (ft-lb)	Muzzle	100	200	300	400	500	-
	2640	2195	1815	1485	1210	980	-
Short-Range Trajectory (yds)	50	100	200	300	-	-	-
	0.0	zero	-4.9	-17.3	-	-	-
Long-Range Trajectory (yds)	50	100	200	300	400	500	-
	1.2	2.4	zero	-10.0	-29.5	-60.7	-

30-06 Spring. (7.62x63mm)

Bullet Style	Soft Point						
Bullet Weight	150 grains.						
Velocity (fps)	Muzzle	100	200	300	400	500	-
	2910	2620	2340	2080	1840	1620	-
Energy (ft-lb)	Muzzle	100	200	300	400	500	-
	2820	2280	1825	1440	1125	875	-
Short-Range Trajectory (yds)	50	100	200	300	-	-	-
	-0.2	zero	-3.6	-13.6	-	-	-
Long-Range Trajectory (yds)	50	100	200	300	400	500	-
	0.7	1.8	zero	-8.2	-24.4	-51.3	-

30-06 Spring. (7.62x63mm)

Bullet Style	Soft Point						
Bullet Weight	180 grains.						
Velocity (fps)	Muzzle	100	200	300	400	500	-
	2700	2470	2250	2050	1850	1670	-
Energy (ft-lb)	Muzzle	100	200	300	400	500	-
	2915	2440	2025	1670	1365	1110	-
Short-Range Trajectory (yds)	50	100	200	300	-	-	-
	-0.1	zero	-4.2	-15.3	-	-	-
Long-Range Trajectory (yds)	50	100	200	300	400	500	-
	1.0	2.1	zero	-9.0	-26.2	-54.0	-

30-06 Spring. (7.62x63mm)

Bullet Style	Soft Point						
Bullet Weight	220 grains.						
Velocity (fps)	Muzzle	100	200	300	400	500	-
	2400	2120	1860	1620	1410	1240	-
Energy (ft-lb)	Muzzle	100	200	300	400	500	-
	2815	2195	1690	1285	975	750	-
Short-Range Trajectory (yds)	50	100	200	300	-	-	-
	0.1	zero	-6.2	-22.7	-	-	-
Long-Range Trajectory (yds)	50	100	200	300	400	500	-
	1.7	3.1	zero	-13.5	-40.0	-84.5	-

300 Win. Magnum

Bullet Style	Soft Point						
Bullet Weight	150 grains.						
Velocity (fps)	Muzzle	100	200	300	400	500	-
	3150	2900	2660	2440	2220	2020	-
Energy (ft-lb)	Muzzle	100	200	300	400	500	-
	3305	2800	2360	1975	1645	1355	-
Short-Range Trajectory (yds)	50	100	200	300	-	-	-
	-0.3	zero	-2.7	-10.2	-	-	-
Long-Range Trajectory (yds)	50	100	200	300	400	500	-
	0.4	1.3	zero	-6.2	-18.3	-37.5	-

300 Win. Magnum

Bullet Style	Soft Point						
Bullet Weight	180 grains.						
Velocity (fps)	Muzzle	100	200	300	400	500	-
	2960	2750	2540	2350	2160	1980	-
Energy (ft-lb)	Muzzle	100	200	300	400	500	-
	3500	3015	2580	2200	1865	1570	-
Short-Range Trajectory (yds)	50	100	200	300	-	-	-
	-0.2	zero	-3.1	-11.6	-	-	-
Long-Range Trajectory (yds)	50	100	200	300	400	500	-
	0.6	1.6	zero	-6.9	-20.3	-41.0	-

300 Win. Short Magnum

Bullet Style	Soft Point						
Bullet Weight	180 grains.						
Velocity (fps)	Muzzle	100	200	300	400	500	-
	2980	2740	2500	2280	2080	1880	-
Energy (ft-lb)	Muzzle	100	200	300	400	500	-
	3550	2990	2505	2085	1720	1410	-
Short-Range Trajectory (yds)	50	100	200	300	-	-	-
	-0.2	zero	-3.2	-11.9	-	-	-
Long-Range Trajectory (yds)	50	100	200	300	400	500	-
	0.6	1.6	zero	-7.1	-21.0	-42.7	-

303 British

Bullet Style	Soft Point						
Bullet Weight	150 grains.						
Velocity (fps)	Muzzle	100	200	300	400	500	-
	2690	2440	2210	1990	1780	1590	-
Energy (ft-lb)	Muzzle	100	200	300	400	500	-
	2410	1985	1625	1315	1055	840	-
Short-Range Trajectory (yds)	50	100	200	300	-	-	-
	-0.1	zero	-4.4	-15.9	-	-	-
Long-Range Trajectory (yds)	50	100	200	300	400	500	-
	1.0	2.2	zero	-9.3	-27.4	-56.9	-

303 British

Bullet Style	Soft Point						
Bullet Weight	180 grains.						
Velocity (fps)	Muzzle	100	200	300	400	500	-
	2460	2210	1970	1740	1540	1360	-
Energy (ft-lb)	Muzzle	100	200	300	400	500	-
	2420	1945	1545	1215	950	740	-
Short-Range Trajectory (yds)	50	100	200	300	-	-	-
	0.1	zero	-5.7	-20.4	-	-	-
Long-Range Trajectory (yds)	50	100	200	300	400	500	-
	1.5	2.8	zero	-11.9	-35.3	-73.6	-

32 Win. Special

Bullet Style	Soft Point FN						
Bullet Weight	170 grains.						
Velocity (fps)	Muzzle	100	200	300	400	500	-
	2250	1920	1630	1380	1180	1050	-
Energy (ft-lb)	Muzzle	100	200	300	400	500	-
	1910	1395	1000	715	525	415	-
Short-Range Trajectory (yds)	50	100	200	300	-	-	-
	0.2	zero	-8.1	-29.3	-	-	-
Long-Range Trajectory (yds)	50	100	200	300	400	500	-
	2.3	4.0	zero	-17.2	-53.1	-114.4	-

8mm Mauser (8x57mm JS Mauser)

Bullet Style	Soft Point						
Bullet Weight	170 grains.						
Velocity (fps)	Muzzle	100	200	300	400	500	-
	2250	2030	1810	1620	1440	1290	-
Energy (ft-lb)	Muzzle	100	200	300	400	500	-
	1910	1550	1240	990	785	630	-
Short-Range Trajectory (yds)	50	100	200	300	-	-	-
	0.2	zero	-6.9	-24.8	-	-	-
Long-Range Trajectory (yds)	50	100	200	300	400	500	-
	1.9	3.5	zero	-14.3	-41.6	-86.1	-

357 Magnum

Bullet Style	Hollow Point						
Bullet Weight	180 grains.						
Velocity (fps)	Muzzle	100	200	300	400	500	-
	1550	1280	1100	980	900	840	-
Energy (ft-lb)	Muzzle	100	200	300	400	500	-
	960	655	480	385	325	285	-
Short-Range Trajectory (yds)	50	100	200	300	-	-	-
	1.5	zero	-19.7	-68.1	-	-	-
Long-Range Trajectory (yds)	50	100	200	300	400	500	-
	-	-	-	-	-	-	-

35 Rem.

Bullet Style	Soft Point RN						
Bullet Weight	200 grains.						
Velocity (fps)	Muzzle	100	200	300	400	500	-
	2080	1700	1370	1140	1000	910	-
Energy (ft-lb)	Muzzle	100	200	300	400	500	-
	1920	1280	840	575	445	370	-
Short-Range Trajectory (yds)	50	100	200	300	-	-	-
	0.5	zero	-10.7	-40.2	-	-	-
Long-Range Trajectory (yds)	50	100	200	300	400	500	-
	3.2	5.4	zero	-24.1	-75.1	-159.2	-

44 Rem. Magnum

Bullet Style	Soft Point						
Bullet Weight	240 grains.						
Velocity (fps)	Muzzle	100	200	300	400	500	-
	1760	1390	1120	980	890	810	-
Energy (ft-lb)	Muzzle	100	200	300	400	500	-
	1650	1025	670	510	415	350	-
Short-Range Trajectory (yds)	50	100	200	300	-	-	-
	1.0	zero	-16.8	-60.9	-	-	-
Long-Range Trajectory (yds)	50	100	200	300	400	500	-
	-	-	-	-	-	-	-

45-70 Government

Bullet Style	Hollow Point						
Bullet Weight	300 grains.						
Velocity (fps)	Muzzle	100	200	300	400	500	-
	1850	1610	1400	1230	1100	1010	-
Energy (ft-lb)	Muzzle	100	200	300	400	500	-
	2280	1730	1305	1000	800	680	-
Short-Range Trajectory (yds)	50	100	200	300	-	-	-
	0.7	zero	-11.9	-41.7	-	-	-
Long-Range Trajectory (yds)	50	100	200	300	400	500	-
	3.7	5.9	zero	-23.9	-71.0	-146.8	-

Winchester Ballistics Tables

SUPREME ELITE & SUPREME RIFLE BALLISTICS

243 Winchester

Bullet Style	XP3®					
Bullet Weight	95 grs.					
Velocity (fps)	Muzzle	100	200	300	400	500
	3100	2864	2641	2428	2225	2032
Energy (ft-lb)	Muzzle	100	200	300	400	500
	2027	1730	1471	1243	1044	871
Short-Range Trajectory (yds)	50	100	200	300	400	500
	-0.3	0	-2.7	-10.5	-24.1	—
Long-Range Trajectory (yds)	50	100	200	300	400	500
	—	1.4	0	-6.4	-18.7	-38

243 Winchester

Bullet Style	Ballistic Silvertip®					
Bullet Weight	95 grs.					
Velocity (fps)	Muzzle	100	200	300	400	500
	3100	2854	2626	2410	2203	2007
Energy (ft-lb)	Muzzle	100	200	300	400	500
	2021	1719	1455	1225	1024	850
Short-Range Trajectory (yds)	50	100	200	300	400	500
	-0.3	0	-2.8	-10.6	-24.4	—
Long-Range Trajectory (yds)	50	100	200	300	400	500
	—	1.4	0	-6.4	-18.9	-38.4

243 WSSM

Bullet Style	XP3®					
Bullet Weight	95 grs.					
Velocity (fps)	Muzzle	100	200	300	400	500
	3150	2912	2686	2471	2266	2071
Energy (ft-lb)	Muzzle	100	200	300	400	500
	2093	1788	1521	1287	1083	904
Short-Range Trajectory (yds)	50	100	200	300	400	500
	-0.3	0	-2.6	-10	-23.2	—
Long-Range Trajectory (yds)	50	100	200	300	400	500
	—	1.3	0	-6.1	-18	-36.6

243 WSSM						
Bullet Style	Ballistic Silvertip®					
Bullet Weight	95 grs.					
Velocity (fps)	Muzzle	100	200	300	400	500
	3150	2905	2674	2453	2244	2045
Energy (ft-lb)	Muzzle	100	200	300	400	500
	2093	1780	1508	1270	1062	882
Short-Range Trajectory (yds)	50	100	200	300	400	500
	-0.3	0	-2.6	-10.1	-23.4	—
Long-Range Trajectory (yds)	50	100	200	300	400	500
	—	1.3	0	-6.2	-18.2	-37.1

25 WSSM						
Bullet Style	AccuBond® CT®					
Bullet Weight	110 grs.					
Velocity (fps)	Muzzle	100	200	300	400	500
	3100	2870	2651	2442	2243	2053
Energy (ft-lb)	Muzzle	100	200	300	400	500
	2347	2011	1716	1456	1228	1029
Short-Range Trajectory (yds)	50	100	200	300	400	500
	-0.3	0	-2.7	-10.4	-24	—
Long-Range Trajectory (yds)	50	100	200	300	400	500
	—	1.4	0	-6.3	-18.5	-37.6

25 WSSM						
Bullet Style	Ballistic Silvertip®					
Bullet Weight	115 grs.					
Velocity (fps)	Muzzle	100	200	300	400	500
	3060	2844	2639	2442	2254	2074
Energy (ft-lb)	Muzzle	100	200	300	400	500
	2392	2066	1778	1523	1298	1099
Short-Range Trajectory (yds)	50	100	200	300	400	500
	-0.3	0	-2.8	-10.6	-24.3	—
Long-Range Trajectory (yds)	50	100	200	300	400	500
	—	1.4	0	-6.4	-18.6	-37.7

25-06 Remington

Bullet Style	AccuBond® CT®					
Bullet Weight	110 grs.					
Velocity (fps)	Muzzle	100	200	300	400	500
	3100	2870	2651	2442	2243	2053
Energy (ft-lb)	Muzzle	100	200	300	400	500
	2347	2011	1716	1456	1228	1029
Short-Range Trajectory (yds)	50	100	200	300	400	500
	-0.3	0	-2.7	-10.4	-24	—
Long-Range Trajectory (yds)	50	100	200	300	400	500
	—	1.4	0	-6.3	-18.5	-37.6

25-06 Remington

Bullet Style	Ballistic Silvertip®					
Bullet Weight	115 grs.					
Velocity (fps)	Muzzle	100	200	300	400	500
	3060	2844	2639	2442	2254	2074
Energy (ft-lb)	Muzzle	100	200	300	400	500
	2392	2066	1778	1523	1298	1099
Short-Range Trajectory (yds)	50	100	200	300	400	500
	-0.3	0	-2.8	-10.6	-24.3	—
Long-Range Trajectory (yds)	50	100	200	300	400	500
	—	1.4	0	-6.4	-18.6	-37.7

270 Winchester

Bullet Style	E-Tip®					
Bullet Weight	130 grs.					
Velocity (fps)	Muzzle	100	200	300	400	500
	3050	2841	2641	2450	2267	2092
Energy (ft-lb)	Muzzle	100	200	300	400	500
	2685	2329	2013	1732	1483	1263
Short-Range Trajectory (yds)	50	100	200	300	400	500
	-0.2	0	-2.8	-10.6	-24.2	—
Long-Range Trajectory (yds)	50	100	200	300	400	500
	—	1.4	0	-6.4	-18.6	-37.6

270 Winchester

Bullet Style	XP3®					
Bullet Weight	130 grs.					
Velocity (fps)	Muzzle	100	200	300	400	500
	3050	2830	2621	2420	2229	2047
Energy (ft-lb)	Muzzle	100	200	300	400	500
	2685	2311	1982	1691	1434	1209
Short-Range Trajectory (yds)	50	100	200	300	400	500
	-0.2	0	-2.8	-11	-25	—
Long-Range Trajectory (yds)	50	100	200	300	400	500
	—	1.4	0	-6.5	-19	-38

270 Winchester

Bullet Style	XP3®					
Bullet Weight	150 grs.					
Velocity (fps)	Muzzle	100	200	300	400	500
	2950	2763	2583	2411	2245	2086
Energy (ft-lb)	Muzzle	100	200	300	400	500
	2898	2542	2223	1936	1679	1449
Short-Range Trajectory (yds)	50	100	200	300	400	500
	-0.2	0	-3.1	-11.3	-25.6	—
Long-Range Trajectory (yds)	50	100	200	300	400	500
	—	1.5	0	-6.7	-19.5	-39.1

270 Winchester

Bullet Style	AccuBond® CT®					
Bullet Weight	140 grs.					
Velocity (fps)	Muzzle	100	200	300	400	500
	2950	2751	2560	2378	2203	2035
Energy (ft-lb)	Muzzle	100	200	300	400	500
	2705	2352	2038	1757	1508	1287
Short-Range Trajectory (yds)	50	100	200	300	400	500
	-0.2	0	-3.1	-11.5	-26.1	—
Long-Range Trajectory (yds)	50	100	200	300	400	500
	—	1.6	0	-6.9	-19.9	-40.1

270 Winchester

Bullet Style	Ballistic Silvertip®					
Bullet Weight	130 grs.					
Velocity (fps)	Muzzle	100	200	300	400	500
	3050	2828	2618	2416	2224	2040
Energy (ft-lb)	Muzzle	100	200	300	400	500
	2685	2309	1978	1685	1428	1202
Short-Range Trajectory (yds)	50	100	200	300	400	500
	-0.2	0	-2.8	-10.8	-24.7	—
Long-Range Trajectory (yds)	50	100	200	300	400	500
	—	1.4	0	-6.5	-18.9	-38.4

270 WSM

Bullet Style	E-Tip®					
Bullet Weight	130 grs.					
Velocity (fps)	Muzzle	100	200	300	400	500
	3275	3055	2845	2645	2454	2271
Energy (ft-lb)	Muzzle	100	200	300	400	500
	3096	2693	2336	2020	1738	1488
Short-Range Trajectory (yds)	50	100	200	300	400	500
	-0.3	0	-2.3	-8.9	-20.6	—
Long-Range Trajectory (yds)	50	100	200	300	400	500
	—	1.1	0	-5.5	-16.1	-32.7

270 WSM

Bullet Style	XP3®					
Bullet Weight	130 grs.					
Velocity (fps)	Muzzle	100	200	300	400	500
	3275	3043	2824	2614	2415	2224
Energy (ft-lb)	Muzzle	100	200	300	400	500
	3096	2673	2301	1973	1683	1427
Short-Range Trajectory (yds)	50	100	200	300	400	500
	-0.3	0	-2.6	-9.8	-22.3	—
Long-Range Trajectory (yds)	50	100	200	300	400	500
	—	1.3	0	-5.9	-17.1	-34.5

270 WSM

Bullet Style	XP3®					
Bullet Weight	150 grs.					
Velocity (fps)	Muzzle	100	200	300	400	500
	3120	2926	2740	2561	2389	2224
Energy (ft-lb)	Muzzle	100	200	300	400	500
	3242	2850	2499	2184	1901	1648
Short-Range Trajectory (yds)	50	100	200	300	400	500
	-0.3	0	-2.4	-9.3	-21.3	—
Long-Range Trajectory (yds)	50	100	200	300	400	500
	—	1.2	0	-5.7	-16.5	-33.3

270 WSM

Bullet Style	Ballistic Silvertip®					
Bullet Weight	130 grs.					
Velocity (fps)	Muzzle	100	200	300	400	500
	3275	3041	2820	2609	2408	2215
Energy (ft-lb)	Muzzle	100	200	300	400	500
	3096	2669	2295	1964	1673	1416
Short-Range Trajectory (yds)	50	100	200	300	400	500
	-0.3	0	-2.6	-9.8	-22.4	—
Long-Range Trajectory (yds)	50	100	200	300	400	500
	—	1.3	0	-5.9	-17.2	-34.7

270 WSM

Bullet Style	Ballistic Silvertip®					
Bullet Weight	150 grs.					
Velocity (fps)	Muzzle	100	200	300	400	500
	3120	2923	2734	2554	2380	2213
Energy (ft-lb)	Muzzle	100	200	300	400	500
	3242	2845	2490	2172	1886	1613
Short-Range Trajectory (yds)	50	100	200	300	400	500
	-0.2	0	-2.8	-10.6	-24	—
Long-Range Trajectory (yds)	50	100	200	300	400	500
	—	1.4	0	-6.3	-18.4	-37

280 Remington

Bullet Style	Ballistic Silvertip®					
Bullet Weight	140 grs.					
Velocity (fps)	Muzzle	100	200	300	400	500
	3040	2842	2653	2471	2297	2130
Energy (ft-lb)	Muzzle	100	200	300	400	500
	2872	2511	2187	1898	1640	1410
Short-Range Trajectory (yds)	50	100	200	300	400	500
	-0.1	0	-3.8	-13.7	-30.8	—
Long-Range Trajectory (yds)	50	100	200	300	400	500
	—	1.9	0	-8	-23.2	-46.9

7mm-08 Remington

Bullet Style	Ballistic Silvertip®					
Bullet Weight	140 grs.					
Velocity (fps)	Muzzle	100	200	300	400	500
	2770	2572	2382	2200	2026	1860
Energy (ft-lb)	Muzzle	100	200	300	400	500
	2386	2056	1764	1504	1276	1076
Short-Range Trajectory (yds)	50	100	200	300	400	500
	-0.3	0	-2.5	-9.5	-21.8	—
Long-Range Trajectory (yds)	50	100	200	300	400	500
	—	1.2	0	-5.8	-16.8	-33.9

7mm WSM

Bullet Style	E-Tip®					
Bullet Weight	140 grs.					
Velocity (fps)	Muzzle	100	200	300	400	500
	3150	2952	2763	2582	2408	2241
Energy (ft-lb)	Muzzle	100	200	300	400	500
	3304	2903	2543	2220	1931	1672
Short-Range Trajectory (yds)	50	100	200	300	400	500
	-0.3	0	-2.7	-10.3	-23.5	—
Long-Range Trajectory (yds)	50	100	200	300	400	500
	—	1.4	0	-6.2	-18	-36.1

7mm WSM

Bullet Style	XP3®					
Bullet Weight	160 grs.					
Velocity (fps)	Muzzle	100	200	300	400	500
	3050	2862	2682	2509	2342	2182
Energy (ft-lb)	Muzzle	100	200	300	400	500
	3304	2910	2555	2235	1948	1691
Short-Range Trajectory (yds)	50	100	200	300	400	500
	-0.3	0	-2.3	-9.1	-21.2	—
Long-Range Trajectory (yds)	50	100	200	300	400	500
	—	1.2	0	-5.6	-16.4	-33.1

7mm WSM

Bullet Style	AccuBond® CT®					
Bullet Weight	140 grs.					
Velocity (fps)	Muzzle	100	200	300	400	500
	3225	3008	2801	2604	2415	2233
Energy (ft-lb)	Muzzle	100	200	300	400	500
	3233	2812	2439	2107	1812	1550
Short-Range Trajectory (yds)	50	100	200	300	400	500
	-0.3	0	-2.7	-10.3	-23.5	—
Long-Range Trajectory (yds)	50	100	200	300	400	500
	—	1.4	0	-6.2	-17.9	-36

7mm WSM

Bullet Style	Ballistic Silvertip®					
Bullet Weight	140 grs.					
Velocity (fps)	Muzzle	100	200	300	400	500
	3225	3008	2810	2603	2414	2233
Energy (ft-lb)	Muzzle	100	200	300	400	500
	3233	2812	2438	2106	1812	1550
Short-Range Trajectory (yds)	50	100	200	300	400	500
	-0.3	0	-2.6	-10	-22.7	—
Long-Range Trajectory (yds)	50	100	200	300	400	500
	—	1.3	0	-6	-17.5	-35.1

7mm Remington Mag.

Bullet Style	E-Tip®					
Bullet Weight	140 grs.					
Velocity (fps)	Muzzle	100	200	300	400	500
	3100	2905	2718	2538	2366	2200
Energy (ft-lb)	Muzzle	100	200	300	400	500
	3200	2809	2459	2145	1864	1612
Short-Range Trajectory (yds)	50	100	200	300	400	500
	-0.2	0	-3	-11.3	-25.5	—
Long-Range Trajectory (yds)	50	100	200	300	400	500
	—	1.5	0	-6.7	-19.4	-38.9

7mm Remington Mag.

Bullet Style	XP3®					
Bullet Weight	160 grs.					
Velocity (fps)	Muzzle	100	200	300	400	500
	2950	2766	2590	2420	2257	2100
Energy (ft-lb)	Muzzle	100	200	300	400	500
	3091	2718	2382	2080	1809	1599
Short-Range Trajectory (yds)	50	100	200	300	400	500
	-0.3	0	-2.5	-9.5	-21.8	—
Long-Range Trajectory (yds)	50	100	200	300	400	500
	—	1.2	0	-5.8	-16.9	-34.2

7mm Remington Mag.

Bullet Style	AccuBond® CT®					
Bullet Weight	140 grs.					
Velocity (fps)	Muzzle	100	200	300	400	500
	3180	2965	2760	2565	2377	2197
Energy (ft-lb)	Muzzle	100	200	300	400	500
	3143	2733	2368	2044	1756	1501
Short-Range Trajectory (yds)	50	100	200	300	400	500
	-0.2	0	-3	-11.3	-25.5	—
Long-Range Trajectory (yds)	50	100	200	300	400	500
	—	1.5	0	-6.7	-19.4	-38.9

7mm Remington Mag.

Bullet Style	Ballistic Silvertip®					
Bullet Weight	140 grs.					
Velocity (fps)	Muzzle	100	200	300	400	500
	3110	2899	2697	2504	2319	2142
Energy (ft-lb)	Muzzle	100	200	300	400	500
	3008	2612	2261	1949	1671	1426
Short-Range Trajectory (yds)	50	100	200	300	400	500
	-0.3	0	-2.6	-10	-22.8	—
Long-Range Trajectory (yds)	50	100	200	300	400	500
	—	1.3	0	-6	-17.5	-35.1

7mm Remington Mag.

Bullet Style	Ballistic Silvertip®					
Bullet Weight	150 grs.					
Velocity (fps)	Muzzle	100	200	300	400	500
	3100	2903	2714	2533	2359	2192
Energy (ft-lb)	Muzzle	100	200	300	400	500
	3200	2806	2453	2136	1853	1600
Short-Range Trajectory (yds)	50	100	200	300	400	500
	0.4	0	-7.5	-27	-63	—
Long-Range Trajectory (yds)	50	100	200	300	400	500
	—	3.8	0	-15.6	-47.9	—

30-30 Winchester

Bullet Style	Ballistic Silvertip®					
Bullet Weight	150 grs.					
Velocity (fps)	Muzzle	100	200	300	400	500
	2390	2040	1723	1447	1225	1072
Energy (ft-lb)	Muzzle	100	200	300	400	500
	1902	1386	989	697	499	383
Short-Range Trajectory (yds)	50	100	200	300	400	500
	0.4	0	-7.5	-27.0	-63.0	—
Long-Range Trajectory (yds)	50	100	200	300	400	500
	—	3.8	0	-15.6	-47.9	—

30-06 Springfield

Bullet Style	XP3®					
Bullet Weight	180 grs.					
Velocity (fps)	Muzzle	100	200	300	400	500
	2750	2579	2414	2280	2103	1957
Energy (ft-lb)	Muzzle	100	200	300	400	500
	3022	2658	2330	2034	1768	1530
Short-Range Trajectory (yds)	50	100	200	300	400	500
	-0.1	0	-3.7	-13.4	-30	—
Long-Range Trajectory (yds)	50	100	200	300	400	500
	—	1.9	0	-7.8	-22.5	-45.1

30-06 Springfield

Bullet Style	XP3®					
Bullet Weight	150 grs.					
Velocity (fps)	Muzzle	100	200	300	400	500
	2925	2712	2508	2313	2127	1950
Energy (ft-lb)	Muzzle	100	200	300	400	500
	2849	2448	2095	1782	1507	1266
Short-Range Trajectory (yds)	50	100	200	300	400	500
	-0.2	0	-3.2	-12	-27.3	—
Long-Range Trajectory (yds)	50	100	200	300	400	500
	—	1.6	0	-7.2	-20.8	-42.2

30-06 Springfield

Bullet Style	Ballistic Silvertip®					
Bullet Weight	150 grs.					
Velocity (fps)	Muzzle	100	200	300	400	500
	2900	2687	2483	2289	2103	1926
Energy (ft-lb)	Muzzle	100	200	300	400	500
	2801	2404	2054	1745	1473	1236
Short-Range Trajectory (yds)	50	100	200	300	400	500
	-0.2	0	-3.3	-12.3	-27.9	—
Long-Range Trajectory (yds)	50	100	200	300	400	500
	—	1.7	0	-7.3	-21.2	-43

30-06 Springfield

Bullet Style	Ballistic Silvertip®					
Bullet Weight	168 grs.					
Velocity (fps)	Muzzle	100	200	300	400	500
	2790	2599	2416	2240	2072	1911
Energy (ft-lb)	Muzzle	100	200	300	400	500
	2903	2520	2177	1872	1601	1362
Short-Range Trajectory (yds)	50	100	200	300	400	500
	-0.2	0	-3.6	-13.3	-29.8	—
Long-Range Trajectory (yds)	50	100	200	300	400	500
	—	1.8	0	-7.8	-22.5	-45.2

30-06 Springfield

Bullet Style	Ballistic Silvertip®					
Bullet Weight	180 grs.					
Velocity (fps)	Muzzle	100	200	300	400	500
	2750	2572	2402	2237	2080	1928
Energy (ft-lb)	Muzzle	100	200	300	400	500
	3022	2644	2305	2001	1728	1486
Short-Range Trajectory (yds)	50	100	200	300	400	500
	-0.1	0	-3.8	-13.6	-30.3	—
Long-Range Trajectory (yds)	50	100	200	300	400	500
	—	1.9	0	-7.9	-22.8	-45.7

300 WSM

Bullet Style	XP3®					
Bullet Weight	180 grs.					
Velocity (fps)	Muzzle	100	200	300	400	500
	3010	2829	2655	2488	2326	2171
Energy (ft-lb)	Muzzle	100	200	300	400	500
	3621	3198	2817	2473	2162	1883
Short-Range Trajectory (yds)	50	100	200	300	400	500
	-0.2	0	-2.8	-10.6	-24	—
Long-Range Trajectory (yds)	50	100	200	300	400	500
	—	1.4	0	-6.4	-18.3	-36.8

300 WSM

Bullet Style	XP3®					
Bullet Weight	150 grs.					
Velocity (fps)	Muzzle	100	200	300	400	500
	3300	3068	2847	2637	2437	2246
Energy (ft-lb)	Muzzle	100	200	300	400	500
	3626	3134	2699	2316	1978	1679
Short-Range Trajectory (yds)	50	100	200	300	400	500
	-0.3	0	-2.2	-8.7	-20.2	—
Long-Range Trajectory (yds)	50	100	200	300	400	500
	—	1.1	0	-5.4	-16	-32

300 WSM

Bullet Style	Ballistic Silvertip®					
Bullet Weight	150 grs.					
Velocity (fps)	Muzzle	100	200	300	400	500
	3300	3061	2834	2619	2414	2218
Energy (ft-lb)	Muzzle	100	200	300	400	500
	3628	3121	2676	2285	1941	1638
Short-Range Trajectory (yds)	50	100	200	300	400	500
	-0.3	0	-2.2	-8.8	-20.4	—
Long-Range Trajectory (yds)	50	100	200	300	400	500
	—	1.1	0	-5.4	-15.9	-32.4

300 Winchester Mag.

Bullet Style	XP3®					
Bullet Weight	180 grs.					
Velocity (fps)	Muzzle	100	200	300	400	500
	3000	2819	2646	2479	2318	2163
Energy (ft-lb)	Muzzle	100	200	300	400	500
	3597	3176	2797	2455	2147	1869
Short-Range Trajectory (yds)	50	100	200	300	400	500
	-0.2	0	-2.9	-10.7	-24.2	—
Long-Range Trajectory (yds)	50	100	200	300	400	500
	—	1.4	0	-6.4	-18.5	-37

300 Winchester Mag.

Bullet Style	XP3®					
Bullet Weight	150 grs.					
Velocity (fps)	Muzzle	100	200	300	400	500
	3260	3030	2811	2603	2404	2214
Energy (ft-lb)	Muzzle	100	200	300	400	500
	3539	3057	2632	2256	1925	1633
Short-Range Trajectory (yds)	50	100	200	300	400	500
	-0.3	0	-2.3	-9	-20.8	—
Long-Range Trajectory (yds)	50	100	200	300	400	500
	—	1.1	0	-5.6	-16.2	-33

308 Winchester

Bullet Style	XP3®					
Bullet Weight	150 grs.					
Velocity (fps)	Muzzle	100	200	300	400	500
	2825	2616	2417	2226	2044	1871
Energy (ft-lb)	Muzzle	100	200	300	400	500
	2658	2279	1945	1650	1392	1166
Short-Range Trajectory (yds)	50	100	200	300	400	500
	-0.2	0	-3.6	-13.1	-29.7	—
Long-Range Trajectory (yds)	50	100	200	300	400	500
	—	1.8	0	-7.8	-22.6	-45.7

308 Winchester

Bullet Style	Ballistic Silvertip®					
Bullet Weight	150 grs.					
Velocity (fps)	Muzzle	100	200	300	400	500
	2810	2601	2401	2211	2028	1856
Energy (ft-lb)	Muzzle	100	200	300	400	500
	2629	2253	1920	1627	1370	1147
Short-Range Trajectory (yds)	50	100	200	300	400	500
	-0.2	0	-3.6	-13.3	-30.2	—
Long-Range Trajectory (yds)	50	100	200	300	400	500
	—	1.8	0	-7.8	-22.8	-46.2

308 Winchester

Bullet Style	Ballistic Silvertip®					
Bullet Weight	168 grs.					
Velocity (fps)	Muzzle	100	200	300	400	500
	2670	2484	2306	2134	1971	1815
Energy (ft-lb)	Muzzle	100	200	300	400	500
	2659	2301	1983	1699	1449	1229
Short-Range Trajectory (yds)	50	100	200	300	400	500
	-0.1	0	-4.1	-14.8	-33.2	—
Long-Range Trajectory (yds)	50	100	200	300	400	500
	—	2.1	0	-8.6	-24.8	-50

308 Winchester Match

Bullet Style	Sierra MatchKing™ BTHP					
Bullet Weight	168 grs.					
Velocity (fps)	Muzzle	100	200	300	400	500
	2680	2485	2297	2118	1948	1786
Energy (ft-lb)	Muzzle	100	200	300	400	500
	2680	2303	1970	1674	1415	1190
Short-Range Trajectory (yds)	50	100	200	300	400	500
	-0.1	0	-4.1	-14.9	-33.4	—
Long-Range Trajectory (yds)	50	100	200	300	400	500
	—	2.1	0	-8.7	-25.1	-50.7

357 Magnum

Bullet Style	Partition Gold®					
Bullet Weight	180 grs.					
Velocity (fps)	Muzzle	100	200	300	400	500
	1550	1160	965	854	769	698
Energy (ft-lb)	Muzzle	100	200	300	400	500
	960	538	372	291	237	195
Short-Range Trajectory (yds)	50	100	200	300	400	500
	2	0	-24.9	-87.1	—	—
Long-Range Trajectory (yds)	50	100	200	300	400	500
	—	12.2	0	-49.4	—	—

41 Remington Mag.

Bullet Style	Platinum Tip®					
Bullet Weight	240 grs.					
Velocity (fps)	Muzzle	100	200	300	400	500
	1830	1488	1219	1047	945	870
Energy (ft-lb)	Muzzle	100	200	300	400	500
	1784	1179	792	584	475	403
Short-Range Trajectory (yds)	50	100	200	300	400	500
	1.1	0	-15	-53.5	—	—
Long-Range Trajectory (yds)	50	100	200	300	400	500
	—	7.2	0	-30.7	-92.9	—

44 Remington Mag.

Bullet Style	Platinum Tip®					
Bullet Weight	250 grs.					
Velocity (fps)	Muzzle	100	200	300	400	500
	1830	1475	1202	1032	931	857
Energy (ft-lb)	Muzzle	100	200	300	400	500
	1859	1208	801	592	481	408
Short-Range Trajectory (yds)	50	100	200	300	400	500
	1.2	0	-15.4	-55.1	—	—
Long-Range Trajectory (yds)	50	100	200	300	400	500
	—	7.3	0	-31.5	-95.4	—

44 Remington Mag.

Bullet Style	Partition Gold®					
Bullet Weight	250 grs.					
Velocity (fps)	Muzzle	100	200	300	400	500
	1810	1456	1188	1025	926	853
Energy (ft-lb)	Muzzle	100	200	300	400	500
	1818	1176	783	583	476	404
Short-Range Trajectory (yds)	50	100	200	300	400	500
	1.2	0	-15.4	-55.1	—	—
Long-Range Trajectory (yds)	50	100	200	300	400	500
	—	7.4	0	-32.1	-97.2	—

SUPER-X RIFLE BALLISTICS

22-250 Remington

Bullet Style	Power-Point®					
Bullet Weight	64 grs.					
Velocity (fps)	Muzzle	100	200	300	400	500
	3500	3086	2708	2360	2038	1744
Energy (ft-lb)	Muzzle	100	200	300	400	500
	1741	1353	1042	791	590	432
Short-Range Trajectory (yds)	50	100	200	300	400	500
	-0.3	0	-2.2	-9.1	-22.4	—
Long-Range Trajectory (yds)	50	100	200	300	400	500
	—	1.1	0	-5.9	-18	-38.6

223 Remington

Bullet Style	Power-Point®					
Bullet Weight	64 grs.					
Velocity (fps)	Muzzle	100	200	300	400	500
	3020	2656	2320	2009	1724	1473
Energy (ft-lb)	Muzzle	100	200	300	400	500
	1296	1003	765	574	423	308
Short-Range Trajectory (yds)	50	100	200	300	400	500
	-0.2	0	-3.5	-13.4	-32.1	—
Long-Range Trajectory (yds)	50	100	200	300	400	500
	—	1.7	0	-8.2	-25.1	-53.6

223 WSSM

Bullet Style	Power-Point®					
Bullet Weight	64 grs.					
Velocity (fps)	Muzzle	100	200	300	400	500
	3600	3144	2732	2356	2011	1698
Energy (ft-lb)	Muzzle	100	200	300	400	500
	1841	1404	1061	789	574	410
Short-Range Trajectory (yds)	50	100	200	300	400	500
	-0.4	0	-2	-8.8	-21.8	—
Long-Range Trajectory (yds)	50	100	200	300	400	500
	—	1	0	-5.7	-17.7	-38.5

243 Winchester

Bullet Style	Power Max Bonded®					
Bullet Weight	100 grs.					
Velocity (fps)	Muzzle	100	200	300	400	500
	2960	2708	2470	2244	2031	1829
Energy (ft-lb)	Muzzle	100	200	300	400	500
	1945	1628	1355	1118	915	743
Short-Range Trajectory (yds)	50	100	200	300	400	500
	-0.2	0	-3.3	-12.2	-28.1	—
Long-Range Trajectory (yds)	50	100	200	300	400	500
	—	1.6	0	-7.3	-21.6	-44.3

243 Winchester

Bullet Style	Power-Point®					
Bullet Weight	100 grs.					
Velocity (fps)	Muzzle	100	200	300	400	500
	2960	2697	2449	2215	1993	1786
Energy (ft-lb)	Muzzle	100	200	300	400	500
	1945	1615	1332	1089	882	708
Short-Range Trajectory (yds)	50	100	200	300	400	500
	-0.2	0	-3.3	-12.4	-28.6	—
Long-Range Trajectory (yds)	50	100	200	300	400	500
	—	1.9	0	-7.8	-22.6	-46.3

243 WSSM

Bullet Style	Power-Point®					
Bullet Weight	100 grs.					
Velocity (fps)	Muzzle	100	200	300	400	500
	3110	2838	2583	2341	2112	1897
Energy (ft-lb)	Muzzle	100	200	300	400	500
	2147	1789	1481	1217	991	799
Short-Range Trajectory (yds)	50	100	200	300	400	500
	-0.3	0	-2.8	-10.9	-25.3	—
Long-Range Trajectory (yds)	50	100	200	300	400	500
	—	1.4	0	-6.6	-19.7	-40.5

6mm Remington

Bullet Style	Power-Point®					
Bullet Weight	100 grs.					
Velocity (fps)	Muzzle	100	200	300	400	500
	3100	2829	2573	2332	2104	1889
Energy (ft-lb)	Muzzle	100	200	300	400	500
	2133	1777	1470	1207	983	792
Short-Range Trajectory (yds)	50	100	200	300	400	500
	-0.3	0	-2.9	-11	-25.5	—
Long-Range Trajectory (yds)	50	100	200	300	400	500
	—	1.7	0	-7	-20.4	-41.7

25 WSSM

Bullet Style	Positive Exp. Point					
Bullet Weight	120 grs.					
Velocity (fps)	Muzzle	100	200	300	400	500
	2990	2717	2459	2216	1987	1773
Energy (ft-lb)	Muzzle	100	200	300	400	500
	2383	1967	1612	1309	1053	838
Short-Range Trajectory (yds)	50	100	200	300	400	500
	-0.2	0	-3.2	-12.2	-28.3	—
Long-Range Trajectory (yds)	50	100	200	300	400	500
	—	1.6	0	-7.4	-21.8	-45.1

25-06 Remington

Bullet Style	Positive Exp. Point					
Bullet Weight	120 grs.					
Velocity (fps)	Muzzle	100	200	300	400	500
	2990	2717	2459	2216	1987	1773
Energy (ft-lb)	Muzzle	100	200	300	400	500
	2382	1967	1612	1309	1053	838
Short-Range Trajectory (yds)	50	100	200	300	400	500
	-0.2	0	-3.2	-12.2	-28.3	—
Long-Range Trajectory (yds)	50	100	200	300	400	500
	—	1.6	0	-7.4	-21.8	-45.1

25-20 Winchester

Bullet Style	Soft Point					
Bullet Weight	117 grs.					
Velocity (fps)	Muzzle	100	200	300	400	500
	2230	1866	1545	1281	1096	984
Energy (ft-lb)	Muzzle	100	200	300	400	500
	1292	904	620	426	312	252
Short-Range Trajectory (yds)	50	100	200	300	400	500
	0.6	0	-9.2	-33.2	-78.4	—
Long-Range Trajectory (yds)	50	100	200	300	400	500
	—	4.3	0	-19	-59.4	—

250 Savage

Bullet Style	Silvertip®					
Bullet Weight	100 grs.					
Velocity (fps)	Muzzle	100	200	300	400	500
	2820	2467	2140	1839	1569	1339
Energy (ft-lb)	Muzzle	100	200	300	400	500
	1765	1351	1017	751	547	398
Short-Range Trajectory (yds)	50	100	200	300	400	500
	-0.1	0	-4.3	-16.2	-38.4	—
Long-Range Trajectory (yds)	50	100	200	300	400	500
	—	2.4	0	-10.1	-30.5	-65.2

257 Roberts +P

Bullet Style	Power-Point®					
Bullet Weight	117 grs.					
Velocity (fps)	Muzzle	100	200	300	400	500
	2780	2411	2071	1761	1488	1263
Energy (ft-lb)	Muzzle	100	200	300	400	500
	2009	1511	1115	806	576	415
Short-Range Trajectory (yds)	50	100	200	300	400	500
	-0.1	0	-4.5	-17.2	-41.3	—
Long-Range Trajectory (yds)	50	100	200	300	400	500
	—	2.6	0	-10.8	-33	-70

264 Winchester Mag.

Bullet Style	Power-Point®					
Bullet Weight	140 grs.					
Velocity (fps)	Muzzle	100	200	300	400	500
	3030	2782	2548	2326	2114	1914
Energy (ft-lb)	Muzzle	100	200	300	400	500
	2854	2406	2018	1682	1389	1139
Short-Range Trajectory (yds)	50	100	200	300	400	500
	-0.2	0	-3	-11.4	-26.2	—
Long-Range Trajectory (yds)	50	100	200	300	400	500
	—	1.8	0	-7.2	-20.8	-42.2

6.5 x 55 Swedish

Bullet Style	Soft Point					
Bullet Weight	140 grs.					
Velocity (fps)	Muzzle	100	200	300	400	500
	2550	2359	2176	2002	1836	1680
Energy (ft-lb)	Muzzle	100	200	300	400	500
	2021	1730	1472	1246	1048	877
Short-Range Trajectory (yds)	50	100	200	300	400	500
	0	0	-4.8	-16.9	-37.7	—
Long-Range Trajectory (yds)	50	100	200	300	400	500
	—	2.4	0	-9.7	-28.2	-56.9

270 Winchester

Bullet Style	Power Max Bonded®					
Bullet Weight	130 grs.					
Velocity (fps)	Muzzle	100	200	300	400	500
	3060	2779	2515	2266	2032	1814
Energy (ft-lb)	Muzzle	100	200	300	400	500
	2702	2229	1826	1482	1191	950
Short-Range Trajectory (yds)	50	100	200	300	400	500
	-0.2	0	-3	-11.5	-26.9	—
Long-Range Trajectory (yds)	50	100	200	300	400	500
	—	1.5	0	-7	-20.8	-42.6

270 Winchester

Bullet Style	Power-Point®					
Bullet Weight	130 grs.					
Velocity (fps)	Muzzle	100	200	300	400	500
	3060	2802	2559	2329	2110	1904
Energy (ft-lb)	Muzzle	100	200	300	400	500
	2702	2267	1890	1565	1285	1046
Short-Range Trajectory (yds)	50	100	200	300	400	500
	-0.2	0	-2.9	-11.2	-25.9	—
Long-Range Trajectory (yds)	50	100	200	300	400	500
	—	1.8	0	-7.1	-20.6	-42

270 Winchester

Bullet Style	Silvertip®					
Bullet Weight	130 grs.					
Velocity (fps)	Muzzle	100	200	300	400	500
	3060	2776	2510	2259	2022	1801
Energy (ft-lb)	Muzzle	100	200	300	400	500
	2702	2225	1818	1472	1180	936
Short-Range Trajectory (yds)	50	100	200	300	400	500
	-0.2	0	-3	-11.6	-27	—
Long-Range Trajectory (yds)	50	100	200	300	400	500
	—	1.8	0	-7.4	-21.6	-44.3

270 Winchester

Bullet Style	Power-Point®					
Bullet Weight	150 grs.					
Velocity (fps)	Muzzle	100	200	300	400	500
	2850	2585	2336	2100	1879	1673
Energy (ft-lb)	Muzzle	100	200	300	400	500
	2705	2226	1817	1468	1175	932
Short-Range Trajectory (yds)	50	100	200	300	400	500
	-0.2	0	-3.7	-13.8	-31.9	—
Long-Range Trajectory (yds)	50	100	200	300	400	500
	—	2.2	0	-8.6	-25	-51.4

270 WSM

Bullet Style	Power-Point®					
Bullet Weight	150 grs.					
Velocity (fps)	Muzzle	100	200	300	400	500
	3150	2867	2601	2350	2113	1890
Energy (ft-lb)	Muzzle	100	200	300	400	500
	3304	2737	2252	1839	1487	1190
Short-Range Trajectory (yds)	50	100	200	300	400	500
	-0.3	0	-2.7	-10.6	-24.9	—
Long-Range Trajectory (yds)	50	100	200	300	400	500
	—	1.4	0	-6.5	-19.4	-40.1

270 WSM

Bullet Style	Power Max Bonded®					
Bullet Weight	130 grs.					
Velocity (fps)	Muzzle	100	200	300	400	500
	3275	2980	2704	2445	2200	1968
Energy (ft-lb)	Muzzle	100	200	300	400	500
	3096	2563	2111	1725	1396	1119
Short-Range Trajectory (yds)	50	100	200	300	400	500
	-0.3	0	-2.4	-9.6	-22.7	—
Long-Range Trajectory (yds)	50	100	200	300	400	500
	—	1.2	0	-6	-17.8	-36.8

7mm-08 Remington

Bullet Style	Power-Point®					
Bullet Weight	140 grs.					
Velocity (fps)	Muzzle	100	200	300	400	500
	2800	2549	2312	2087	1876	1679
Energy (ft-lb)	Muzzle	100	200	300	400	500
	2437	2020	1661	1354	1094	876
Short-Range Trajectory (yds)	50	100	200	300	400	500
	-0.1	0	-3.9	-14.3	-32.7	—
Long-Range Trajectory (yds)	50	100	200	300	400	500
	—	1.9	0	-8.5	-24.9	-51.3

7mm Mauser (7 x 57)

Bullet Style	Power-Point®					
Bullet Weight	145 grs.					
Velocity (fps)	Muzzle	100	200	300	400	500
	2660	2413	2180	1960	1754	1565
Energy (ft-lb)	Muzzle	100	200	300	400	500
	2278	1875	1530	1236	990	788
Short-Range Trajectory (yds)	50	100	200	300	400	500
	-0.1	0	-4.5	-16.3	-37.2	—
Long-Range Trajectory (yds)	50	100	200	300	400	500
	—	2.2	0	-9.6	-28.3	-58.3

7mm WSM

Bullet Style	Power Max Bonded®					
Bullet Weight	150 grs.					
Velocity (fps)	Muzzle	100	200	300	400	500
	3200	2948	2710	2484	2270	2066
Energy (ft-lb)	Muzzle	100	200	300	400	500
	3410	2894	2446	2055	1716	1421
Short-Range Trajectory (yds)	50	100	200	300	400	500
	-0.3	0	-2.5	-9.8	-22.7	—
Long-Range Trajectory (yds)	50	100	200	300	400	500
	—	1.3	0	-6	-17.6	-36.1

7mm WSM

Bullet Style	Power-Point®					
Bullet Weight	150 grs.					
Velocity (fps)	Muzzle	100	200	300	400	500
	3200	2915	2648	2396	2157	1933
Energy (ft-lb)	Muzzle	100	200	300	400	500
	3410	2830	2335	1911	1550	1245
Short-Range Trajectory (yds)	50	100	200	300	400	500
	-0.3	0	-2.6	-10.2	-23.8	—
Long-Range Trajectory (yds)	50	100	200	300	400	500
	—	1.3	0	-6.3	-18.6	-38.5

7mm Remington Mag.

Bullet Style	Power Max Bonded®					
Bullet Weight	150 grs.					
Velocity (fps)	Muzzle	100	200	300	400	500
	3090	2844	2612	2391	2181	1981
Energy (ft-lb)	Muzzle	100	200	300	400	500
	3180	2694	2272	1904	1584	1307
Short-Range Trajectory (yds)	50	100	200	300	400	500
	-0.3	0	-2.8	-10.7	-24.7	—
Long-Range Trajectory (yds)	50	100	200	300	400	500
	—	-1.5	0	-6.5	-19.1	-39.1

7mm Remington Mag.

Bullet Style	Power-Point®					
Bullet Weight	150 grs.					
Velocity (fps)	Muzzle	100	200	300	400	500
	3090	2831	2587	2356	2136	1929
Energy (ft-lb)	Muzzle	100	200	300	400	500
	3180	2670	2229	1848	1520	1239
Short-Range Trajectory (yds)	50	100	200	300	400	500
	-0.3	0	-2.8	-10.9	-25.2	—
Long-Range Trajectory (yds)	50	100	200	300	400	500
	—	1.4	0	-6.6	-19.5	-40.1

7.62 x 39mm

Bullet Style	Soft Point					
Bullet Weight	123 grs.					
Velocity (fps)	Muzzle	100	200	300	400	500
	2365	2033	1731	1465	1248	1093
Energy (ft-lb)	Muzzle	100	200	300	400	500
	1527	1129	818	586	425	327
Short-Range Trajectory (yds)	50	100	200	300	400	500
	0.2	0	-7	-25.7	-60.7	—
Long-Range Trajectory (yds)	50	100	200	300	400	500
	—	3.8	0	-15.4	-46.3	-98.4

30-30 Winchester

Bullet Style	Power Max Bonded®					
Bullet Weight	150 grs.					
Velocity (fps)	Muzzle	100	200	300	400	500
	2390	2028	1702	1420	1198	1052
Energy (ft-lb)	Muzzle	100	200	300	400	500
	1902	1370	965	672	478	368
Short-Range Trajectory (yds)	50	100	200	300	400	500
	0.4	0	-7.6	-27.4	-64.6	—
Long-Range Trajectory (yds)	50	100	200	300	400	500
	—	0	-7.6	-27.4	-64.6	—

30-30 Winchester

Bullet Style	Hollow Point					
Bullet Weight	150 grs.					
Velocity (fps)	Muzzle	100	200	300	400	500
	2390	2019	1685	1398	1178	1036
Energy (ft-lb)	Muzzle	100	200	300	400	500
	1902	1357	945	651	462	357
Short-Range Trajectory (yds)	50	100	200	300	400	500
	0.5	0	-7.7	-27.9	-65.9	—
Long-Range Trajectory (yds)	50	100	200	300	400	500
	—	3.6	0	-16	-49.9	—

30-30 Winchester

Bullet Style	Power-Point®					
Bullet Weight	150 grs.					
Velocity (fps)	Muzzle	100	200	300	400	500
	2390	2019	1685	1398	1178	1036
Energy (ft-lb)	Muzzle	100	200	300	400	500
	1902	1357	945	651	462	357
Short-Range Trajectory (yds)	50	100	200	300	400	500
	0.5	0	-7.7	-27.9	-65.9	—
Long-Range Trajectory (yds)	50	100	200	300	400	500
	—	3.6	0	-16	-49.9	—

30-30 Winchester

Bullet Style	Silvertip®					
Bullet Weight	150 grs.					
Velocity (fps)	Muzzle	100	200	300	400	500
	2390	2019	1685	1398	1178	1036
Energy (ft-lb)	Muzzle	100	200	300	400	500
	1902	1357	945	651	462	357
Short-Range Trajectory (yds)	50	100	200	300	400	500
	0.5	0	-7.7	-27.9	-65.9	—
Long-Range Trajectory (yds)	50	100	200	300	400	500
	—	3.6	0	-16	-49.9	—

30-30 Winchester

Bullet Style	Power-Point®					
Bullet Weight	170 grs.					
Velocity (fps)	Muzzle	100	200	300	400	500
	2200	1879	1591	1346	1158	1034
Energy (ft-lb)	Muzzle	100	200	300	400	500
	1827	1332	955	683	506	404
Short-Range Trajectory (yds)	50	100	200	300	400	500
	0.6	0	-9	-32	-74.2	—
Long-Range Trajectory (yds)	50	100	200	300	400	500
	—	4.2	0	-18.1	-55.5	—

30-30 Winchester

Bullet Style	Silvertip®					
Bullet Weight	170 grs.					
Velocity (fps)	Muzzle	100	200	300	400	500
	2200	1920	1664	1438	1250	1110
Energy (ft-lb)	Muzzle	100	200	300	400	500
	1827	1391	1045	781	590	465
Short-Range Trajectory (yds)	50	100	200	300	400	500
	0.6	0	-8.6	-29.8	-68	—
Long-Range Trajectory (yds)	50	100	200	300	400	500
	—	4	0	-16.6	-50.2	—

30-06 Springfield

Bullet Style	Power Max Bonded®					
Bullet Weight	150 grs.					
Velocity (fps)	Muzzle	100	200	300	400	500
	2920	2636	2368	2117	1882	1664
Energy (ft-lb)	Muzzle	100	200	300	400	500
	2839	2313	1868	1492	1179	922
Short-Range Trajectory (yds)	50	100	200	300	400	500
	-0.2	0	-3.5	-13.3	-30.8	—
Long-Range Trajectory (yds)	50	100	200	300	400	500
	—	1.8	0	-8	-23.8	-49.4

30-06 Springfield

Bullet Style	Power-Point®					
Bullet Weight	150 grs.					
Velocity (fps)	Muzzle	100	200	300	400	500
	2920	2607	2314	2041	1788	1558
Energy (ft-lb)	Muzzle	100	200	300	400	500
	2839	2263	1783	1387	1064	808
Short-Range Trajectory (yds)	50	100	200	300	400	500
	-0.2	0	-3.6	-13.8	-32.4	—
Long-Range Trajectory (yds)	50	100	200	300	400	500
	—	1.8	0	-8.3	-25.1	-52.8

30-06 Springfield

Bullet Style	Silvertip®					
Bullet Weight	150 grs.					
Velocity (fps)	Muzzle	100	200	300	400	500
	2910	2617	2342	2083	1843	1622
Energy (ft-lb)	Muzzle	100	200	300	400	500
	2820	2281	1827	1445	1131	876
Short-Range Trajectory (yds)	50	100	200	300	400	500
	-0.2	0	-3.6	-13.6	-31.6	—
Long-Range Trajectory (yds)	50	100	200	300	400	500
	—	2.1	0	-8.5	-25	-51.8

30-06 Springfield

Bullet Style	Pointed Soft Point					
Bullet Weight	165 grs.					
Velocity (fps)	Muzzle	100	200	300	400	500
	2800	2536	2286	2051	1831	1627
Energy (ft-lb)	Muzzle	100	200	300	400	500
	2872	2355	1915	1541	1228	970
Short-Range Trajectory (yds)	50	100	200	300	400	500
	-0.1	0	-3.9	-14.5	-33.4	—
Long-Range Trajectory (yds)	50	100	200	300	400	500
	—	2	0	-8.6	-25.6	-53

30-06 Springfield

Bullet Style	Power Max Bonded®					
Bullet Weight	180 grs.					
Velocity (fps)	Muzzle	100	200	300	400	500
	2700	2475	2262	2058	1866	1687
Energy (ft-lb)	Muzzle	100	200	300	400	500
	2913	2448	2044	1693	1392	1137
Short-Range Trajectory (yds)	50	100	200	300	400	500
	-0.1	0	-4.2	-15.2	-34.4	—
Long-Range Trajectory (yds)	50	100	200	300	400	500
	—	2.1	0	-8.9	-26.1	-53.2

30-06 Springfield

Bullet Style	Power-Point®					
Bullet Weight	180 grs.					
Velocity (fps)	Muzzle	100	200	300	400	500
	2700	2468	2247	2038	1840	1657
Energy (ft-lb)	Muzzle	100	200	300	400	500
	2913	2433	2018	1659	1354	1097
Short-Range Trajectory (yds)	50	100	200	300	400	500
	-0.1	0	-4.2	-15.4	-34.9	—
Long-Range Trajectory (yds)	50	100	200	300	400	500
	—	2.1	0	-9	-26.4	-54.2

30-40 Krag

Bullet Style	Power-Point®					
Bullet Weight	180 grs.					
Velocity (fps)	Muzzle	100	200	300	400	500
	2430	2218	2017	1828	1651	1489
Energy (ft-lb)	Muzzle	100	200	300	400	500
	2360	1967	1626	1335	1089	886
Short-Range Trajectory (yds)	50	100	200	300	400	500
	0.4	0	-6.2	-20.9	-46.1	—
Long-Range Trajectory (yds)	50	100	200	300	400	500
	—	2.8	0	-11.4	-33.2	-67.8

300 WSM

Bullet Style	Power Max Bonded®					
Bullet Weight	150 grs.					
Velocity (fps)	Muzzle	100	200	300	400	500
	3270	2962	2675	2406	2152	1914
Energy (ft-lb)	Muzzle	100	200	300	400	500
	3561	2922	2384	1927	1542	1220
Short-Range Trajectory (yds)	50	100	200	300	400	500
	-0.3	0	-2.5	-9.8	-23.2	—
Long-Range Trajectory (yds)	50	100	200	300	400	500
	—	1.2	0	-6.1	-18.3	-37.9

300 WSM

Bullet Style	Power-Point®					
Bullet Weight	150 grs.					
Velocity (fps)	Muzzle	100	200	300	400	500
	3270	2931	2617	2324	2050	1796
Energy (ft-lb)	Muzzle	100	200	300	400	500
	3561	2861	2281	1798	1399	1074
Short-Range Trajectory (yds)	50	100	200	300	400	500
	-0.3	0	-2.6	-10.2	-24.4	—
Long-Range Trajectory (yds)	50	100	200	300	400	500
	—	1.3	0	-6.4	-19.2	-40.4

300 Winchester Mag.

Bullet Style	Power Max Bonded®					
Bullet Weight	150 grs.					
Velocity (fps)	Muzzle	100	200	300	400	500
	3290	2981	2693	2422	2168	1929
Energy (ft-lb)	Muzzle	100	200	300	400	500
	3605	2959	2415	1954	1565	1239
Short-Range Trajectory (yds)	50	100	200	300	400	500
	-0.3	0	-2.4	-9.7	-22.9	—
Long-Range Trajectory (yds)	50	100	200	300	400	500
	—	1.2	0	-6	-18	-37.4

300 Winchester Mag.

Bullet Style	Power-Point®					
Bullet Weight	150 grs.					
Velocity (fps)	Muzzle	100	200	300	400	500
	3290	2950	2634	2340	2065	1813
Energy (ft-lb)	Muzzle	100	200	300	400	500
	3605	2898	2311	1824	1420	1095
Short-Range Trajectory (yds)	50	100	200	300	400	500
	-0.3	0	-2.5	-10.1	-24	—
Long-Range Trajectory (yds)	50	100	200	300	400	500
	—	1.3	0	-6.3	-19	-39.3

300 Savage

Bullet Style	Power-Point®					
Bullet Weight	150 grs.					
Velocity (fps)	Muzzle	100	200	300	400	500
	2630	2336	2061	1810	1575	1372
Energy (ft-lb)	Muzzle	100	200	300	400	500
	2303	1817	1415	1091	826	627
Short-Range Trajectory (yds)	50	100	200	300	400	500
	0	0	-4.9	-17.3	-41.9	—
Long-Range Trajectory (yds)	50	100	200	300	400	500
	—	2.5	0	-10	-32.1	-67.6

307 Winchester

Bullet Style	Power-Point®					
Bullet Weight	180 grs.					
Velocity (fps)	Muzzle	100	200	300	400	500
	2510	2179	1874	1599	1363	1177
Energy (ft-lb)	Muzzle	100	200	300	400	500
	2518	1897	1403	1022	742	554
Short-Range Trajectory (yds)	50	100	200	300	400	500
	0	0	-5.9	-21.8	-51.3	—
Long-Range Trajectory (yds)	50	100	200	300	400	500
	—	2.9	0	-12.9	-39.6	-85.1

308 Winchester

Bullet Style	Power Max Bonded®					
Bullet Weight	150 grs.					
Velocity (fps)	Muzzle	100	200	300	400	500
	2820	2542	2280	2034	1808	1594
Energy (ft-lb)	Muzzle	100	200	300	400	500
	2648	2152	1731	1378	1089	846
Short-Range Trajectory (yds)	50	100	200	300	400	500
	-0.1	0	-3.9	-14.5	-32.9	—
Long-Range Trajectory (yds)	50	100	200	300	400	500
	—	2	0	-8.7	-25.1	-53.6

308 Winchester

Bullet Style	Power-Point®					
Bullet Weight	150 grs.					
Velocity (fps)	Muzzle	100	200	300	400	500
	2820	2513	2227	1960	1713	1492
Energy (ft-lb)	Muzzle	100	200	300	400	500
	2648	2104	1651	1279	977	742
Short-Range Trajectory (yds)	50	100	200	300	400	500
	-0.1	0	-4	-15.1	-35.3	—
Long-Range Trajectory (yds)	50	100	200	300	400	500
	—	2	0	-9.1	-27.2	-57.3

308 Winchester

Bullet Style	Power-Point®					
Bullet Weight	180 grs.					
Velocity (fps)	Muzzle	100	200	300	400	500
	2620	2392	2176	1971	1779	1600
Energy (ft-lb)	Muzzle	100	200	300	400	500
	2743	2287	1892	1553	1264	1023
Short-Range Trajectory (yds)	50	100	200	300	400	500
	-0.1	0	-4.6	-16.6	-37.5	—
Long-Range Trajectory (yds)	50	100	200	300	400	500
	—	2.3	0	-9.7	-28.3	-58

32 Winchester Special

Bullet Style	Power-Point®					
Bullet Weight	170 grs.					
Velocity (fps)	Muzzle	100	200	300	400	500
	2250	1870	1537	1266	1081	971
Energy (ft-lb)	Muzzle	100	200	300	400	500
	1911	1320	891	605	441	356
Short-Range Trajectory (yds)	50	100	200	300	400	500
	0.6	0	-9.2	-33.3	-79.1	—
Long-Range Trajectory (yds)	50	100	200	300	400	500
	—	4.3	0	-19.2	-60.2	—

8mm Mauser (8 x 57)

Bullet Style	Power-Point®					
Bullet Weight	170 grs.					
Velocity (fps)	Muzzle	100	200	300	400	500
	2360	1970	1623	1333	1123	997
Energy (ft-lb)	Muzzle	100	200	300	400	500
	2102	1464	994	671	476	375
Short-Range Trajectory (yds)	50	100	200	300	400	500
	0.2	0	-7.6	-28.5	-69.2	—
Long-Range Trajectory (yds)	50	100	200	300	400	500
	—	3.8	0	-17.2	-54.1	—

35 Remington

Bullet Style	Power-Point®					
Bullet Weight	200 grs.					
Velocity (fps)	Muzzle	100	200	300	400	500
	2020	1646	1335	1114	985	901
Energy (ft-lb)	Muzzle	100	200	300	400	500
	1812	1203	791	551	431	360
Short-Range Trajectory (yds)	50	100	200	300	400	500
	0.9	0	-12.1	-43.9	—	—
Long-Range Trajectory (yds)	50	100	200	300	400	500
	—	5.8	0	-25.4	-78.7	—

356 Winchester

Bullet Style	Power-Point®					
Bullet Weight	200 grs.					
Velocity (fps)	Muzzle	100	200	300	400	500
	2460	2114	1797	1517	1284	1113
Energy (ft-lb)	Muzzle	100	200	300	400	500
	2688	1985	1434	1022	732	550
Short-Range Trajectory (yds)	50	100	200	300	400	500
	0.4	0	-7	-24.8	-57.9	—
Long-Range Trajectory (yds)	50	100	200	300	400	500
	—	3.2	0	-14.1	-43.4	-93.9

357 Magnum

Bullet Style	Jacketed H.P.					
Bullet Weight	158 grs.					
Velocity (fps)	Muzzle	100	200	300	400	500
	1830	1427	1138	980	883	809
Energy (ft-lb)	Muzzle	100	200	300	400	500
	1175	715	454	337	274	229
Short-Range Trajectory (yds)	50	100	200	300	400	500
	1.2	0	-16.4	-59.6	—	—
Long-Range Trajectory (yds)	50	100	200	300	400	500
	—	7.9	0	-34.7	—	—

357 Magnum

Bullet Style	Jacketed Soft Point					
Bullet Weight	158 grs.					
Velocity (fps)	Muzzle	100	200	300	400	500
	1830	1427	1138	980	883	809
Energy (ft-lb)	Muzzle	100	200	300	400	500
	1175	715	454	337	274	229
Short-Range Trajectory (yds)	50	100	200	300	400	500
	1.2	0	-16.4	-59.6	—	—
Long-Range Trajectory (yds)	50	100	200	300	400	500
	—	7.9	0	-34.7	—	—

375 Winchester

Bullet Style	Power-Point®					
Bullet Weight	200 grs.					
Velocity (fps)	Muzzle	100	200	300	400	500
	2200	1841	1526	1268	1089	980
Energy (ft-lb)	Muzzle	100	200	300	400	500
	2150	1506	1034	714	527	427
Short-Range Trajectory (yds)	50	100	200	300	400	500
	3.4	0	-33.8	—	—	—
Long-Range Trajectory (yds)	50	100	200	300	400	500
	—	16.6	0	-59.4	—	—

38-40 Winchester

Bullet Style	Soft Point					
Bullet Weight	180 grs.					
Velocity (fps)	Muzzle	100	200	300	400	500
	1160	999	901	827	764	710
Energy (ft-lb)	Muzzle	100	200	300	400	500
	538	399	324	273	233	201
Short-Range Trajectory (yds)	50	100	200	300	400	500
	2.3	0	-23.7	-76.5	—	—
Long-Range Trajectory (yds)	50	100	200	300	400	500
	—	11.5	0	-40.7	—	—

38-55 Winchester

Bullet Style	Soft Point					
Bullet Weight	255 grs.					
Velocity (fps)	Muzzle	100	200	300	400	500
	1320	1190	1091	1018	963	917
Energy (ft-lb)	Muzzle	100	200	300	400	500
	987	802	674	587	525	476
Short-Range Trajectory (yds)	50	100	200	300	400	500
	3.2	0	-33.2	—	—	—
Long-Range Trajectory (yds)	50	100	200	300	400	500
	—	16.3	0	-59.2	—	—

44 Remington Mag.

Bullet Style	Hollow Soft Point					
Bullet Weight	240 grs.					
Velocity (fps)	Muzzle	100	200	300	400	500
	1760	1362	1094	953	861	789
Energy (ft-lb)	Muzzle	100	200	300	400	500
	1650	988	638	484	395	332
Short-Range Trajectory (yds)	50	100	200	300	400	500
	1	0	-12.2	-42	-94.6	—
Long-Range Trajectory (yds)	50	100	200	300	400	500
	—	5.8	0	-23.3	-69.5	—

44-40 Winchester

Bullet Style	Soft Point					
Bullet Weight	200 grs.					
Velocity (fps)	Muzzle	100	200	300	400	500
	1190	1006	900	822	756	699
Energy (ft-lb)	Muzzle	100	200	300	400	500
	629	449	360	300	254	217
Short-Range Trajectory (yds)	50	100	200	300	400	500
	0.5	0	-9.7	-34.4	-79.1	—
Long-Range Trajectory (yds)	50	100	200	300	400	500
	—	4.8	0	-19.9	-59.8	—

45-70 Government						
Bullet Style	Jacketed H.P.					
Bullet Weight	300 grs.					
Velocity (fps)	Muzzle	100	200	300	400	500
	1880	1650	1425	1235	1105	1010
Energy (ft-lb)	Muzzle	100	200	300	400	500
	2355	1815	1355	1015	810	680
Short-Range Trajectory (yds)	50	100	200	300	400	500
	1.0	0	-12.2	-42.0	-94.6	—
Long-Range Trajectory (yds)	50	100	200	300	400	500
	—	5.8	0	-23.3	-69.5	—

USA BRAND RIFLE BALLISTICS

223 Remington						
Bullet Style	Jacketed H.P.					
Bullet Weight	45 grs.					
Velocity (fps)	Muzzle	100	200	300	400	500
	3600	3033	2533	2085	1687	1356
Energy (ft-lb)	Muzzle	100	200	300	400	500
	1295	919	641	434	284	184
Short-Range Trajectory (yds)	50	100	200	300	400	500
	-0.4	0	-2.3	-10.1	-26.1	—
Long-Range Trajectory (yds)	50	100	200	300	400	500
	—	1.2	0	-6.7	-21.4	-48.7

223 Remington						
Bullet Style	Full Metal Jacket					
Bullet Weight	55 grs.					
Velocity (fps)	Muzzle	100	200	300	400	500
	3240	2854	2499	2172	1869	1597
Energy (ft-lb)	Muzzle	100	200	300	400	500
	1282	995	763	576	427	311
Short-Range Trajectory (yds)	50	100	200	300	400	500
	-0.3	0	-2.8	-11.2	-27	—
Long-Range Trajectory (yds)	50	100	200	300	400	500
	—	1.4	0	-7	-21.4	-45.9

223 Remington

Bullet Style	Full Metal Jacket					
Bullet Weight	62 grs.					
Velocity (fps)	Muzzle	100	200	300	400	500
	3100	2762	2448	2155	1884	1636
Energy (ft-lb)	Muzzle	100	200	300	400	500
	1323	1050	825	640	488	368
Short-Range Trajectory (yds)	50	100	200	300	400	500
	-0.2	0	-3.1	-12	-28.4	—
Long-Range Trajectory (yds)	50	100	200	300	400	500
	—	1.5	0	-7.4	-22.3	-47.1

22-250 Remington

Bullet Style	Jacketed H.P.					
Bullet Weight	45 grs.					
Velocity (fps)	Muzzle	100	200	300	400	500
	4000	3346	2781	2281	1837	1458
Energy (ft-lb)	Muzzle	100	200	300	400	500
	1598	1118	773	520	337	212
Short-Range Trajectory (yds)	50	100	200	300	400	500
	-0.4	0	-1.6	-7.8	-20.8	—
Long-Range Trajectory (yds)	50	100	200	300	400	500
	—	0.8	0	-5.4	-17.5	-40.2

5.56mm

Bullet Style	Full Metal Jacket					
Bullet Weight	55 grs.					
Velocity (fps)	Muzzle	100	200	300	400	500
	3270	2898	2555	2238	1943	1675
Energy (ft-lb)	Muzzle	100	200	300	400	500
	1306	1025	797	611	461	342
Short-Range Trajectory (yds)	50	100	200	300	400	500
	-0.3	0	-2.7	-10.7	-25.7	—
Long-Range Trajectory (yds)	50	100	200	300	400	500
	—	1.6	0	-7	-21	-44.2

30 Carbine

Bullet Style	Full Metal Jacket					
Bullet Weight	110 grs.					
Velocity (fps)	Muzzle	100	200	300	400	500
	1990	1596	1279	1070	952	870
Energy (ft-lb)	Muzzle	100	200	300	400	500
	967	622	399	280	221	185
Short-Range Trajectory (yds)	50	100	200	300	400	500
	0.9	0	-13	-47.4	—	—
Long-Range Trajectory (yds)	50	100	200	300	400	500
	—	6.5	0	-27.9	-86	—

7.62 x 39mm

Bullet Style	Full Metal Jacket					
Bullet Weight	123 grs.					
Velocity (fps)	Muzzle	100	200	300	400	500
	2355	2026	1726	1463	1247	1093
Energy (ft-lb)	Muzzle	100	200	300	400	500
	1515	1121	814	584	425	326
Short-Range Trajectory (yds)	50	100	200	300	400	500
	0.2	0	-7	-25.9	-61.1	—
Long-Range Trajectory (yds)	50	100	200	300	400	500
	—	3.8	0	-15.6	-47.6	—

30-06 Springfield

Bullet Style	Full Metal Jacket					
Bullet Weight	147 grs.					
Velocity (fps)	Muzzle	100	200	300	400	500
	3020	2794	2579	2374	2178	1992
Energy (ft-lb)	Muzzle	100	200	300	400	500
	2976	2548	2171	1839	1549	1295
Short-Range Trajectory (yds)	50	100	200	300	400	500
	-0.2	0	-3	-11.2	-25.5	—
Long-Range Trajectory (yds)	50	100	200	300	400	500
	—	1.5	0	-6.7	-19.6	-39.9

308 Winchester

Bullet Style	Full Metal Jacket					
Bullet Weight	147 grs.					
Velocity (fps)	Muzzle	100	200	300	400	500
	2800	2582	2374	2176	1987	1812
Energy (ft-lb)	Muzzle	100	200	300	400	500
	2559	2176	1840	1545	1289	1072
Short-Range Trajectory (yds)	50	100	200	300	400	500
	-0.1	0	-3.7	-13.6	-30.9	—
Long-Range Trajectory (yds)	50	100	200	300	400	500
	—	1.9	0	-8	-23.5	-46.6

7.62 x 54R

Bullet Style	Full Metal Jacket					
Bullet Weight	180 grs.					
Velocity (fps)	Muzzle	100	200	300	400	500
	2580	2401	2230	2066	1909	1760
Energy (ft-lb)	Muzzle	100	200	300	400	500
	2658	2304	1987	1706	1457	1238
Short-Range Trajectory (yds)	50	100	200	300	400	500
	0	0	-4.5	-16.1	-35.8	—
Long-Range Trajectory (yds)	50	100	200	300	400	500
	—	2.6	0	-9.6	-27.3	-54.6

7.62 x 54R

Bullet Style	Soft Point					
Bullet Weight	180 grs.					
Velocity (fps)	Muzzle	100	200	300	400	500
	2625	2302	2003	1729	1485	1281
Energy (ft-lb)	Muzzle	100	200	300	400	500
	2751	2117	1603	1195	882	655
Short-Range Trajectory (yds)	50	100	200	300	400	500
	0	0	-5.1	-18.9	-44.5	—
Long-Range Trajectory (yds)	50	100	200	300	400	500
	—	2.9	0	-11.6	-34.9	-74.1

Remington®

Remington Ballistics Tables

6mm Remington

Bullet Style	Core-Lokt® Pointed Soft Point						
Bullet Weight	100 grains						
Velocity (fps)	Muzzle	100	200	300	400	500	-
	3100	2829	2573	2573	2104	1889	-
Energy (ft-lb)	Muzzle	100	200	300	400	500	-
	2133	1777	1470	1207	983	792	-
Short-Range Trajectory (yds)	50	100	150	200	250	300	-
	0	0.6	zero	-1.8	-4.8	-9.3	-
Long-Range Trajectory (yds)	100	150	200	250	300	400	500
	1.4	1.3	zero	-2.6	-6.7	-19.8	-40.8

243 Win.

Bullet Style	AccuTip-V Boat Tail						
Bullet Weight	75 grains						
Velocity (fps)	Muzzle	100	200	300	400	500	-
	3375	3065	2775	2775	2248	2008	-
Energy (ft-lb)	Muzzle	100	200	300	400	500	-
	1897	1564	1282	1044	842	671	-
Short-Range Trajectory (yds)	50	100	150	200	250	300	-
	0	0.4	zero	-1.4	-4	-7.8	-
Long-Range Trajectory (yds)	100	150	200	250	300	400	500
	2	2.4	1.8	zero	-3	-13.3	-30.6

243 Win.

Bullet Style	Pointed Soft Point						
Bullet Weight	80 grains						
Velocity (fps)	Muzzle	100	200	300	400	500	-
	3350	2955	2593	2593	1951	1670	-
Energy (ft-lb)	Muzzle	100	200	300	400	500	-
	1993	1551	1194	906	676	495	-
Short-Range Trajectory (yds)	50	100	150	200	250	300	-
	0	0.5	zero	-1.6	-4.5	-8.8	-
Long-Range Trajectory (yds)	100	150	200	250	300	400	500
	2.2	2.7	2	zero	-3.5	-15.8	-37.3

243 Win.

Bullet Style	Power-Lokt® Hollow Point						
Bullet Weight	80 grains						
Velocity (fps)	Muzzle	100	200	300	400	500	-
	3350	2955	2593	2593	1951	1670	-
Energy (ft-lb)	Muzzle	100	200	300	400	500	-
	1993	1551	1194	906	676	495	-
Short-Range Trajectory (yds)	50	100	150	200	250	300	-
	0	0.5	zero	-1.6	-4.5	-8.8	-
Long-Range Trajectory (yds)	100	150	200	250	300	400	500
	2.2	2.7	2	zero	-3.5	-15.8	-37.3

243 Win.

Bullet Style	Copper Solid Tipped						
Bullet Weight	80 grains						
Velocity (fps)	Muzzle	100	200	300	400	500	-
	3350	3011	2696	2696	2128	1872	-
Energy (ft-lb)	Muzzle	100	200	300	400	500	-
	1993	1610	1291	1025	804	622	-
Short-Range Trajectory (yds)	50	100	150	200	250	300	-
	-0.1	0.4	zero	-1.5	-4.2	-8.2	-
Long-Range Trajectory (yds)	100	150	200	250	300	400	500
	2.1	2.5	1.9	zero	-3.2	-14.3	-33.1

243 Win.

Bullet Style	Swift Scirocco™ Bonded						
Bullet Weight	90 grains						
Velocity (fps)	Muzzle	100	200	300	400	500	-
	3120	2871	2635	2635	2199	1997	-
Energy (ft-lb)	Muzzle	100	200	300	400	500	-
	1946	1647	1388	1162	966	797	-
Short-Range Trajectory (yds)	50	100	150	200	250	300	-
	0	0.5	zero	-1.7	-4.5	-8.9	-
Long-Range Trajectory (yds)	100	150	200	250	300	400	500
	1.4	1.3	zero	-2.5	-6.4	-18.8	-38.3

243 Win.

Bullet Style	AccuTip						
Bullet Weight	95 grains						
Velocity (fps)	Muzzle	100	200	300	400	500	-
	3120	2847	2590	2590	2118	1902	-
Energy (ft-lb)	Muzzle	100	200	300	400	500	-
	2053	1710	1415	1162	946	763	-
Short-Range Trajectory (yds)	50	100	150	200	250	300	-
	0	0.5	zero	-1.7	-4.6	-9.2	-
Long-Range Trajectory (yds)	100	150	200	250	300	400	500
	0.5	1.3	zero	-2.7	-6.6	-19.5	-40.2

243 Win.

Bullet Style	Core-Lokt® Ultra Bonded™						
Bullet Weight	100 grains						
Velocity (fps)	Muzzle	100	200	300	400	500	-
	2960	2709	2471	2471	2033	1832	-
Energy (ft-lb)	Muzzle	100	200	300	400	500	-
	1945	1629	1356	1120	917	745	-
Short-Range Trajectory (yds)	50	100	150	200	250	300	-
	0	0.5	zero	-2.0	-5.3	-10.3	-
Long-Range Trajectory (yds)	100	150	200	250	300	400	500
	1.6	1.5	zero	-2.9	-7.3	-21.6	-44.3

243 Win.

Bullet Style	Core-Lokt® Pointed Soft Point						
Bullet Weight	100 grains						
Velocity (fps)	Muzzle	100	200	300	400	500	-
	2960	2697	2449	2449	1993	1786	-
Energy (ft-lb)	Muzzle	100	200	300	400	500	-
	1945	1615	1332	1089	882	708	-
Short-Range Trajectory (yds)	50	100	150	200	250	300	-
	0.1	0.7	zero	-2.0	-5.4	-10.4	-
Long-Range Trajectory (yds)	100	150	200	250	300	400	500
	1.6	1.5	zero	-2.9	-7.5	-22.1	-45.4

25-06 Remington

Bullet Style	Core-Lokt® Pointed Soft Point						
Bullet Weight	100 grains						
Velocity (fps)	Muzzle	100	200	300	400	500	-
	3230	2893	2580	2580	2014	1762	-
Energy (ft-lb)	Muzzle	100	200	300	400	500	-
	2316	1858	1478	1161	901	689	-
Short-Range Trajectory (yds)	50	100	150	200	250	300	-
	0	0.5	zero	-1.7	-4.6	-9.1	-
Long-Range Trajectory (yds)	100	150	200	250	300	400	500
	1.3	1.3	zero	-2.6	-6.6	-19.8	-41.7

25-06 Remington

Bullet Style	Core-Lokt® Ultra Bonded™						
Bullet Weight	115 grains						
Velocity (fps)	Muzzle	100	200	300	400	500	-
	3000	2751	2516	2516	2081	1881	-
Energy (ft-lb)	Muzzle	100	200	300	400	500	-
	2298	1933	1616	1342	1106	903	-
Short-Range Trajectory (yds)	50	100	150	200	250	300	-
	0.1	0.6	zero	-1.9	-5.1	-9.9	-
Long-Range Trajectory (yds)	100	150	200	250	300	400	500
	1.6	1.4	zero	-2.8	-7.1	-20.7	-42.5

25-06 Remington

Bullet Style	Core-Lokt® Pointed Soft Point						
Bullet Weight	120 grains						
Velocity (fps)	Muzzle	100	200	300	400	500	-
	2990	2730	2484	2484	2032	1825	-
Energy (ft-lb)	Muzzle	100	200	300	400	500	-
	2382	1985	1644	1351	1100	887	-
Short-Range Trajectory (yds)	50	100	150	200	250	300	-
	0.1	0.6	zero	-1.9	-5.2	-10.1	-
Long-Range Trajectory (yds)	100	150	200	250	300	400	500
	1.6	1.4	zero	-2.8	-7.2	-21.4	-44.1

250 Savage

Bullet Style	Pointed Soft Point						
Bullet Weight	100 grains						
Velocity (fps)	Muzzle	100	200	300	400	500	-
	2820	2504	2210	2210	1684	1461	-
Energy (ft-lb)	Muzzle	100	200	300	400	500	-
	1765	1392	1084	832	630	474	-
Short-Range Trajectory (yds)	50	100	150	200	250	300	-
	0	zero	-1.3	-4.1	-8.7	-15.3	-
Long-Range Trajectory (yds)	100	150	200	250	300	400	500
	2	1.8	zero	-3.6	-9.2	-27.7	-58.6

257 Roberts

Bullet Style	Core-Lokt® Soft Point						
Bullet Weight	117 grains						
Velocity (fps)	Muzzle	100	200	300	400	500	-
	2650	2291	1961	1961	1404	1199	-
Energy (ft-lb)	Muzzle	100	200	300	400	500	-
	1824	1363	999	718	512	373	-
Short-Range Trajectory (yds)	50	100	150	200	250	300	-
	0	zero	-1.5	-4.8	-9.9	-17	-
Long-Range Trajectory (yds)	100	150	200	250	300	400	500
	2.4	2.1	zero	-3.9	-9.8	-27	-57.8

6.5x55 Swedish

Bullet Style	Core-Lokt® Pointed Soft Point						
Bullet Weight	140 grains						
Velocity (fps)	Muzzle	100	200	300	400	500	-
	3210	2905	2621	2621	2102	1867	-
Energy (ft-lb)	Muzzle	100	200	300	400	500	-
	2745	2248	1830	1475	1177	929	-
Short-Range Trajectory (yds)	50	100	150	200	250	300	-
	0.4	0.7	zero	-1.8	-4.9	-9.5	-
Long-Range Trajectory (yds)	100	150	200	250	300	400	500
	2.7	3	2.1	zero	-3.5	-15.5	-35.3

260 Remington

Bullet Style	AccuTip Boat Tail						
Bullet Weight	120 grains						
Velocity (fps)	Muzzle	100	200	300	400	500	-
	2890	2697	2512	2512	2163	2000	-
Energy (ft-lb)	Muzzle	100	200	300	400	500	-
	2392	2083	1807	1560	1340	1146	-
Short-Range Trajectory (yds)	50	100	150	200	250	300	-
	0.1	0.7	zero	-1.8	-4.9	-9.5	-
Long-Range Trajectory (yds)	100	150	200	250	300	400	500
	1.6	1.5	zero	-2.8	-7.2	-20.7	-41.7

260 Remington

Bullet Style	Core-Lokt® Pointed Soft Point						
Bullet Weight	140 grains						
Velocity (fps)	Muzzle	100	200	300	400	500	-
	2750	2544	2347	2347	1979	1812	-
Energy (ft-lb)	Muzzle	100	200	300	400	500	-
	2351	2011	1712	1448	1217	1021	-
Short-Range Trajectory (yds)	50	100	150	200	250	300	-
	0.3	0.8	zero	-2.3	-6.1	-11.7	-
Long-Range Trajectory (yds)	100	150	200	250	300	400	500
	1.9	1.7	zero	-3.3	-8.3	-24	-47.2

260 Remington

Bullet Style	Core-Lokt® Ultra Bonded™						
Bullet Weight	140 grains						
Velocity (fps)	Muzzle	100	200	300	400	500	-
	2750	2554	2365	2365	2013	1849	-
Energy (ft-lb)	Muzzle	100	200	300	400	500	-
	2351	2027	1739	1484	1260	1063	-
Short-Range Trajectory (yds)	50	100	150	200	250	300	-
	0.3	0.8	zero	-2.2	-6	-11.5	-
Long-Range Trajectory (yds)	100	150	200	250	300	400	500
	1.9	1.7	zero	-3.2	-8.1	-23.6	-47.6

260 Remington

Bullet Style	Core-Lokt® Pointed Soft Point						
Bullet Weight	140 grains						
Velocity (fps)	Muzzle	100	200	300	400	500	-
	2360	2171	1991	1991	1660	1511	-
Energy (ft-lb)	Muzzle	100	200	300	400	500	-
	1731	1465	1232	1029	856	710	-
Short-Range Trajectory (yds)	50	100	150	200	250	300	-
	0.1	zero	-1.9	-5.9	-12	-20.6	-
Long-Range Trajectory (yds)	100	150	200	250	300	400	500
	2.9	2.5	zero	-4.7	-11.7	-34	-68.9

264 Win. Mag.

Bullet Style	Core-Lokt® Pointed Soft Point						
Bullet Weight	140 grains						
Velocity (fps)	Muzzle	100	200	300	400	500	-
	3030	2782	2548	2548	2114	1914	-
Energy (ft-lb)	Muzzle	100	200	300	400	500	-
	2854	2406	2018	1682	1389	1139	-
Short-Range Trajectory (yds)	50	100	150	200	250	300	-
	0.1	0.6	zero	-1.8	-5	-9.6	-
Long-Range Trajectory (yds)	100	150	200	250	300	400	500
	1.5	1.4	zero	-2.7	-6.9	-20.2	-41.3

6.8mm Rem. SPC

Bullet Style	Open Tip Match (OTM)						
Bullet Weight	115 grains						
Velocity (fps)	Muzzle	100	200	300	400	500	-
	2625	2373	2135	2135	1702	1513	-
Energy (ft-lb)	Muzzle	100	200	300	400	500	-
	1759	1437	1163	932	740	584	-
Short-Range Trajectory (yds)	50	100	150	200	250	300	-
	0.4	1	zero	-2.7	-7.3	-14.1	-
Long-Range Trajectory (yds)	100	150	200	250	300	400	500
	2.3	2	zero	-3.9	-10	-29.6	-61.2

6.8mm Rem. SPC

Bullet Style	Metal Case						
Bullet Weight	115 grains						
Velocity (fps)	Muzzle	100	200	300	400	500	-
	2625	2329	2053	2053	1565	1363	-
Energy (ft-lb)	Muzzle	100	200	300	400	500	-
	1759	1385	1076	825	625	474	-
Short-Range Trajectory (yds)	50	100	150	200	250	300	-
	0.5	1	zero	-2.9	-7.8	-15.1	-
Long-Range Trajectory (yds)	100	150	200	250	300	400	500
	2.5	2.1	zero	-4.2	-10.6	-32.4	-68.3

6.8mm Rem. SPC

Bullet Style	MatchKing® BTHP						
Bullet Weight	115 grains						
Velocity (fps)	Muzzle	100	200	300	400	500	-
	2625	2365	2119	2119	1676	1484	-
Energy (ft-lb)	Muzzle	100	200	300	400	500	-
	1759	1428	1147	911	717	562	-
Short-Range Trajectory (yds)	50	100	150	200	250	300	-
	0.5	1	zero	-2.7	-7.4	-14.3	-
Long-Range Trajectory (yds)	100	150	200	250	300	400	500
	2.4	2.1	zero	-4	-10.1	-30.1	-62.5

6.8mm Rem. SPC

Bullet Style	Core-Lokt® Ultra Bonded™						
Bullet Weight	115 grains						
Velocity (fps)	Muzzle	100	200	300	400	500	-
	2625	2332	2058	2058	1574	1372	-
Energy (ft-lb)	Muzzle	100	200	300	400	500	-
	1759	1389	1082	832	633	481	-
Short-Range Trajectory (yds)	50	100	150	200	250	300	-
	0.5	1	zero	-2.8	-7.8	-15	-
Long-Range Trajectory (yds)	100	150	200	250	300	400	500
	2.5	2.1	zero	-4.2	-10.7	-32.2	-67.8

270 Win.

Bullet Style	Pointed Soft Point						
Bullet Weight	100 grains						
Velocity (fps)	Muzzle	100	200	300	400	500	-
	3320	2924	2561	2561	1916	1636	-
Energy (ft-lb)	Muzzle	100	200	300	400	500	-
	2448	1898	1456	1099	815	594	-
Short-Range Trajectory (yds)	50	100	150	200	250	300	-
	0	0.5	zero	-1.6	-4.6	-9.1	-
Long-Range Trajectory (yds)	100	150	200	250	300	400	500
	2.3	2.8	2	zero	-3.6	-16.2	-38.5

270 Win.

Bullet Style	Core-Lokt® Pointed Soft Point						
Bullet Weight	115 grains						
Velocity (fps)	Muzzle	100	200	300	400	500	-
	2710	2412	2133	2133	1636	1425	-
Energy (ft-lb)	Muzzle	100	200	300	400	500	-
	1875	1485	1161	896	683	519	-
Short-Range Trajectory (yds)	50	100	150	200	250	300	-
	0.1	zero	-1.6	-4.8	-10	-17.8	-
Long-Range Trajectory (yds)	100	150	200	250	300	400	500
	1	zero	-2.7	-7.4	-14.2	-35.6	-70.1

270 Win.

Bullet Style	AccuTip Boat Tail						
Bullet Weight	130 grains						
Velocity (fps)	Muzzle	100	200	300	400	500	-
	3060	2845	2639	2639	2254	2076	-
Energy (ft-lb)	Muzzle	100	200	300	400	500	-
	2702	2335	2009	1721	1467	1243	-
Short-Range Trajectory (yds)	50	100	150	200	250	300	-
	0	0.5	zero	-1.7	-4.7	-9	-
Long-Range Trajectory (yds)	100	150	200	250	300	400	500
	1.4	1.3	zero	-2.4	-6.4	-18.6	-37.7

270 Win.

Bullet Style	Swift Scirocco™ Bonded						
Bullet Weight	130 grains						
Velocity (fps)	Muzzle	100	200	300	400	500	-
	3060	2838	2627	2627	2232	2048	-
Energy (ft-lb)	Muzzle	100	200	300	400	500	-
	2702	2325	1991	1697	1438	1211	-
Short-Range Trajectory (yds)	50	100	150	200	250	300	-
	0	0.6	zero	-1.7	-4.7	-9	-
Long-Range Trajectory (yds)	100	150	200	250	300	400	500
	1.4	1.3	zero	-2.5	-6.5	-18.8	-38.2

270 Win.

Bullet Style	Core-Lokt® Pointed Soft Point						
Bullet Weight	130 grains						
Velocity (fps)	Muzzle	100	200	300	400	500	-
	3060	2776	2510	2510	2022	1801	-
Energy (ft-lb)	Muzzle	100	200	300	400	500	-
	2702	2225	1818	1472	1180	936	-
Short-Range Trajectory (yds)	50	100	150	200	250	300	-
	0.1	0.6	zero	-1.8	-5.1	-9.8	-
Long-Range Trajectory (yds)	100	150	200	250	300	400	500
	1.5	1.4	zero	-2.8	-7	-20.9	-43.3

270 Win.

Bullet Style	Bronze Point™						
Bullet Weight	130 grains						
Velocity (fps)	Muzzle	100	200	300	400	500	-
	3060	2802	2559	2559	2110	1904	-
Energy (ft-lb)	Muzzle	100	200	300	400	500	-
	2702	2267	1890	1565	1285	1046	-
Short-Range Trajectory (yds)	50	100	150	200	250	300	-
	0	0.6	zero	-1.8	-4.9	-9.5	-
Long-Range Trajectory (yds)	100	150	200	250	300	400	500
	1.5	1.3	zero	-2.7	-6.8	-20	-41.1

270 Win.

Bullet Style	Copper Solid Tipped						
Bullet Weight	130 grains						
Velocity (fps)	Muzzle	100	200	300	400	500	-
	3060	2837	2625	2625	2229	2044	-
Energy (ft-lb)	Muzzle	100	200	300	400	500	-
	2702	2323	1988	1693	1434	1206	-
Short-Range Trajectory (yds)	50	100	150	200	250	300	-
	0	0.6	zero	-1.7	-4.7	-9.1	-
Long-Range Trajectory (yds)	100	150	200	250	300	400	500
	2.4	2.8	2	zero	-3.4	-14.8	-33.2

270 Win.

Bullet Style	Core-Lokt® Ultra Bonded™						
Bullet Weight	140 grains						
Velocity (fps)	Muzzle	100	200	300	400	500	-
	2925	2667	2424	2424	1975	1771	-
Energy (ft-lb)	Muzzle	100	200	300	400	500	-
	2659	2211	1826	1495	1212	975	-
Short-Range Trajectory (yds)	50	100	150	200	250	300	-
	0.1	0.7	zero	-2.0	-5.5	-10.7	-
Long-Range Trajectory (yds)	100	150	200	250	300	400	500
	1.7	1.5	zero	-3	-7.6	-22.5	-46.4

270 Win.

Bullet Style	Swift A-Frame™ PSP						
Bullet Weight	140 grains						
Velocity (fps)	Muzzle	100	200	300	400	500	-
	2925	2652	2394	2394	1923	1711	-
Energy (ft-lb)	Muzzle	100	200	300	400	500	-
	2659	2186	1782	1439	1150	910	-
Short-Range Trajectory (yds)	50	100	150	200	250	300	-
	0.2	0.7	zero	-2.1	-5.6	-10.9	-
Long-Range Trajectory (yds)	100	150	200	250	300	400	500
	1.7	1.5	zero	-3.1	-7.8	-23.2	-48

270 Win.

Bullet Style	Core-Lokt® Soft Point						
Bullet Weight	150 grains						
Velocity (fps)	Muzzle	100	200	300	400	500	-
	2850	2504	2183	2183	1618	1385	-
Energy (ft-lb)	Muzzle	100	200	300	400	500	-
	2705	2087	1587	1185	872	639	-
Short-Range Trajectory (yds)	50	100	150	200	250	300	-
	0.3	0.8	zero	-2.4	-6.7	-13	-
Long-Range Trajectory (yds)	100	150	200	250	300	400	500
	2	1.8	zero	-3.6	-9.4	-28.6	-61.2

270 WSM

Bullet Style	Core-Lokt® Soft Point						
Bullet Weight	130 grains						
Velocity (fps)	Muzzle	100	200	300	400	500	-
	3285	2986	2707	2707	2196	1963	-
Energy (ft-lb)	Muzzle	100	200	300	400	500	-
	3114	2573	2114	1724	1392	1112	-
Short-Range Trajectory (yds)	50	100	150	200	250	300	-
	-0.1	0.4	zero	-1.5	-4.2	-8.2	-
Long-Range Trajectory (yds)	100	150	200	250	300	400	500
	2.1	2.5	1.9	zero	-3.2	-14.1	-32.2

280 Remington

Bullet Style	AccuTip						
Bullet Weight	140 grains						
Velocity (fps)	Muzzle	100	200	300	400	500	-
	3000	2804	2617	2617	2265	2099	-
Energy (ft-lb)	Muzzle	100	200	300	400	500	-
	2797	2444	2129	1846	1594	1369	-
Short-Range Trajectory (yds)	50	100	150	200	250	300	-
	0.1	0.6	zero	-1.8	-4.8	-9.2	-
Long-Range Trajectory (yds)	100	150	200	250	300	400	500
	2.5	2.9	2.1	zero	-3.4	-14.8	-33

280 Remington

Bullet Style	Core-Lokt® Pointed Soft Point						
Bullet Weight	140 grains						
Velocity (fps)	Muzzle	100	200	300	400	500	-
	3000	2758	2528	2528	2102	1905	-
Energy (ft-lb)	Muzzle	100	200	300	400	500	-
	2797	2363	1986	1657	1373	1128	-
Short-Range Trajectory (yds)	50	100	150	200	250	300	-
	0.1	0.6	zero	-1.9	-5.1	-9.8	-
Long-Range Trajectory (yds)	100	150	200	250	300	400	500
	1.5	1.4	zero	-2.8	-7	-20.5	-42

280 Remington

Bullet Style	Core-Lokt® Pointed Soft Point						
Bullet Weight	150 grains						
Velocity (fps)	Muzzle	100	200	300	400	500	-
	2890	2624	2373	2373	1912	1705	-
Energy (ft-lb)	Muzzle	100	200	300	400	500	-
	2781	2293	1875	1518	1217	968	-
Short-Range Trajectory (yds)	50	100	150	200	250	300	-
	0.2	0.7	zero	-2.1	-5.8	-11.2	-
Long-Range Trajectory (yds)	100	150	200	250	300	400	500
	1.8	1.6	zero	-3.1	-8	-23.6	-48.8

280 Remington

Bullet Style	Core-Lokt® Soft Point						
Bullet Weight	165 grains						
Velocity (fps)	Muzzle	100	200	300	400	500	-
	2820	2510	2220	2220	1701	1479	-
Energy (ft-lb)	Muzzle	100	200	300	400	500	-
	2913	2308	1805	1393	1060	801	-
Short-Range Trajectory (yds)	50	100	150	200	250	300	-
	0	zero	-1.3	-4.1	-8.6	-15.2	-
Long-Range Trajectory (yds)	100	150	200	250	300	400	500
	2	1.8	zero	-3.6	-9.1	-27.4	-57.8

7mm-08 Remington

Bullet Style	Hollow Point						
Bullet Weight	120 grains						
Velocity (fps)	Muzzle	100	200	300	400	500	-
	3000	2725	2467	2223	1992	1778	-
Energy (ft-lb)	Muzzle	100	200	300	400	500	-
	2398	1979	1621	1316	1058	842	-
Short-Range Trajectory (yds)	50	100	150	200	250	300	-
	0.1	0.6	zero	-1.9	-5.3	-10.2	-
Long-Range Trajectory (yds)	100	150	200	250	300	400	500
	1.6	1.4	zero	-2.9	-7.3	-21.7	-44.9

7mm-08 Remington

Bullet Style	Core-Lokt® Pointed Soft Point						
Bullet Weight	140 grains						
Velocity (fps)	Muzzle	100	200	300	400	500	-
	2860	2625	2402	2189	1988	1798	-
Energy (ft-lb)	Muzzle	100	200	300	400	500	-
	2542	2142	1793	1490	1228	1005	-
Short-Range Trajectory (yds)	50	100	150	200	250	300	-
	0.2	0.7	zero	-2.1	-5.7	-11	-
Long-Range Trajectory (yds)	100	150	200	250	300	400	500
	1.8	1.6	zero	-3.1	-7.8	-22.9	-46.8

7mm-08 Remington

Bullet Style	AccuTip Boat Tail						
Bullet Weight	140 grains						
Velocity (fps)	Muzzle	100	200	300	400	500	-
	2860	2670	2489	2314	2146	1986	-
Energy (ft-lb)	Muzzle	100	200	300	400	500	-
	2542	2216	1925	1664	1432	1225	-
Short-Range Trajectory (yds)	50	100	150	200	250	300	-
	0.2	0.7	zero	-2	-5.4	-10.3	-
Long-Range Trajectory (yds)	100	150	200	250	300	400	500
	1.7	1.5	zero	-2.9	-7.3	-21.1	-42.5

7mm-08 Remington

Bullet Style	Core-Lokt® Pointed Soft Point						
Bullet Weight	140 grains						
Velocity (fps)	Muzzle	100	200	300	400	500	-
	2361	2151	1951	1764	1590	1433	-
Energy (ft-lb)	Muzzle	100	200	300	400	500	-
	1732	1437	1183	967	786	638	-
Short-Range Trajectory (yds)	50	100	150	200	250	300	-
	0.1	zero	-2	-6	-12.4	-21.3	-
Long-Range Trajectory (yds)	100	150	200	250	300	400	500
	3	2.5	zero	-4.8	-12.2	-35.6	-72.8

7mm Rem Magnum

Bullet Style	Core-Lokt® Ultra Bonded™						
Bullet Weight	140 grains						
Velocity (fps)	Muzzle	100	200	300	400	500	-
	3175	2934	2707	2490	2283	2086	-
Energy (ft-lb)	Muzzle	100	200	300	400	500	-
	3133	2676	2277	1927	1620	1353	-
Short-Range Trajectory (yds)	50	100	150	200	250	300	-
	0.1	0.5	zero	-1.6	-4.3	-8.4	-
Long-Range Trajectory (yds)	100	150	200	250	300	400	500
	1.3	1.2	zero	-2.4	-6	-17.7	-36

7mm Rem Magnum

Bullet Style	Core-Lokt® Pointed Soft Point						
Bullet Weight	140 grains						
Velocity (fps)	Muzzle	100	200	300	400	500	-
	3175	2923	2684	2458	2243	2039	-
Energy (ft-lb)	Muzzle	100	200	300	400	500	-
	3133	2655	2240	1878	1564	1292	-
Short-Range Trajectory (yds)	50	100	150	200	250	300	-
	0	0.5	zero	-1.6	-4.4	-8.5	-
Long-Range Trajectory (yds)	100	150	200	250	300	400	500
	2.2	2.6	1.9	zero	-3.2	-14.2	-32

7mm Rem Magnum

Bullet Style	Core-Lokt® Ultra Bonded™						
Bullet Weight	160 grains						
Velocity (fps)	Muzzle	100	200	300	400	500	-
	2950	2724	2510	2305	2109	1924	-
Energy (ft-lb)	Muzzle	100	200	300	400	500	-
	3091	2636	2237	1887	1581	1315	-
Short-Range Trajectory (yds)	50	100	150	200	250	300	-
	0.1	0.6	zero	-1.9	-5.2	-10	-
Long-Range Trajectory (yds)	100	150	200	250	300	400	500
	1.6	1.4	zero	-2.8	-7.1	-20.8	-42.4

7mm Rem Magnum

Bullet Style	Core-Lokt® Pointed Soft Point						
Bullet Weight	175 grains						
Velocity (fps)	Muzzle	100	200	300	400	500	-
	2860	2645	2440	2244	2057	1879	-
Energy (ft-lb)	Muzzle	100	200	300	400	500	-
	3178	2718	2313	1956	1644	1372	-
Short-Range Trajectory (yds)	50	100	150	200	250	300	-
	0.2	0.7	zero	-2.1	-5.6	-10.7	-
Long-Range Trajectory (yds)	100	150	200	250	300	400	500
	1.7	1.5	zero	-3	-7.6	-22.1	-44.8

7mm Mauser (7x57)

Bullet Style	Core-Lokt® Pointed Soft Point						
Bullet Weight	140 grains						
Velocity (fps)	Muzzle	100	200	300	400	500	-
	2660	2435	2221	2018	1827	1648	-
Energy (ft-lb)	Muzzle	100	200	300	400	500	-
	2199	1843	1533	1266	1037	844	-
Short-Range Trajectory (yds)	50	100	150	200	250	300	-
	0	zero	-1.4	-4.4	-9.1	-15.8	-
Long-Range Trajectory (yds)	100	150	200	250	300	400	500
	2.2	1.9	zero	-3.6	-9.2	-27.4	-55.3

7mm Remington SA Ultra Mag™

Bullet Style	Core-Lokt® Ultra Bonded™						
Bullet Weight	140 grains						
Velocity (fps)	Muzzle	100	200	300	400	500	-
	3175	2934	2707	2490	2283	2086	-
Energy (ft-lb)	Muzzle	100	200	300	400	500	-
	3133	2676	2277	1927	1620	1353	-
Short-Range Trajectory (yds)	50	100	150	200	250	300	-
	0.1	0.5	zero	-1.6	-4.3	-8.4	-
Long-Range Trajectory (yds)	100	150	200	250	300	400	500
	1.3	1.2	zero	-2.4	-6	-17.7	-36

7mm Remington SA Ultra Mag™

Bullet Style	Core-Lokt® Pointed Soft Point						
Bullet Weight	150 grains						
Velocity (fps)	Muzzle	100	200	300	400	500	-
	3110	2831	2568	2321	2087	1867	-
Energy (ft-lb)	Muzzle	100	200	300	400	500	-
	3221	2669	2197	1793	1450	1161	-
Short-Range Trajectory (yds)	50	100	150	200	250	300	-
	0	0.6	zero	-1.7	-4.8	-9.3	-
Long-Range Trajectory (yds)	100	150	200	250	300	400	500
	2.5	2.9	2.1	zero	-3.6	-15.7	-35.9

7mm Remington SA Ultra Mag™

Bullet Style	Core-Lokt® Ultra Bonded™						
Bullet Weight	160 grains						
Velocity (fps)	Muzzle	100	200	300	400	500	-
	2960	2733	2518	2313	2117	1931	-
Energy (ft-lb)	Muzzle	100	200	300	400	500	-
	3112	2654	2252	1900	1592	1323	-
Short-Range Trajectory (yds)	50	100	150	200	250	300	-
	0.1	0.6	zero	-1.9	-5.2	-9.9	-
Long-Range Trajectory (yds)	100	150	200	250	300	400	500
	2.7	3.1	2.2	zero	-3.7	-16.2	-36.5

7mm Rem Ultra Mag™ Power Level III

Bullet Style	Core-Lokt® Ultra Bonded™						
Bullet Weight	140 grains						
Velocity (fps)	Muzzle	100	200	300	400	500	-
	3425	3170	2929	2701	2485	2278	-
Energy (ft-lb)	Muzzle	100	200	300	400	500	-
	3646	3123	2667	2268	1919	1613	-
Short-Range Trajectory (yds)	50	100	150	200	250	300	-
	-0.2	0.3	zero	-1.3	-3.6	-7	-
Long-Range Trajectory (yds)	100	150	200	250	300	400	500
	1.8	2.2	1.6	zero	-2.7	-11.7	-26.4

7mm Rem Ultra Mag™ Power Level III

Bullet Style	Swift Scirocco™ Bonded						
Bullet Weight	150 grains						
Velocity (fps)	Muzzle	100	200	300	400	500	-
	3325	3132	2948	2771	2602	2438	-
Energy (ft-lb)	Muzzle	100	200	300	400	500	-
	3682	3267	2894	2558	2254	1979	-
Short-Range Trajectory (yds)	50	100	150	200	250	300	-
	-0.1	0.4	zero	-1.3	-3.6	-7	-
Long-Range Trajectory (yds)	100	150	200	250	300	400	500
	1.8	2.2	1.6	zero	-2.6	-11.4	-25.3

7mm Rem Ultra Mag™ Power Level III

Bullet Style	Swift A-Frame™ PSP						
Bullet Weight	175 grains						
Velocity (fps)	Muzzle	100	200	300	400	500	-
	3025	2831	2645	2467	2296	2212	-
Energy (ft-lb)	Muzzle	100	200	300	400	500	-
	3555	3114	2718	2364	2047	1764	-
Short-Range Trajectory (yds)	50	100	150	200	250	300	-
	0	0.6	zero	-1.7	-4.7	-9	-
Long-Range Trajectory (yds)	100	150	200	250	300	400	500
	2.4	2.8	2	zero	-3.4	-14.5	-32.2

7mm Rem Ultra Mag™ Power Level II

Bullet Style	Core-Lokt® Ultra Bonded™						
Bullet Weight	160 grains						
Velocity (fps)	Muzzle	100	200	300	400	500	-
	2950	2724	2508	2303	2108	1922	-
Energy (ft-lb)	Muzzle	100	200	300	400	500	-
	3091	2635	2235	1884	1578	1312	-
Short-Range Trajectory (yds)	50	100	150	200	250	300	-
	0.1	0.6	zero	-1.9	-5.2	-10	-
Long-Range Trajectory (yds)	100	150	200	250	300	400	500
	1.6	1.4	zero	-2.8	-7.1	-20.8	-42.4

7mm Rem Ultra Mag™ Power Level I

Bullet Style	Core-Lokt® Pointed Soft Point						
Bullet Weight	140 grains						
Velocity (fps)	Muzzle	100	200	300	400	500	-
	3000	2768	2549	2339	2139	1950	-
Energy (ft-lb)	Muzzle	100	200	300	400	500	-
	2797	23882	2019	1700	1422	1181	-
Short-Range Trajectory (yds)	50	100	150	200	250	300	-
	0.1	0.6	zero	-1.8	-5	-9.6	-
Long-Range Trajectory (yds)	100	150	200	250	300	400	500
	2.6	3	2.2	zero	-3.6	-15.8	-35.6

30 Carbine

Bullet Style	UMC® Metal Case						
Bullet Weight	110 grains						
Velocity (fps)	Muzzle	100	200	300	400	500	-
	1990	1567	1236	1035	923	842	-
Energy (ft-lb)	Muzzle	100	200	300	400	500	-
	967	600	373	262	208	173	-
Short-Range Trajectory (yds)	50	100	150	200	250	300	-
	0.6	zero	-4.2	-12.9	-27.2	-48.6	-
Long-Range Trajectory (yds)	100	150	200	250	300	400	500
	2.8	zero	-7.3	-20.4	-40.3	-105.6	-211.8

30 Carbine

Bullet Style	Soft Point						
Bullet Weight	110 grains						
Velocity (fps)	Muzzle	100	200	300	400	500	-
	1990	1567	1236	1035	923	842	-
Energy (ft-lb)	Muzzle	100	200	300	400	500	-
	967	600	373	262	208	173	-
Short-Range Trajectory (yds)	50	100	150	200	250	300	-
	0.6	zero	-4.2	-12.9	-27.2	-48.6	-
Long-Range Trajectory (yds)	100	150	200	250	300	400	500
	zero	-4.2	-12.9	-27.2	-48.6	-117.1	-225.5

30 Remington AR

Bullet Style	AccuTip Boat Tail						
Bullet Weight	125 grains						
Velocity (fps)	Muzzle	100	200	300	400	500	-
	2800	2531	2278	2039	1816	1610	-
Energy (ft-lb)	Muzzle	100	200	300	400	500	-
	2176	1778	1440	1153	915	719	-
Short-Range Trajectory (yds)	50	100	150	200	250	300	-
	0.3	0.8	zero	-2.3	-6.3	-12.2	-
Long-Range Trajectory (yds)	100	150	200	250	300	400	500
	2	1.7	zero	-3.4	-8.7	-25.8	-53.5

30 Remington AR

Bullet Style	Core-Lokt® Pointed Soft Point						
Bullet Weight	125 grains						
Velocity (fps)	Muzzle	100	200	300	400	500	-
	2800	2465	2154	1867	1606	1380	-
Energy (ft-lb)	Muzzle	100	200	300	400	500	-
	2176	1686	1288	967	716	529	-
Short-Range Trajectory (yds)	50	100	150	200	250	300	-
	0.3	0.9	zero	-2.5	-6.9	-13.4	-
Long-Range Trajectory (yds)	100	150	200	250	300	400	500
	2.1	1.9	zero	-3.8	-9.7	-29.4	-62.7

30 Remington AR

Bullet Style	Core-Lokt® Pointed Soft Point						
Bullet Weight	150 grains						
Velocity (fps)	Muzzle	100	200	300	400	500	-
	2575	2302	2047	N/A	N/A	N/A	-
Energy (ft-lb)	Muzzle	100	200	300	400	500	-
	2208	1765	1395	N/A	N/A	N/A	-
Short-Range Trajectory (yds)	50	100	150	200	250	300	-
	0	zero	-1.6	-5.1	-10.6	-18.5	-
Long-Range Trajectory (yds)	100	150	200	250	300	400	500
	2.5	2.2	zero	-4.3	-10.9	-32.5	-67.9

30 Remington AR

Bullet Style	Metal Case						
Bullet Weight	123 grains						
Velocity (fps)	Muzzle	100	200	300	400	500	-
	2800	2464	2152	1864	1603	1376	-
Energy (ft-lb)	Muzzle	100	200	300	400	500	-
	2141	1658	1264	948	701	517	-
Short-Range Trajectory (yds)	50	100	150	200	250	300	-
	0.3	0.9	zero	-2.5	-6.9	-13.5	-
Long-Range Trajectory (yds)	100	150	200	250	300	400	500
	2.1	1.9	zero	-3.8	-9.7	-29.5	-62.9

30-30 Win.

Bullet Style	Core-Lokt® Pointed Soft Point						
Bullet Weight	125 grains						
Velocity (fps)	Muzzle	100	200	300	400	500	-
	2175	1820	1508	1255	1082	975	-
Energy (ft-lb)	Muzzle	100	200	300	400	500	-
	1313	919	631	437	325	264	-
Short-Range Trajectory (yds)	50	100	150	200	250	300	-
	0.3	zero	-3	-9.1	-19.1	-33.7	-
Long-Range Trajectory (yds)	100	150	200	250	300	400	500
	2	zero	-5.2	-14.1	-27.8	-72.5	-146.9

30-30 Win.

Bullet Style	Core-Lokt® Soft Point						
Bullet Weight	150 grains						
Velocity (fps)	Muzzle	100	200	300	400	500	-
	2390	1973	1605	1303	1095	974	-
Energy (ft-lb)	Muzzle	100	200	300	400	500	-
	1902	1296	858	565	399	316	-
Short-Range Trajectory (yds)	50	100	150	200	250	300	-
	0.2	zero	-2.4	-7.6	-16.1	-28.8	-
Long-Range Trajectory (yds)	100	150	200	250	300	400	500
	1.6	zero	-4.3	-12.1	-24	-64.2	-133.2

30-30 Win.

Bullet Style	Copper Solid Tipped						
Bullet Weight	150 grains						
Velocity (fps)	Muzzle	100	200	300	400	500	-
	2220	1806	1448	1185	1022	924	-
Energy (ft-lb)	Muzzle	100	200	300	400	500	-
	1641	1086	698	468	348	284	-
Short-Range Trajectory (yds)	50	100	150	200	250	300	-
	0.5	zero	-3.6	-10.3	-21.2	-37.3	-
Long-Range Trajectory (yds)	100	150	200	250	300	400	500
	5.2	4.2	zero	-8.3	-21.8	-68.6	-149

30-30 Win.

Bullet Style	Core-Lokt® Soft Point						
Bullet Weight	170 grains						
Velocity (fps)	Muzzle	100	200	300	400	500	-
	2200	1895	1619	1381	1191	1061	-
Energy (ft-lb)	Muzzle	100	200	300	400	500	-
	1827	1355	989	720	535	425	-
Short-Range Trajectory (yds)	50	100	150	200	250	300	-
	0.3	zero	-2.7	-8.3	-17.1	-29.9	-
Long-Range Trajectory (yds)	100	150	200	250	300	400	500
	1.8	zero	-4.6	-12.6	-24.5	-62.6	-125.3

30-30 Win.

Bullet Style	Core-Lokt® Hollow Point						
Bullet Weight	170 grains						
Velocity (fps)	Muzzle	100	200	300	400	500	-
	2200	1895	1619	1381	1191	1061	-
Energy (ft-lb)	Muzzle	100	200	300	400	500	-
	1827	1355	989	720	535	425	-
Short-Range Trajectory (yds)	50	100	150	200	250	300	-
	0.3	zero	-2.7	-8.3	-17.1	-29.9	-
Long-Range Trajectory (yds)	100	150	200	250	300	400	500
	1.8	zero	-4.6	-12.6	-24.5	-62.6	-125.3

30-40 Krag

Bullet Style	Core-Lokt® Pointed Soft Point						
Bullet Weight	180 grains						
Velocity (fps)	Muzzle	100	200	300	400	500	-
	2430	2213	2007	1813	1632	1468	-
Energy (ft-lb)	Muzzle	100	200	300	400	500	-
	2360	1957	1610	1314	1064	861	-
Short-Range Trajectory (yds)	50	100	150	200	250	300	-
	0.1	zero	-1.8	-5.6	-11.6	-19.9	-
Long-Range Trajectory (yds)	100	150	200	250	300	400	500
	1.2	zero	-3.2	-8.5	-16.2	-39.9	-76.7

30-06 Springfield

Bullet Style	Pointed Soft Point						
Bullet Weight	125 grains						
Velocity (fps)	Muzzle	100	200	300	400	500	-
	3140	2780	2447	2138	1853	1595	-
Energy (ft-lb)	Muzzle	100	200	300	400	500	-
	2736	2145	1662	1269	953	706	-
Short-Range Trajectory (yds)	50	100	150	200	250	300	-
	0	0.6	zero	-1.9	-5.2	-10.1	-
Long-Range Trajectory (yds)	100	150	200	250	300	400	500
	1.5	1.4	zero	-2.8	-7.4	-22.4	-47.6

30-06 Springfield

Bullet Style	Core-Lokt® Pointed Soft Point						
Bullet Weight	125 grains						
Velocity (fps)	Muzzle	100	200	300	400	500	-
	2660	2335	2034	1757	1509	1300	-
Energy (ft-lb)	Muzzle	100	200	300	400	500	-
	1964	1513	1148	856	632	469	-
Short-Range Trajectory (yds)	50	100	150	200	250	300	-
	-0.1	zero	-1.5	-4.9	-10.4	-18.3	-
Long-Range Trajectory (yds)	100	150	200	250	300	400	500
	1	zero	-2.9	-7.8	-15.2	-38.9	-78

30-06 Springfield

Bullet Style	UMC® Metal Case						
Bullet Weight	150 grains						
Velocity (fps)	Muzzle	100	200	300	400	500	-
	2910	2617	2342	2084	1843	1622	-
Energy (ft-lb)	Muzzle	100	200	300	400	500	-
	2820	2281	1827	1446	1131	876	-
Short-Range Trajectory (yds)	50	100	150	200	250	300	-
	-0.2	zero	-1.1	-3.6	-7.7	-13.6	-
Long-Range Trajectory (yds)	100	150	200	250	300	400	500
	1.6	1.6	zero	-3.2	-8.2	-24.4	-50.9

30-06 Springfield

Bullet Style	Swift Scirocco™ Bonded						
Bullet Weight	150 grains						
Velocity (fps)	Muzzle	100	200	300	400	500	-
	2910	2696	2492	2298	2111	1934	-
Energy (ft-lb)	Muzzle	100	200	300	400	500	-
	2820	2421	2069	1758	1485	1246	-
Short-Range Trajectory (yds)	50	100	150	200	250	300	-
	0.1	0.7	zero	-2	-5.3	-10.2	-
Long-Range Trajectory (yds)	100	150	200	250	300	400	500
	1.6	1.5	zero	-2.9	-7.3	-21.1	-42.3

30-06 Springfield

Bullet Style	AccuTip Boat Tail						
Bullet Weight	150 grains						
Velocity (fps)	Muzzle	100	200	300	400	500	-
	2910	2686	2473	2270	2077	1893	-
Energy (ft-lb)	Muzzle	100	200	300	400	500	-
	2820	2403	2037	1716	1436	1193	-
Short-Range Trajectory (yds)	50	100	150	200	250	300	-
	0.1	0.7	zero	-2	-5.4	-10.3	-
Long-Range Trajectory (yds)	100	150	200	250	300	400	500
	1.7	1.5	zero	-2.9	-7.4	-21.5	-43.7

30-06 Springfield

Bullet Style	Core-Lokt® Pointed Soft Point						
Bullet Weight	150 grains						
Velocity (fps)	Muzzle	100	200	300	400	500	-
	2910	2617	2342	2083	1843	1622	-
Energy (ft-lb)	Muzzle	100	200	300	400	500	-
	2820	2281	1827	1445	1131	876	-
Short-Range Trajectory (yds)	50	100	150	200	250	300	-
	0.2	0.7	zero	-2.2	-5.9	-11.4	-
Long-Range Trajectory (yds)	100	150	200	250	300	400	500
	1.8	1.6	zero	-3.2	-8.2	-24.4	-50.9

30-06 Springfield

Bullet Style	Bronze Point™						
Bullet Weight	150 grains						
Velocity (fps)	Muzzle	100	200	300	400	500	-
	2910	2656	2416	2189	1974	1773	-
Energy (ft-lb)	Muzzle	100	200	300	400	500	-
	2820	2349	1944	1596	1298	1047	-
Short-Range Trajectory (yds)	50	100	150	200	250	300	-
	0.2	0.7	zero	-2	-5.6	-10.8	-
Long-Range Trajectory (yds)	100	150	200	250	300	400	500
	1.7	1.5	zero	-3	-7.7	-22.7	-46.6

30-06 Springfield

Bullet Style	Core-Lokt® Ultra Bonded™						
Bullet Weight	150 grains						
Velocity (fps)	Muzzle	100	200	300	400	500	-
	2910	2631	2368	2121	1889	1674	-
Energy (ft-lb)	Muzzle	100	200	300	400	500	-
	2820	2305	1868	1498	1188	933	-
Short-Range Trajectory (yds)	50	100	150	200	250	300	-
	0.2	0.7	zero	-2.1	-5.8	-11.2	-
Long-Range Trajectory (yds)	100	150	200	250	300	400	500
	1.8	1.6	zero	-3.1	-8	-23.8	-49.3

30-06 Springfield

Bullet Style	Copper Solid Tipped						
Bullet Weight	150 grains						
Velocity (fps)	Muzzle	100	200	300	400	500	-
	2910	2678	2458	2248	2048	1860	-
Energy (ft-lb)	Muzzle	100	200	300	400	500	-
	2820	2388	2012	1683	1397	1152	-
Short-Range Trajectory (yds)	50	100	150	200	250	300	-
	0.1	0.7	zero	-2	-5.4	-10.4	-
Long-Range Trajectory (yds)	100	150	200	250	300	400	500
	1.7	1.5	zero	-2.9	-7.4	-21.8	-44.5

30-06 Springfield

Bullet Style	Copper Solid Tipped						
Bullet Weight	165 grains						
Velocity (fps)	Muzzle	100	200	300	400	500	-
	2800	2597	2403	2217	2039	1870	-
Energy (ft-lb)	Muzzle	100	200	300	400	500	-
	2872	2470	2115	1800	1523	1281	-
Short-Range Trajectory (yds)	50	100	150	200	250	300	-
	0.1	zero	-1.4	-4.3	-8.6	-14.6	-
Long-Range Trajectory (yds)	100	150	200	250	300	400	500
	2.1	1.8	zero	-3.3	-8.2	-23.4	-47.1

30-06 Springfield

Bullet Style	AccuTip Boat Tail						
Bullet Weight	165 grains						
Velocity (fps)	Muzzle	100	200	300	400	500	-
	2800	2597	2403	2217	2039	1870	-
Energy (ft-lb)	Muzzle	100	200	300	400	500	-
	2872	2470	2115	1800	1523	1281	-
Short-Range Trajectory (yds)	50	100	150	200	250	300	-
	0.2	0.8	zero	-2.1	-5.9	-11.1	-
Long-Range Trajectory (yds)	100	150	200	250	300	400	500
	1.8	1.6	zero	-3.2	-7.9	-22.8	-46.2

30-06 Springfield

Bullet Style	Core-Lokt® Pointed Soft Point						
Bullet Weight	165 grains						
Velocity (fps)	Muzzle	100	200	300	400	500	-
	2800	2534	2283	2047	1825	1621	-
Energy (ft-lb)	Muzzle	100	200	300	400	500	-
	2872	2352	1909	1534	1220	963	-
Short-Range Trajectory (yds)	50	100	150	200	250	300	-
	0.3	0.8	zero	-2.3	-6.3	-12.1	-
Long-Range Trajectory (yds)	100	150	200	250	300	400	500
	2	1.7	zero	-3.4	-8.7	-25.9	-53.2

30-06 Springfield

Bullet Style	Core-Lokt® Ultra Bonded™						
Bullet Weight	168 grains						
Velocity (fps)	Muzzle	100	200	300	400	500	-
	2800	2546	2306	2079	1866	1668	-
Energy (ft-lb)	Muzzle	100	200	300	400	500	-
	2924	2418	1984	1613	1299	1037	-
Short-Range Trajectory (yds)	50	100	150	200	250	300	-
	0.3	0.8	zero	-2.3	-6.2	-11.9	-
Long-Range Trajectory (yds)	100	150	200	250	300	400	500
	1.9	1.7	zero	-3.3	-8.5	-25.1	-51.7

30-06 Springfield

Bullet Style	AccuTip Boat Tail						
Bullet Weight	180 grains						
Velocity (fps)	Muzzle	100	200	300	400	500	-
	2725	2539	2360	2188	2024	1867	-
Energy (ft-lb)	Muzzle	100	200	300	400	500	-
	2967	2576	2226	1914	1637	1393	-
Short-Range Trajectory (yds)	50	100	150	200	250	300	-
	0.3	0.8	zero	-2.3	-6.1	-11.6	-
Long-Range Trajectory (yds)	100	150	200	250	300	400	500
	0.9	2	zero	-3.3	-8.2	-23.7	-47.7

30-06 Springfield

Bullet Style	Swift A-Frame™ PSP						
Bullet Weight	180 grains						
Velocity (fps)	Muzzle	100	200	300	400	500	-
	2700	2465	2243	2032	1833	1648	-
Energy (ft-lb)	Muzzle	100	200	300	400	500	-
	2913	2429	2010	1650	1343	1085	-
Short-Range Trajectory (yds)	50	100	150	200	250	300	-
	0	zero	-1.3	-4.2	-8.9	-15.4	-
Long-Range Trajectory (yds)	100	150	200	250	300	400	500
	2.1	1.8	zero	-3.6	-9.1	-26.6	-54.4

30-06 Springfield

Bullet Style	Core-Lokt® Ultra Bonded™						
Bullet Weight	180 grains						
Velocity (fps)	Muzzle	100	200	300	400	500	-
	2700	2480	2270	2070	1882	1704	-
Energy (ft-lb)	Muzzle	100	200	300	400	500	-
	2913	2457	2059	1713	1415	1161	-
Short-Range Trajectory (yds)	50	100	150	200	250	300	-
	0	zero	-1.3	-4.2	-8.7	-15.1	-
Long-Range Trajectory (yds)	100	150	200	250	300	400	500
	2.1	1.8	zero	-3.5	-8.9	-25.8	-52.7

30-06 Springfield

Bullet Style	Swift Scirocco™ Bonded						
Bullet Weight	180 grains						
Velocity (fps)	Muzzle	100	200	300	400	500	-
	2700	2522	2351	2186	2028	1878	-
Energy (ft-lb)	Muzzle	100	200	300	400	500	-
	2913	2542	2208	1910	1644	1409	-
Short-Range Trajectory (yds)	50	100	150	200	250	300	-
	0	zero	-1.3	-4	-8.3	-14.2	-
Long-Range Trajectory (yds)	100	150	200	250	300	400	500
	2	1.7	zero	-3.3	-8.3	-23.9	-47.9

30-06 Springfield

Bullet Style	Core-Lokt® Soft Point						
Bullet Weight	180 grains						
Velocity (fps)	Muzzle	100	200	300	400	500	-
	2700	2348	2023	1727	1466	1251	-
Energy (ft-lb)	Muzzle	100	200	300	400	500	-
	2913	2203	1635	1192	859	625	-
Short-Range Trajectory (yds)	50	100	150	200	250	300	-
	0	zero	-1.5	-4.9	-10.3	-18.3	-
Long-Range Trajectory (yds)	100	150	200	250	300	400	500
	2.4	2.1	zero	-4.3	-11	-33.8	-72.8

30-06 Springfield

Bullet Style	Core-Lokt® Pointed Soft Point						
Bullet Weight	180 grains						
Velocity (fps)	Muzzle	100	200	300	400	500	-
	2700	2469	2250	2042	1846	1663	-
Energy (ft-lb)	Muzzle	100	200	300	400	500	-
	2913	2436	2023	1666	1362	1105	-
Short-Range Trajectory (yds)	50	100	150	200	250	300	-
	0	zero	-1.3	-4.2	-8.8	-15.4	-
Long-Range Trajectory (yds)	100	150	200	250	300	400	500
	2.1	1.8	zero	-3.5	-9	-26.3	-54

30-06 Springfield

Bullet Style	Bronze Point™						
Bullet Weight	180 grains						
Velocity (fps)	Muzzle	100	200	300	400	500	-
	2700	2485	2280	2084	1899	1725	-
Energy (ft-lb)	Muzzle	100	200	300	400	500	-
	2913	2468	2077	1736	1441	1189	-
Short-Range Trajectory (yds)	50	100	150	200	250	300	-
	0	zero	-1.3	-4.2	-8.7	-15	-
Long-Range Trajectory (yds)	100	150	200	250	300	400	500
	2.1	1.8	zero	-3.5	-8.8	-25.5	-52

30-06 Springfield

Bullet Style	Core-Lokt® Soft Point						
Bullet Weight	220 grains						
Velocity (fps)	Muzzle	100	200	300	400	500	-
	2410	2130	1870	1632	1422	1246	-
Energy (ft-lb)	Muzzle	100	200	300	400	500	-
	2837	2216	1708	1301	988	758	-
Short-Range Trajectory (yds)	50	100	150	200	250	300	-
	0.1	zero	-2	-6.2	-12.9	-22.4	-
Long-Range Trajectory (yds)	100	150	200	250	300	400	500
	1.3	zero	-3.5	-9.5	-18.4	-46.4	-91.6

300 Savage

Bullet Style	Core-Lokt® Pointed Soft Point						
Bullet Weight	150 grains						
Velocity (fps)	Muzzle	100	200	300	400	500	-
	2630	2354	2095	1853	1631	1432	-
Energy (ft-lb)	Muzzle	100	200	300	400	500	-
	2303	1845	1462	1143	886	685	-
Short-Range Trajectory (yds)	50	100	150	200	250	300	-
	0	zero	-1.5	-4.8	-10.1	-17.6	-
Long-Range Trajectory (yds)	100	150	200	250	300	400	500
	2.4	2.1	zero	-4.1	-10.4	-30.9	-64.6

300 Win Mag

Bullet Style	Core-Lokt® Pointed Soft Point						
Bullet Weight	150 grains						
Velocity (fps)	Muzzle	100	200	300	400	500	-
	3290	2950	2634	2340	2065	1810	-
Energy (ft-lb)	Muzzle	100	200	300	400	500	-
	3605	2897	2311	1823	1420	1091	-
Short-Range Trajectory (yds)	50	100	150	200	250	300	-
	0	0.5	zero	-1.6	-4.4	-8.7	-
Long-Range Trajectory (yds)	100	150	200	250	300	400	500
	1.3	1.2	zero	-2.4	-6.3	-18.9	-39.8

300 Win Mag

Bullet Style	Core-Lokt® Pointed Soft Point						
Bullet Weight	150 grains						
Velocity (fps)	Muzzle	100	200	300	400	500	-
	2650	2373	2113	1870	1646	1446	-
Energy (ft-lb)	Muzzle	100	200	300	400	500	-
	2339	1875	1486	1164	902	696	-
Short-Range Trajectory (yds)	50	100	150	200	250	300	-
	-0.1	zero	-1.5	-4.7	-9.9	-17.2	-
Long-Range Trajectory (yds)	100	150	200	250	300	400	500
	1	zero	-2.7	-7.4	-14.3	-35.8	-70.3

300 Win Mag

Bullet Style	Core-Lokt® Ultra Bonded™						
Bullet Weight	150 grains						
Velocity (fps)	Muzzle	100	200	300	400	500	-
	3290	2967	2666	2384	2120	1873	-
Energy (ft-lb)	Muzzle	100	200	300	400	500	-
	3605	2931	2366	1893	1496	1168	-
Short-Range Trajectory (yds)	50	100	150	200	250	300	-
	-0.1	0.5	zero	-1.6	-4.3	-8.5	-
Long-Range Trajectory (yds)	100	150	200	250	300	400	500
	1.2	1.2	zero	-2.4	-6.1	-18.4	-38.5

300 Win Mag

Bullet Style	Copper Solid Tipped						
Bullet Weight	150 grains						
Velocity (fps)	Muzzle	100	200	300	400	500	-
	3290	3037	2799	2572	2357	2152	-
Energy (ft-lb)	Muzzle	100	200	300	400	500	-
	3605	3072	2608	2204	1850	1542	-
Short-Range Trajectory (yds)	50	100	150	200	250	300	-
	-0.1	0.4	zero	-1.4	-4	-7.7	-
Long-Range Trajectory (yds)	100	150	200	250	300	400	500
	2	2.4	1.8	zero	-3	-12.9	-29.2

300 Win Mag

Bullet Style	Copper Solid Tipped						
Bullet Weight	165 grains						
Velocity (fps)	Muzzle	100	200	300	400	500	-
	3260	3035	2821	2617	2422	2235	-
Energy (ft-lb)	Muzzle	100	200	300	400	500	-
	3893	3373	2915	2508	2148	1830	-
Short-Range Trajectory (yds)	50	100	150	200	250	300	-
	0	zero	-0.9	-2.9	-5.9	-10.1	-
Long-Range Trajectory (yds)	100	150	200	250	300	400	500
	1.4	1.2	zero	-2.3	-5.8	-16.7	-33.6

300 Win Mag

Bullet Style	Swift Scirocco™ Bonded						
Bullet Weight	180 grains						
Velocity (fps)	Muzzle	100	200	300	400	500	-
	2960	2774	2595	2424	2259	2100	-
Energy (ft-lb)	Muzzle	100	200	300	400	500	-
	3501	3075	2692	2348	2039	1762	-
Short-Range Trajectory (yds)	50	100	150	200	250	300	-
	0.1	0.6	zero	-1.8	-4.9	-9.4	-
Long-Range Trajectory (yds)	100	150	200	250	300	400	500
	1.5	1.4	zero	-2.6	-6.7	-19.3	-38.7

300 Win Mag

Bullet Style	Core-Lokt® Ultra Bonded™						
Bullet Weight	180 grains						
Velocity (fps)	Muzzle	100	200	300	400	500	-
	2960	2774	2505	2294	2093	1903	-
Energy (ft-lb)	Muzzle	100	200	300	400	500	-
	3501	2971	2508	2103	1751	1448	-
Short-Range Trajectory (yds)	50	100	150	200	250	300	-
	0.1	0.6	zero	-1.9	-5.2	-10	-
Long-Range Trajectory (yds)	100	150	200	250	300	400	500
	2.7	3.1	2.2	zero	-3.8	-16.4	-37

300 Win Mag

Bullet Style	AccuTip Boat Tail						
Bullet Weight	180 grains						
Velocity (fps)	Muzzle	100	200	300	400	500	-
	2960	2764	2577	2397	2224	2058	-
Energy (ft-lb)	Muzzle	100	200	300	400	500	-
	3501	3053	2653	2295	1976	1693	-
Short-Range Trajectory (yds)	50	100	150	200	250	300	-
	0.1	0.6	zero	-1.8	-4.9	-9.5	-
Long-Range Trajectory (yds)	100	150	200	250	300	400	500
	1.5	1.4	zero	-2.7	-6.8	-19.6	-39.5

300 Win Mag

Bullet Style	Core-Lokt® Pointed Soft Point						
Bullet Weight	180 grains						
Velocity (fps)	Muzzle	100	200	300	400	500	-
	2960	2715	2482	2262	2052	1856	-
Energy (ft-lb)	Muzzle	100	200	300	400	500	-
	3501	2945	2463	2044	1683	1375	-
Short-Range Trajectory (yds)	50	100	150	200	250	300	-
	-0.1	0.5	zero	-1.6	-4.3	-8.5	-
Long-Range Trajectory (yds)	100	150	200	250	300	400	500
	1.7	1.5	zero	-2.9	-7.4	-21.3	-43.7

300 Win Mag

Bullet Style	Swift A-Frame™ PSP						
Bullet Weight	200 grains						
Velocity (fps)	Muzzle	100	200	300	400	500	-
	2825	2595	2377	2169	1971	1786	-
Energy (ft-lb)	Muzzle	100	200	300	400	500	-
	3544	2990	2508	2088	1726	1416	-
Short-Range Trajectory (yds)	50	100	150	200	250	300	-
	0.2	0.8	zero	-2.2	-5.9	-11.2	-
Long-Range Trajectory (yds)	100	150	200	250	300	400	500
	1.8	1.6	zero	-3.2	-8	-23.4	-47.8

300 Win Mag

Bullet Style	Core-Lokt® Pointed Soft Point						
Bullet Weight	150 grains						
Velocity (fps)	Muzzle	100	200	300	400	500	-
	3320	2977	2660	2364	2087	1830	-
Energy (ft-lb)	Muzzle	100	200	300	400	500	-
	3671	2952	2356	1861	1451	1116	-
Short-Range Trajectory (yds)	50	100	150	200	250	300	-
	-0.1	0.4	zero	-1.5	-4.3	-8.5	-
Long-Range Trajectory (yds)	100	150	200	250	300	400	500
	1.2	1.2	zero	-2.4	-6.2	-18.6	-39

300 WSM

Bullet Style	AccuTip Boat Tail						
Bullet Weight	180 grains						
Velocity (fps)	Muzzle	100	200	300	400	500	-
	3010	2812	2622	2440	2265	2097	-
Energy (ft-lb)	Muzzle	100	200	300	400	500	-
	3621	3159	2746	2378	2050	1757	-
Short-Range Trajectory (yds)	50	100	150	200	250	300	-
	0.1	0.6	zero	-1.8	-4.8	-9.1	-
Long-Range Trajectory (yds)	100	150	200	250	300	400	500
	2.5	2.9	2.1	zero	-3.4	-14.8	-32.9

300 WSM

Bullet Style	Swift Scirocco™ Bonded						
Bullet Weight	180 grains						
Velocity (fps)	Muzzle	100	200	300	400	500	-
	2980	2793	2614	2442	2276	2116	-
Energy (ft-lb)	Muzzle	100	200	300	400	500	-
	3549	3118	2730	2382	2070	1790	-
Short-Range Trajectory (yds)	50	100	150	200	250	300	-
	0.1	0.6	zero	-1.8	-4.8	-9.2	-
Long-Range Trajectory (yds)	100	150	200	250	300	400	500
	1.5	1.3	zero	-2.6	-6.6	-19	-38.1

300 WSM

Bullet Style	Soft Point						
Bullet Weight	150 grains						
Velocity (fps)	Muzzle	100	200	300	400	500	-
	2725	2275	1871	1519	1239	1057	-
Energy (ft-lb)	Muzzle	100	200	300	400	500	-
	2473	1724	1166	768	511	372	-
Short-Range Trajectory (yds)	50	100	150	200	250	300	-
	0	zero	-1.6	-5.3	-11.5	-20.7	-
Long-Range Trajectory (yds)	100	150	200	250	300	400	500
	2.7	2.3	zero	-4.8	-12.7	-40.8	-91.5

308 Marlin Express

Bullet Style	Core-Lokt® Pointed Soft Point						
Bullet Weight	125 grains						
Velocity (fps)	Muzzle	100	200	300	400	500	-
	2660	2382	2121	1878	1653	1453	-
Energy (ft-lb)	Muzzle	100	200	300	400	500	-
	1964	1575	1249	978	759	586	-
Short-Range Trajectory (yds)	50	100	150	200	250	300	-
	-0.1	zero	-1.5	-4.7	-9.8	-17.1	-
Long-Range Trajectory (yds)	100	150	200	250	300	400	500
	1	zero	-2.7	-7.3	-14.1	-35.5	-69.6

308 Win.

Bullet Style	UMC® Metal Case						
Bullet Weight	150 grains						
Velocity (fps)	Muzzle	100	200	300	400	500	-
	2820	2533	2263	2010	1775	1561	-
Energy (ft-lb)	Muzzle	100	200	300	400	500	-
	2648	2137	1705	1345	1049	811	-
Short-Range Trajectory (yds)	50	100	150	200	250	300	-
	-0.1	zero	-1.2	-3.9	-8.4	-14.7	-
Long-Range Trajectory (yds)	100	150	200	250	300	400	500
	2	1.7	zero	-3.4	-8.8	-26.2	-54.8

308 Win.

Bullet Style	Swift Scirocco™ Bonded						
Bullet Weight	150 grains						
Velocity (fps)	Muzzle	100	200	300	400	500	-
	2820	2611	2410	2219	2037	1863	-
Energy (ft-lb)	Muzzle	100	200	300	400	500	-
	2648	2269	1935	1640	1381	1156	-
Short-Range Trajectory (yds)	50	100	150	200	250	300	-
	0	zero	-1.1	-3.6	-7.6	-13.2	-
Long-Range Trajectory (yds)	100	150	200	250	300	400	500
	1.8	1.6	zero	-3.1	-7.8	-22.7	-46

308 Win.

Bullet Style	Core-Lokt® Ultra Bonded™						
Bullet Weight	150 grains						
Velocity (fps)	Muzzle	100	200	300	400	500	-
	2820	2546	2288	2046	1819	1611	-
Energy (ft-lb)	Muzzle	100	200	300	400	500	-
	2648	2159	1744	1394	1102	864	-
Short-Range Trajectory (yds)	50	100	150	200	250	300	-
	0.2	zero	-1.2	-3.9	-8.2	-14.4	-
Long-Range Trajectory (yds)	100	150	200	250	300	400	500
	1.9	1.7	zero	-3.4	-8.6	-25.5	-53.1

308 Win.

Bullet Style	Core-Lokt® Pointed Soft Point						
Bullet Weight	150 grains						
Velocity (fps)	Muzzle	100	200	300	400	500	-
	2820	2533	2263	2009	1774	1560	-
Energy (ft-lb)	Muzzle	100	200	300	400	500	-
	2648	2137	1705	1344	1048	810	-
Short-Range Trajectory (yds)	50	100	150	200	250	300	-
	0	zero	-1.2	-3.9	-8.4	-14.7	-
Long-Range Trajectory (yds)	100	150	200	250	300	400	500
	2	1.7	zero	-3.4	-8.8	-26.2	-54.8

308 Win.

Bullet Style	Copper Solid Tipped						
Bullet Weight	150 grains						
Velocity (fps)	Muzzle	100	200	300	400	500	-
	2820	2593	2376	2171	1975	1791	-
Energy (ft-lb)	Muzzle	100	200	300	400	500	-
	2648	2238	1881	1569	1299	1068	-
Short-Range Trajectory (yds)	50	100	150	200	250	300	-
	0.2	0.8	zero	-2.2	-5.9	-11.3	-
Long-Range Trajectory (yds)	100	150	200	250	300	400	500
	1.8	1.6	zero	-3.2	-8	-23.4	-47.8

308 Win.

Bullet Style	AccuTip Boat Tail						
Bullet Weight	150 grains						
Velocity (fps)	Muzzle	100	200	300	400	500	-
	2700	2501	2311	2129	1956	1792	-
Energy (ft-lb)	Muzzle	100	200	300	400	500	-
	2670	2292	1957	1661	1401	1176	-
Short-Range Trajectory (yds)	50	100	150	200	250	300	-
	-0.1	zero	-1.3	-4.1	-8.5	-14.7	-
Long-Range Trajectory (yds)	100	150	200	250	300	400	500
	2	1.8	zero	-3.4	-8.6	-24.8	-50.1

308 Win.

Bullet Style	MatchKing® BTHP						
Bullet Weight	168 grains						
Velocity (fps)	Muzzle	100	200	300	400	500	-
	2680	2493	2314	2143	1979	1823	-
Energy (ft-lb)	Muzzle	100	200	300	400	500	-
	2678	2318	1998	1713	1460	1239	-
Short-Range Trajectory (yds)	50	100	150	200	250	300	-
	0	zero	-1.3	-4.1	-8.5	-14.7	-
Long-Range Trajectory (yds)	100	150	200	250	300	400	500
	2.1	1.8	zero	-3.4	-8.6	-24.7	-49.9

308 Win.

Bullet Style	MatchKing® BTHP						
Bullet Weight	175 grains						
Velocity (fps)	Muzzle	100	200	300	400	500	-
	2609	2433	2264	2102	1946	1798	-
Energy (ft-lb)	Muzzle	100	200	300	400	500	-
	2644	2300	1992	1716	1472	1256	-
Short-Range Trajectory (yds)	50	100	150	200	250	300	-
	0.4	0.9	zero	-2.5	-6.7	-12.8	-
Long-Range Trajectory (yds)	100	150	200	250	300	400	500
	2.2	1.9	zero	-3.6	-9	-25.9	-51.9

308 Win.

Bullet Style	Core-Lokt® Ultra Bonded™						
Bullet Weight	180 grains						
Velocity (fps)	Muzzle	100	200	300	400	500	-
	2620	2404	2198	2002	1818	1644	-
Energy (ft-lb)	Muzzle	100	200	300	400	500	-
	2743	2309	1930	1601	1320	1080	-
Short-Range Trajectory (yds)	50	100	150	200	250	300	-
	0	zero	-1.4	-4.5	-9.4	-16.3	-
Long-Range Trajectory (yds)	100	150	200	250	300	400	500
	2.3	2	zero	-3.8	-9.5	-27.7	-56.4

308 Win.

Bullet Style	Core-Lokt® Soft Point						
Bullet Weight	180 grains						
Velocity (fps)	Muzzle	100	200	300	400	500	-
	2620	2274	1955	1666	1414	1212	-
Energy (ft-lb)	Muzzle	100	200	300	400	500	-
	2743	2066	1527	1109	799	587	-
Short-Range Trajectory (yds)	50	100	150	200	250	300	-
	0	zero	-1.7	-5.3	-11.2	-19.7	-
Long-Range Trajectory (yds)	100	150	200	250	300	400	500
	2.6	2.3	zero	-4.6	-11.8	-36.3	-78.2

308 Win.

Bullet Style	Core-Lokt® Pointed Soft Point						
Bullet Weight	180 grains						
Velocity (fps)	Muzzle	100	200	300	400	500	-
	2620	2393	2178	1974	1782	1604	-
Energy (ft-lb)	Muzzle	100	200	300	400	500	-
	2743	2288	1896	1557	1269	1028	-
Short-Range Trajectory (yds)	50	100	150	200	250	300	-
	0	zero	-1.5	-4.6	-9.5	-16.5	-
Long-Range Trajectory (yds)	100	150	200	250	300	400	500
	2.3	2	zero	-3.8	-9.7	-28.3	-57.8

300 Wby. Mag.

Bullet Style	Core-Lokt® Pointed Soft Point						
Bullet Weight	180 grains						
Velocity (fps)	Muzzle	100	200	300	400	500	-
	3120	2866	2626	2398	2181	1976	-
Energy (ft-lb)	Muzzle	100	200	300	400	500	-
	3890	3282	2755	2298	1902	1561	-
Short-Range Trajectory (yds)	50	100	150	200	250	300	-
	0	0.5	zero	-1.7	-4.6	-9	-
Long-Range Trajectory (yds)	100	150	200	250	300	400	500
	1.4	1.3	zero	-2.5	-6.4	-18.9	-38.7

303 British

Bullet Style	UMC® Metal Case						
Bullet Weight	174 grains						
Velocity (fps)	Muzzle	100	200	300	400	500	-
	2475	2209	1960	1729	1520	1338	-
Energy (ft-lb)	Muzzle	100	200	300	400	500	-
	2366	1885	1484	1155	893	692	-
Short-Range Trajectory (yds)	50	100	150	200	250	300	-
	0.1	zero	-1.9	-5.9	-12.2	-21.4	-
Long-Range Trajectory (yds)	100	150	200	250	300	400	500
	2.8	2.4	zero	-4.7	-11.9	-35.6	-74.3

303 British

Bullet Style	Core-Lokt® Soft Point						
Bullet Weight	180 grains						
Velocity (fps)	Muzzle	100	200	300	400	500	-
	2460	2124	1817	1542	1311	1137	-
Energy (ft-lb)	Muzzle	100	200	300	400	500	-
	2418	1803	1319	950	687	517	-
Short-Range Trajectory (yds)	50	100	150	200	250	300	-
	0.1	zero	-2	-6.3	-13.2	-23.1	-
Long-Range Trajectory (yds)	100	150	200	250	300	400	500
	1.3	zero	-3.6	-9.8	-19.1	-49.4	-99.9

7.62x39mm

Bullet Style	UMC® Metal Case						
Bullet Weight	123 grains						
Velocity (fps)	Muzzle	100	200	300	400	500	-
	2365	2060	1780	1529	1315	1150	-
Energy (ft-lb)	Muzzle	100	200	300	400	500	-
	1527	1159	865	638	472	361	-
Short-Range Trajectory (yds)	50	100	150	200	250	300	-
	0.1	zero	-2.2	-6.8	-14.1	-24.5	-
Long-Range Trajectory (yds)	100	150	200	250	300	400	500
	1.5	zero	-3.8	-10.4	-20.2	-51.5	-103

7.62x39mm

Bullet Style	Pointed Soft Point						
Bullet Weight	125 grains						
Velocity (fps)	Muzzle	100	200	300	400	500	-
	2365	2062	1783	1533	1320	1154	-
Energy (ft-lb)	Muzzle	100	200	300	400	500	-
	1552	1180	882	652	483	370	-
Short-Range Trajectory (yds)	50	100	150	200	250	300	-
	0.1	zero	-2.2	-6.7	-14	-24.5	-
Long-Range Trajectory (yds)	100	150	200	250	300	400	500
	1.5	zero	-3.8	-10.4	-20.1	-51.3	-102.5

300 Remington Short Action Ultra Mag™

Bullet Style	Core-Lokt® Ultra Bonded™						
Bullet Weight	150 grains						
Velocity (fps)	Muzzle	100	200	300	400	500	-
	3200	2901	2622	2359	2112	1880	-
Energy (ft-lb)	Muzzle	100	200	300	400	500	-
	3410	2803	2290	1854	1485	1177	-
Short-Range Trajectory (yds)	50	100	150	200	250	300	-
	0.1	0.5	zero	-1.6	-4.6	-8.9	-
Long-Range Trajectory (yds)	100	150	200	250	300	400	500
	1.3	1.2	zero	-2.5	-6.4	-19.1	-39.6

300 Remington Short Action Ultra Mag™

Bullet Style	Core-Lokt® Poined Soft Point						
Bullet Weight	165 grains						
Velocity (fps)	Muzzle	100	200	300	400	500	-
	3075	2792	2527	2276	2040	1819	-
Energy (ft-lb)	Muzzle	100	200	300	400	500	-
	3464	2856	2339	1898	1525	1213	-
Short-Range Trajectory (yds)	50	100	150	200	250	300	-
	0.1	0.6	zero	-1.8	-5	-9.7	-
Long-Range Trajectory (yds)	100	150	200	250	300	400	500
	1.5	1.4	zero	-2.7	-7	-20.7	-42.1

300 Remington Short Action Ultra Mag™

Bullet Style	Core-Lokt® Ultra Bonded™						
Bullet Weight	180 grains						
Velocity (fps)	Muzzle	100	200	300	400	500	-
	2960	2727	2506	2295	2094	1904	-
Energy (ft-lb)	Muzzle	100	200	300	400	500	-
	3501	2972	2509	2105	1753	1449	-
Short-Range Trajectory (yds)	50	100	150	200	250	300	-
	0.1	0.6	zero	-1.9	-5.2	-10	-
Long-Range Trajectory (yds)	100	150	200	250	300	400	500
	1.6	1.4	zero	-2.8	-7.1	-20.9	-42.6

300 Remington Short Action Ultra Mag™

Bullet Style	MatchKing® BTHP						
Bullet Weight	190 grains						
Velocity (fps)	Muzzle	100	200	300	400	500	-
	2900	2725	2557	2395	2239	2089	-
Energy (ft-lb)	Muzzle	100	200	300	400	500	-
	3547	3133	2758	2420	2115	1840	-
Short-Range Trajectory (yds)	50	100	150	200	250	300	-
	0.1	0.6	zero	-1.9	-5.1	-9.8	-
Long-Range Trajectory (yds)	100	150	200	250	300	400	500
	1.6	1.4	zero	-2.7	-6.9	-19.9	-39.8

300 Remington Ultra Mag™ Power Level III

Bullet Style	Swift Scirocco™ Bonded						
Bullet Weight	150 grains						
Velocity (fps)	Muzzle	100	200	300	400	500	-
	3450	3208	2980	2762	2556	2358	-
Energy (ft-lb)	Muzzle	100	200	300	400	500	-
	3964	3427	2956	2541	2175	1852	-
Short-Range Trajectory (yds)	50	100	150	200	250	300	-
	0	0.3	zero	-1.2	-3.4	-6.7	-
Long-Range Trajectory (yds)	100	150	200	250	300	400	500
	1.7	2.1	1.5	zero	-2.6	-11.2	-25.3

300 Remington Ultra Mag™ Power Level III

Bullet Style	Swift Scirocco™ Bonded						
Bullet Weight	180 grains						
Velocity (fps)	Muzzle	100	200	300	400	500	-
	3250	3048	2856	2672	2495	2325	-
Energy (ft-lb)	Muzzle	100	200	300	400	500	-
	4221	3714	3260	2853	2487	2160	-
Short-Range Trajectory (yds)	50	100	150	200	250	300	-
	0	0.4	zero	-1.4	-3.9	-7.5	-
Long-Range Trajectory (yds)	100	150	200	250	300	400	500
	2	2.3	1.7	zero	-2.8	-12.3	-27.3

300 Remington Ultra Mag™ Power Level III

Bullet Style	Copper Solid Tipped						
Bullet Weight	165 grains						
Velocity (fps)	Muzzle	100	200	300	400	500	-
	3260	3035	2821	2617	2422	2235	-
Energy (ft-lb)	Muzzle	100	200	300	400	500	-
	3893	3373	2915	2617	2422	2235	-
Short-Range Trajectory (yds)	50	100	150	200	250	300	-
	0	zero	-0.9	-2.9	-5.9	-10.1	-
Long-Range Trajectory (yds)	100	150	200	250	300	400	500
	1.4	1.2	zero	-2.3	-.5.8	-16.7	-33.6

300 Remington Ultra Mag™ Power Level III

Bullet Style	Core-Lokt® Ultra Bonded™						
Bullet Weight	180 grains						
Velocity (fps)	Muzzle	100	200	300	400	500	-
	3250	2988	2742	2508	2287	2076	-
Energy (ft-lb)	Muzzle	100	200	300	400	500	-
	4221	3568	3003	2513	2088	1721	-
Short-Range Trajectory (yds)	50	100	150	200	250	300	-
	0	0.4	zero	-1.5	-4.2	-8.1	-
Long-Range Trajectory (yds)	100	150	200	250	300	400	500
	2.1	2.5	1.8	zero	-3.1	-13.6	-30.7

300 Remington Ultra Mag™ Power Level III

Bullet Style	Swift A-Frame™ PSP						
Bullet Weight	200 grains						
Velocity (fps)	Muzzle	100	200	300	400	500	-
	3032	2791	2562	2345	2138	1942	-
Energy (ft-lb)	Muzzle	100	200	300	400	500	-
	4083	3459	2916	2442	2030	1675	-
Short-Range Trajectory (yds)	50	100	150	200	250	300	-
	0.1	0.6	zero	-1.8	-4.9	-9.5	-
Long-Range Trajectory (yds)	100	150	200	250	300	400	500
	1.5	1.4	zero	-2.7	-6.8	-19.9	-40.7

300 Remington Ultra Mag™ Power Level II

Bullet Style	Core-Lokt® Ultra Bonded™						
Bullet Weight	180 grains						
Velocity (fps)	Muzzle	100	200	300	400	500	-
	2980	2742	2515	2300	2096	1902	-
Energy (ft-lb)	Muzzle	100	200	300	400	500	-
	3549	3004	2528	2114	1755	1445	-
Short-Range Trajectory (yds)	50	100	150	200	250	300	-
	0.1	0.6	zero	-1.9	-5.1	-9.9	-
Long-Range Trajectory (yds)	100	150	200	250	300	400	500
	1.6	1.4	zero	-2.8	-7.1	-20.7	-42.4

300 Remington Ultra Mag™ Power Level II

Bullet Style	Swift Scirocco™ Bonded						
Bullet Weight	180 grains						
Velocity (fps)	Muzzle	100	200	300	400	500	-
	2980	2793	2614	2442	2276	2116	-
Energy (ft-lb)	Muzzle	100	200	300	400	500	-
	3549	3118	2730	2382	2070	1790	-
Short-Range Trajectory (yds)	50	100	150	200	250	300	-
	0.1	0.6	zero	-1.8	-4.8	-9.2	-
Long-Range Trajectory (yds)	100	150	200	250	300	400	500
	1.5	1.3	zero	-2.6	-6.6	-19	-38.1

300 Remington Ultra Mag™ Power Level I

Bullet Style	AccuTip Boat Tail						
Bullet Weight	150 grains						
Velocity (fps)	Muzzle	100	200	300	400	500	-
	2910	2686	2473	2270	2077	1893	-
Energy (ft-lb)	Muzzle	100	200	300	400	500	-
	2820	2403	2037	1716	1436	1193	-
Short-Range Trajectory (yds)	50	100	150	200	250	300	-
	0.1	0.7	zero	-2	-5.4	-10.3	-
Long-Range Trajectory (yds)	100	150	200	250	300	400	500
	1.7	1.5	zero	-2.9	-7.4	-21.5	-43.7

300 Remington Ultra Mag™ Power Level I

Bullet Style	Core-Lokt® Pointed Soft Point						
Bullet Weight	150 grains						
Velocity (fps)	Muzzle	100	200	300	400	500	-
	2910	2617	2342	2083	1843	1622	-
Energy (ft-lb)	Muzzle	100	200	300	400	500	-
	2820	2281	1827	1445	1131	876	-
Short-Range Trajectory (yds)	50	100	150	200	250	300	-
	0.2	0.7	zero	-2.2	-5.9	-11.4	-
Long-Range Trajectory (yds)	100	150	200	250	300	400	500
	1.8	1.6	zero	-3.2	-8.2	-24.4	-50.9

300 Remington Ultra Mag™ Power Level I

Bullet Style	Core-Lokt® Pointed Soft Point						
Bullet Weight	150 grains						
Velocity (fps)	Muzzle	100	200	300	400	500	-
	2815	2528	2258	2005	1770	1556	-
Energy (ft-lb)	Muzzle	100	200	300	400	500	-
	2639	2127	1698	1339	1043	806	-
Short-Range Trajectory (yds)	50	100	150	200	250	300	-
	0.3	0.8	zero	-2.3	-6.4	-12.3	-
Long-Range Trajectory (yds)	100	150	200	250	300	400	500
	2	1.8	zero	-3.5	-8.8	-26.4	-55.1

32-20 Win.

Bullet Style	Lead						
Bullet Weight	100 grains						
Velocity (fps)	Muzzle	100	200	300	400	500	-
	1210	1021	913	834	769	712	-
Energy (ft-lb)	Muzzle	100	200	300	400	500	-
	325	231	185	154	131	113	-
Short-Range Trajectory (yds)	50	100	150	200	250	300	-
	zero	-5.7	-19.7	-43.1	-76.9	-122.2	-
Long-Range Trajectory (yds)	100	150	200	250	300	400	500
	zero	-11.2	-31.7	-62.7	-105.2	-228.5	-410.8

32 Win. Special

Bullet Style	Core-Lokt® Soft Point						
Bullet Weight	170 grains						
Velocity (fps)	Muzzle	100	200	300	400	500	-
	2250	1921	1626	1372	1175	1044	-
Energy (ft-lb)	Muzzle	100	200	300	400	500	-
	1911	1393	998	710	521	411	-
Short-Range Trajectory (yds)	50	100	150	200	250	300	-
	0.3	zero	-2.6	-8	-16.7	-29.3	-
Long-Range Trajectory (yds)	100	150	200	250	300	400	500
	1.7	zero	-4.5	-12.4	-24.1	-62.1	-125.3

8mm Rem. Magnum

Bullet Style	Swift A-Frame™ PSP						
Bullet Weight	200 grains						
Velocity (fps)	Muzzle	100	200	300	400	500	-
	2900	2623	2361	2115	1885	1672	-
Energy (ft-lb)	Muzzle	100	200	300	400	500	-
	3734	3054	2476	1987	1577	1241	-
Short-Range Trajectory (yds)	50	100	150	200	250	300	-
	0.2	0.7	zero	-2.1	-5.8	-11.2	-
Long-Range Trajectory (yds)	100	150	200	250	300	400	500
	1.8	1.6	zero	-3.1	-8	-23.9	-49.6

8mm Mauser

Bullet Style	Core-Lokt® Soft Point						
Bullet Weight	170 grains						
Velocity (fps)	Muzzle	100	200	300	400	500	-
	2360	1969	1622	1333	1123	997	-
Energy (ft-lb)	Muzzle	100	200	300	400	500	-
	2102	1463	993	671	476	375	-
Short-Range Trajectory (yds)	50	100	150	200	250	300	-
	0.2	zero	-2.4	-7.6	-16.1	-28.6	-
Long-Range Trajectory (yds)	100	150	200	250	300	400	500
	1.6	zero	-4.4	-12	-23.7	-62.8	-128.9

35 Remington

Bullet Style	Core-Lokt® Pointed Soft Point						
Bullet Weight	150 grains						
Velocity (fps)	Muzzle	100	200	300	400	500	-
	2300	1874	1506	1218	1039	934	-
Energy (ft-lb)	Muzzle	100	200	300	400	500	-
	1762	1169	755	494	359	291	-
Short-Range Trajectory (yds)	50	100	150	200	250	300	-
	0.3	zero	-2.7	-8.6	-18.2	-32.6	-
Long-Range Trajectory (yds)	100	150	200	250	300	400	500
	1.8	zero	-4.9	-13.7	-27.1	-73	-150.8

35 Remington

Bullet Style	Core-Lokt® Soft Point						
Bullet Weight	200 grains						
Velocity (fps)	Muzzle	100	200	300	400	500	-
	2080	1698	1376	1140	1001	911	-
Energy (ft-lb)	Muzzle	100	200	300	400	500	-
	1921	1280	841	577	445	369	-
Short-Range Trajectory (yds)	50	100	150	200	250	300	-
	0.5	zero	-3.5	-10.7	-22.6	-40.1	-
Long-Range Trajectory (yds)	100	150	200	250	300	400	500
	2.3	zero	-6.1	-16.7	-33	-86.6	-174.8

350 Remington Mag

Bullet Style	Core-Lokt® Pointed Soft Point						
Bullet Weight	200 grains						
Velocity (fps)	Muzzle	100	200	300	400	500	-
	2775	2471	2186	1921	1678	1461	-
Energy (ft-lb)	Muzzle	100	200	300	400	500	-
	3419	2711	2122	1639	1250	947	-
Short-Range Trajectory (yds)	50	100	150	200	250	300	-
	-0.1	zero	-1.3	-4.2	-9	-15.8	-
Long-Range Trajectory (yds)	100	150	200	250	300	400	500
	2.1	1.8	zero	-3.6	-9.4	-28.3	-59.7

44 Rem. Magnum

Bullet Style	Soft Point						
Bullet Weight	240 grains						
Velocity (fps)	Muzzle	100	200	300	400	500	-
	1760	1380	1114	970	878	806	-
Energy (ft-lb)	Muzzle	100	200	300	400	500	-
	1650	1015	661	501	411	346	-
Short-Range Trajectory (yds)	50	100	150	200	250	300	-
	zero	-2.1	-8.7	-21.2	-40.6	-68.2	-
Long-Range Trajectory (yds)	100	150	200	250	300	400	500
	zero	-5.6	-17	-35.4	-61.9	-143.8	-270.9

44 Rem. Magnum

Bullet Style	Semi-Jacketed Hollow Point						
Bullet Weight	240 grains						
Velocity (fps)	Muzzle	100	200	300	400	500	-
	1760	1380	1114	970	878	806	-
Energy (ft-lb)	Muzzle	100	200	300	400	500	-
	1650	1015	661	501	411	346	-
Short-Range Trajectory (yds)	50	100	150	200	250	300	-
	zero	-2.1	-8.7	-21.2	-40.6	-68.2	-
Long-Range Trajectory (yds)	100	150	200	250	300	400	500
	zero	-5.6	-17	-35.4	-61.9	-143.8	-270.9

444 Mar.

Bullet Style	Soft Point						
Bullet Weight	240 grains						
Velocity (fps)	Muzzle	100	200	300	400	500	-
	2350	1815	1377	1087	941	846	-
Energy (ft-lb)	Muzzle	100	200	300	400	500	-
	2942	1755	1010	630	472	381	-
Short-Range Trajectory (yds)	50	100	150	200	250	300	-
	0.3	zero	-2.9	-9.3	-20.4	-37.4	-
Long-Range Trajectory (yds)	100	150	200	250	300	400	500
	1.9	zero	-5.4	-15.5	-31.5	-86.8	-181.5

45-70 Government

Bullet Style	Semi-Jacketed Hollow Point						
Bullet Weight	300 grains						
Velocity (fps)	Muzzle	100	200	300	400	500	-
	1810	1497	1244	1073	969	895	-
Energy (ft-lb)	Muzzle	100	200	300	400	500	-
	2182	1492	1031	767	625	533	-
Short-Range Trajectory (yds)	50	100	150	200	250	300	-
	zero	-1.7	-7.3	-17.6	-33.5	-56	-
Long-Range Trajectory (yds)	100	150	200	250	300	400	500
	zero	-4.7	-14.2	-29.2	-50.9	-117.6	-221.3

45-70 Government

Bullet Style	Soft Point						
Bullet Weight	405 grains						
Velocity (fps)	Muzzle	100	200	300	400	500	-
	1330	1168	1055	977	918	869	-
Energy (ft-lb)	Muzzle	100	200	300	400	500	-
	1590	1227	1001	858	758	679	-
Short-Range Trajectory (yds)	50	100	150	200	250	300	-
	zero	-4.1	-14.6	-32.2	-57.6	-91.4	-
Long-Range Trajectory (yds)	100	150	200	250	300	400	500
	zero	-8.4	-24	-47.3	-79	-170.4	-303

450 Bushmaster							
Bullet Style	Soft Point						
Bullet Weight	250 grains						
Velocity (fps)	Muzzle	100	200	300	400	500	-
	2200	1831	1508	148	1073	967	-
Energy (ft-lb)	Muzzle	100	200	300	400	500	-
	2686	1860	1262	864	639	519	-
Short-Range Trajectory (yds)	50	100	150	200	250	300	-
	0.3	zero	-2.9	-9	-18.9	-33.5	-
Long-Range Trajectory (yds)	100	150	200	250	300	400	500
	2	zero	-5.1	-14	-27.6	-72.6	-147.6

450 Bushmaster							
Bullet Style	AccuTip						
Bullet Weight	250 grains						
Velocity (fps)	Muzzle	100	200	300	400	500	-
	2180	1665	1263	N/A	N/A	N/A	-
Energy (ft-lb)	Muzzle	100	200	300	400	500	-
	2743	1601	921	N/A	N/A	N/A	-
Short-Range Trajectory (yds)	50	100	150	200	250	300	-
	0.4	zero	-3.6	-11.4	-24.6	-44.7	-
Long-Range Trajectory (yds)	100	150	200	250	300	400	500
	2.4	zero	-6.6	-18.6	-37.5	-101.3	-207.5

*Note: These ballistics reflected a test barrel length of 24"
except those for 30 Carbine and 44 Remington Magnum which
are 20" barrels. Specifications are nominal. Ballistics figures
established in test barrels. Individual rifles may vary from
test barrel results. "zero" indicates yardage at which rifle was
sighted in.*

Most professional hunters consider 1200 ft.lbs. of energy is required for a bullet to put down a large white-tailed buck.

Range in Yards at Which Deer Cartridges Retain 1200 Ft.Lbs. of Energy

Cartridges Ft.Lbs.	Bullet Weight (Yds.)	Muzzle Velocity (Gr.)	Yards (FPS)
.243 Win.	100	2960	250
.243 WSSM	100	3110	300
.25-06 Rem.	120	2990	360
.270 Win.	130	3060	390
.270 Win.	150	2850	295
.270 WSM	150	3150	450
7mm-08 Rem.	140	2860	400
7 x 57 Mauser	140	2650	300
.280 Rem.	150	2970	435
.280 Rem.	160	2840	500
7mm WSM	150	3200	500
7mm Rem.Mag.	150	3110	485
7mm Rem.Mag.	175	2860	575
7mm Rem. SA/UM	140	3175	500
7mm Rem. UM	140	3425	500
.30-30 Win.	170	2200	140
.308 Win.	150	2820	345
.308 Win.	180	2620	425
.30-06 Spng.	150	2910	435

Cartridges Ft.Lbs.	Bullet Weight (Yds.)	Muzzle Velocity (Gr.)	Yards (FPS)
.30-06 Spng.	180	2700	460
.300 WSM	150	3300	500
.300 Rem SA/UM	150	3200	450
.300 Rem SA	150	3450	500
.300 Win. Mag	180	2960	645
.375 Win.	200	2200	175
.444 Marlin	269	2335	250
.450 Hornady	350	2100	250
.45-70 Govt	300	1880	225

Sight-In Deer Rifle with Six Shots

1. From a sandbag rest, fire three carefully aimed shots at a target 100 yards downrange.

2. With the rifle unloaded, go to the target and mark each of the three holes with a black marker so they can be seen easily.

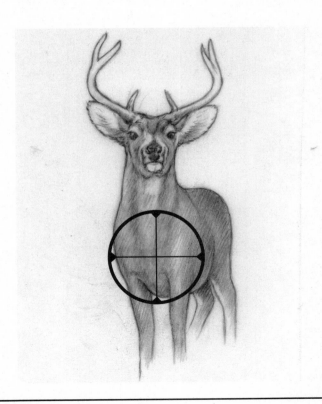

3. Return to the shooting bench and aim the unloaded rifle at the target again. Holding the rifle steady, look through the scope and move the vertical cross wire from the bull's eye to the center of the three-shot group.

4. Next, move the horizontal cross wire from the bull's eye until it is in the center of the three-shot group. It is essential that the rifle be held securely during these adjustments. A helper or a shooting vise will probably make this easier.

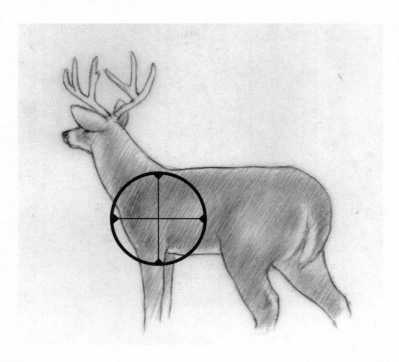

5. Now load and shoot one more carefully aimed shot. It should be in or near the bull's eye.

6. If not, do the same adjustment – carefully adjust the cross wires from the bull's eye to the hole.

7. Now your rifle should be dead-on at 100 yards.

Vital Areas of a Deer

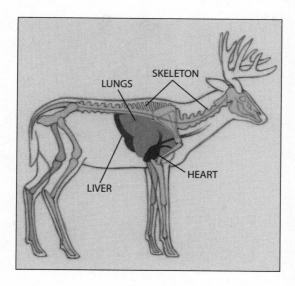

A deer's vital areas must be studied if humane one-shot kills are expected.

SECTION 7

SAFETY

10 Commandments of Firearm Safety

1. Always keep the muzzle pointed in a safe direction.

2. Firearms should be unloaded when not actually in use.

3. Don't rely on your gun's safety.

4. Be sure of your target and what's beyond it.

5. Use proper ammunition.

6. If your gun fails to fire when the trigger is pulled, handle with care.

7. Always wear eye and ear protection when shooting.

8. Be sure the barrel is clear of obstructions before shooting.

9. Don't alter or modify your gun and have it serviced regularly.

10. Learn the mechanical and handling characteristics of the firearm you are using.

Elevated Stand Safety

BEFORE THE HUNT

- Read and understand your elevated stand manufacturer's instruction and warnings before you use your stand and Full-body Harness (FBH).

- Check stands every season and also before each use for signs of wear, fatigue, cracks, loose or missing nuts or bolts and replace as necessary.

- Practice at ground level with your stand and FBH with another person with you before the hunt.

- Learn how to properly use your FBH with a suspended release device.

Tree selection

- Select a healthy, straight tree that is the right size for your treestand.

- Check the tree for insect nests or animal dens.

- Avoid climbing stands on smooth barked trees, especially during icy or wet conditions.

- Clear debris from the tree to minimize injury from a fall and to ensure a safe base if using a ladder stand.

Alternate ground blind

- Be prepared for weather conditions and changes such as lightning, rain, and high wind that might make it unsafe to hunt from an elevated stand.

- Know and admit to your limitations. If you feel sleepy or unsure about the climb go to a ground blind.

Have a plan

- Let a responsible adult know where you will be hunting, when you plan on returning and who is with you. Plans and maps marked with your stand location make rescue easier if necessary. Carry a cell phone, whistle or other signal devices.

DURING THE HUNT

Wear a Full Body Harness!

- Always wear and use a FBH.

- Make sure your FBH is attached to the tree as soon as you begin to climb using climbing stands or climbing aids such as steps.

- In the case of ladder stands, attach the FBH before securing the platform to the tree or stepping onto it.

Don't take chances

- When climbing a ladder, keep three points of contact with the ladder at all times. Both hands and a foot or both feet and one hand should be used to support your body weight when using a ladder.

- Use boots with non-slip soles to avoid slipping.

- When using a platform stand, climb higher than the stand and then step down onto the platform. Slowly put your weight onto your stand to be sure of your balance.

- Never carry gear when climbing. Always use a haul line to raise and lower gear.

IN THE STAND

- Whether sitting or standing, keep the tether line distance as short as possible with no slack in the tether while in the seated position. This keeps fall distance to a minimum.

- Always raise and lower your firearm, bow or other equipment with a haul line.

- Make sure your firearms are unloaded before attaching to a haul rope and do not attach the haul line near the trigger or trigger guard.

- Make sure broadheads are covered prior to raising or lowering.

The 3 R's of a fall – Recover, relief, and rescue

- Attempt to recover and return to your stand. If this is not possible, exercise your legs by pushing against the tree, using another form of motion or suspension relief device until help arrives.

- Don't take chances.

- Call for help immediately.

Avoiding Hypothermia

(1) **Stay dry**. When clothing gets wet it may lose 90 percent of its insulating value. Even sweating can bring on hypothermia.

(2) **Beware of the wind chill**. A slight breeze carries heat away from bare skin faster than still air. It turns wet clothing into a refrigerator due to evaporation.

(3) **Understand cold**. Most hypothermia cases develop in air temperatures that are considered mild, wind chill temperatures in the 40s and 50s. Most people do not believe such temperatures can be dangerous.

(4) **Terminate exposure**. When you cannot stay warm and dry in existing weather conditions, either get a fire going at a natural shelter out of the wind or set up your tube tent and get into the emergency bag. Get out of the wind and dampness, and get warm, as fast as possible.

(5) **Never ignore shivering**. Persistent or violent shivering is clear warning that you are in the early stages of hypothermia.

As the body core temperature drops here is how hypothermia affects you:

98.6° to 96°   Uncontrolled shivering, ability to perform complex tasks impaired.

95° to 91°   Violent shivering, difficulty in speaking.

90° to 86°   Shivering decreases, muscles begin to stiffen, lose coordination. Mind becomes dull; in some cases, amnesia occurs.

85° to 81°   Victim becomes irrational, drifts into stupor. Pulse and respiration are slowed. Muscular rigidity continues.

80° to 78°   Unconsciousness. Reflexes cease to function and heartbeat becomes erratic.

Below 78°   Total failure of cardiac and respiration systems. Death occurs.

Treatment

When hypothermia symptoms are noticed, treatment should begin immediately.

- First get the victim out of the weather and remove his wet clothing.

- If the victim is only mildly impaired, give him warm drinks and get him into dry clothing and a tube tent and emergency bag.

- If the victim is semi-conscious or worse, he does not have the capability of regaining his body temperature without outside help. Keep him awake, give him warm drinks, and if possible get him into a warm bath.

- If possible strip the victim and put him into an emergency bag with another person. Skin to skin contact is an effective treatment.

Water Submersion Hypothermia Survival Time

Water temperature (degrees F)	Exhaustion or unconsciousness	Expected time of survival
32.5	Under 15 min.	under 15 -45 min.
32.5 – 40	15 – 30 min.	30 – 90 min.
40 – 50	30 – 60 min.	1 – 3 hours
50 – 60	1 – 2 hours	1 – 6 hours
60 – 70	2 – 7 hours	2 – 40 hours
70 – 80	3 – 12 hours	3 hours. – indefinite
Over 80	Indefinite	Indefinite

Wind Chill Chart

COOLING POWER OF WIND EXPRESSED AS "EQUIVALENT CHILL TEMPERATURE"

TEMPERATURE (°F)

WIND SPEED KNOTS	MPH	40	35	30	25	20	15	10	5	0	-5	-10	-15	-20	-25	-30	-35	-40	-45	-50	-55	-60
CALM	CALM	40	35	30	25	20	15	10	5	0	-5	-10	-15	-20	-25	-30	-35	-40	-45	-50	-55	-60
3-6	5	35	30	25	20	15	10	5	0	-5	-10	-15	-20	-25	-30	-35	-40	-45	-50	-55	-65	-70
7-10	10	30	20	15	10	5	0	-10	-15	-20	-25	-35	-40	-45	-50	-60	-65	-70	-75	-80	-90	-95
11-15	15	25	15	10	0	-5	-10	-20	-25	-30	-40	-45	-50	-60	-65	-70	-80	-85	-90	-100	-105	-110
16-19	20	20	10	5	0	-10	-15	-25	-30	-35	-45	-50	-60	-65	-75	-80	-85	-95	-100	-110	-115	-120
20-23	25	15	10	0	-5	-15	-20	-30	-35	-45	-50	-60	-65	-75	-80	-90	-95	-105	-110	-120	-125	-135
24-28	30	10	5	0	-10	-20	-25	-30	-40	-50	-55	-65	-70	-80	-85	-95	-100	-110	-115	-125	-130	-140
29-32	35	10	5	-5	-10	-20	-30	-35	-40	-50	-60	-65	-75	-80	-90	-100	-105	-115	-120	-130	-135	-145
33-36	40	10	0	-5	-15	-20	-30	-35	-45	-55	-60	-70	-75	-85	-95	-100	-110	-115	-125	-130	-140	-150

EQUIVALENT CHILL TEMPERATURE

LITTLE DANGER

INCREASING DANGER (Flesh may freeze within 1 minute)

GREAT DANGER (Flesh may freeze within 30 seconds)

DANGER OF FREEZING EXPOSED FLESH FOR PROPERLY CLOTHED PERSONS

WINDS ABOVE 40 HAVE LITTLE ADDITIONAL EFFECT.

Beaufort Wind Scale

Beaufort Number or Force	Wind Speed			Description	Effects Land / Sea
	mph	km/hr	knots		
0	<1	<1	<1	Calm	Still, calm air, smoke will rise vertically. Water is mirror-like.
1	1-3 mph	1-5 kph	1-3 knots	Light Air	Rising smoke drifts, wind vane is inactive. Small ripples appear on water surface.
2	4-7 mph	6-11 kph	4-6 knots	Light Breeze	Leaves rustle, can feel wind on your face, wind vanes begin to move. Small wavelets develop, crests are glassy.
3	8-12 mph	12-19 kph	7-10 knots	Gentle Breeze	Leaves and small twigs move, light weight flags extend. Large wavelets, crests start to break, some whitecaps.
4	13-18 mph	20-28 kph	11-16 knots	Moderate Breeze	Small branches move, raises dust, leaves and paper. Small waves develop, becoming longer, whitecaps.

Beaufort Number or Force	Wind Speed			Description	Effects Land / Sea
	mph	km/hr	knots		
5	19-24 mph	29-38 kph	17-21 knots	Fresh Breeze	Small trees sway. White crested wavelets (whitecaps) form, some spray.
6	25-31 mph	39-49 kph	22-27 knots	Strong Breeze	Large tree branches move, telephone wires begin to "whistle," umbrellas are difficult to keep under control. Larger waves form, whitecaps prevalent, spray.
7	32-38 mph	50-61 kph	28-33 knots	Moderate or Near Gale	Large trees sway, becoming difficult to walk. Larger waves develop, white foam from breaking waves begins to be blown.
8	39-46 mph	62-74 kph	34-40 knots	Gale or Fresh Gale	Twigs and small branches are broken from trees, walking is difficult. Moderately large waves with blown foam.

Beaufort Number or Force	Wind Speed			Description	Effects Land / Sea
	mph	km/hr	knots		
9	47-54 mph	75-88 kph	41-47 knots	Strong Gale	Slight damage occurs to buildings, shingles are blown off of roofs. High waves (6 meters), rolling seas, dense foam, Blowing spray reduces visibility.
10	55-63 mph	89-102 kph	48-55 knots	Whole Gale or Storm	Trees are broken or uprooted, building damage is considerable. Large waves (6-9 meters), overhanging crests, sea becomes white with foam, heavy rolling, reduced visibility.
11	64-72 mph	103-117 kph	56-63 knots	Violent Storm	Extensive widespread damage. Large waves (9-14 meters), white foam, visibility further reduced.
12	73+ mph	118+ kph	64+ knots	Hurricane	Extreme destruction, devastation. Large waves over 14 meters, air filled with foam, sea white with foam and driving spray, little visibility.

Lightning Rules When Deer Hunting

Remember, there is NO safe place outside in a thunderstorm. If you absolutely can't get to safety, this section may help you slightly lessen the threat of being struck by lightning while outside. Don't kid yourself—you are NOT safe outside.

Being stranded outdoors when lightning is striking nearby is a harrowing experience. Your first and only truly safe choice is to get to a safe building or vehicle. If you are camping, climbing, on a motorcycle or bicycle, boating, scuba diving, or enjoying other outdoor activities and cannot get to a safe vehicle or building, follow these **last resort** tips. They will *not* prevent you from being struck by lightning, but may *slightly* lessen the odds.

- Know the weather patterns of the area. For example, in mountainous areas, thunderstorms typically develop in the early afternoon, so plan to hike early in the day and be down the mountain by noon.

- Listen to the weather forecast for the outdoor area you plan to visit. The forecast may be very different from the one near your home. If there is a high chance of thunderstorms, stay home.

These actions may *slightly* reduce your risk of being struck by lightning:

- If camping, hiking, etc., far from a safe vehicle or building, avoid open fields, the top of a hill or a ridge top.

- Stay away from tall, isolated trees or other tall objects. If you are in a forest, stay near a lower stand of trees.

- If you are camping in an open area, set up camp in a valley, ravine or other low area. Remember, a tent offers NO protection from lighting.

- Stay away from water, wet items (such as ropes) and metal objects (such as fences and poles). Water and metal are excellent conductors of electricity. The current from a lightning flash will easily travel for long distances.

CPR

Every hunter should have
formal CPR training

- Check the victim for unresponsiveness. If there is no response, call 911 and return to the victim. 911 can assist you with CPR.

- Tilt the head back and listen for breathing. If not breathing normally, pinch the nose and cover the mouth with yours and blow until you see the chest rise. Give two breaths. Each breath should take 1 second.

- If the victim is still not breathing normally, coughing or moving, began chest compressions. Push down on the chest 1 ½ to 2 inches 30 times right between the nipples. Pump at the rate of 100/minute, faster than once per second.

- Continue with 2 breaths and 30 pumps until medical help arrives.

Heart Attack

Symptoms

- Uncomfortable pressure, fullness, squeezing or pain in the center of the chest lasting more than a few minutes.

- Pain spreading to the shoulders, neck or arms. The pain may be mild to intense. It may feel like pressure, tightness, burning, or heavy weight. It may be located in the chest, upper abdomen, neck, jaw, or inside the arms or shoulders.

- Chest discomfort with lightheadedness, fainting, sweating, nausea or shortness of breath.

- Anxiety, nervousness and/or cold, sweaty skin.

- Paleness or pallor.

- Increased or irregular heart rate.

- Feeling of impending doom.

Treatment

- Seek medical attention, call 911. Began CPR if unconscious or heart has stopped.

STROKE

Symptoms

- Sudden numbness or weakness of the face, arm or leg, especially on one side of the body

- Sudden confusion, trouble speaking or understanding

- Sudden trouble seeing in one or both eyes

- Sudden trouble walking, dizziness, loss of balance or coordination

- Sudden, severe headache with no known cause

Treatment

- Keep the victim calm and comfortable.

- Do not allow them to eat or drink.

- Be prepared to give CPR.

- Seek medical attention instantly, call 911.

- Not all the warning signs occur in every stroke. Don't ignore signs of stroke, even if they go away!

- Check the time. When did the first warning sign or symptom start? You'll be asked this important question later.

- If you have one or more stroke symptoms that last more than a few minutes, don't delay! Immediately call 911 or the emergency medical service (EMS) number so an ambulance (ideally with advanced life support) can quickly be sent for you.

- If you're with someone who may be having stroke symptoms, immediately call 911 or the EMS. Expect the person to protest — denial is common. Don't take "no" for an answer. Insist on taking prompt action.

Items For Deer Hunter's Survival Kit

- Tube Tent
- Strike-anywhere kitchen matches in waterproof match safe
- Flashlight, lithium batteries
- Fire starters (tinder)
- Signal mirror
- Police whistle
- MPI Emergency Space bag
- Parachute cord – 50'
- Aluminum foil – 36"X36"
- Insect repellent
- Water purification tablets
- Pocket Survival Guide
- Resealable plastic bag - 1 gallon size

What To Do When Lost

1. Always let a responsible person know where you will be hunting and when you expect to return. They can launch a search quickly if you do not show up on time.

2. Always carry a survival kit, cell phone, and GPS as a part of your hunting gear.

3. Once you realize you are lost or stranded first STOP and try to call for help and be able to give your exact location.

4. If you cannot reach help by cell phone or two-way radio then prepare to WAIT for help to find you. Resist the temptation to walk out. Stay in one place.

5. Select a survival campsite near an open area or your stalled vehicle. You want to be seen easily, especially from the air.

6. Set up a set of signals, with backups, and keep them ready for instant use.

7. Erect your tube tent or construct shelter making it reasonably comfortable without wasting energy.

8. Gather firewood and start a fire.

9. Maintain a positive survival attitude.

10. Dispel fears.

11. Get comfortable, enjoy the unique experience, and get ready to be found. It will not take long. Most lost hunters are found within three or four hours. In a worst case scenario it takes no longer than 72 hours.

How to Search for a Missing Hunter

Attempting to set up your own search is generally a bad idea, since most often untrained people with the best of intentions, usually do more harm than good. They destroy valuable clues and often become lost or hurt themselves. Searching for missing people is a skill best left to those trained.

However, in some specific circumstances, such as when help is hours away or when the tract of land is not large and it is known almost exactly where the missing person is likely to be, fellow outdoorsmen might conduct a limited search. In those exceptional cases follow these guidelines:

1. Get the entire group together to plan to plan your search. To help identify clues that you find, find out what each member knows, such as when and where the missing buddy was last seen, did he file a trip plan, what brand of cigarettes he smokes, what type of sole does he have on his boots and their size, where he is most likely hunting, and so on.

2. Establish someone in the group as leader of the search, and everyone does as he says.

3. Leave someone at the original spot to continue signaling.

4. If a specific hunting spot is known, two hunters should begin the search with a thorough examination of that

immediate area in case there was a health problem or injury. Take care not to destroy any signs. It is important that only one or two do this, as a larger group will destroy clues that might be helpful if a professional search is needed.

5. Look for signs such as tracks, or, in the case of hunters, blood trail markers for an indication of the missing person's direction of travel.

6. Due to the excitement of the moment, searchers often get lost themselves, so mark the trail you take in so you can follow it out.

7. Consider what sounds the missing person can hear: farm, railroad, highway, mill whistle, etc., and send someone to that location. Many lost people rather than sit still will try to walk to sounds such as these.

8. If there are roads around the area, a vehicle should patrol these roads regularly, but do not blow the horn as you travel.

9. If there is a long opening in the area such as a railroad, gas line or electric line right-of-way, or large fields have someone watch these areas with binoculars.

10. Plan a signal or specific time for calling off the search. If the missing person has not been found within a short time, turn the search over to professionals.

SECTION 8

WHERE TO GET INFORMATION

Wildlife Management Assistance

Alabama

Wildlife Biologist
Natural Resources
Conservation Service
Box 311
Auburn, AL 36830
Phone: 334-887-4535

Wildlife Division
Alabama Division of Game
and Fish
64 North Union St.
Montgomery, AL 36130
Phone: 334-242-3465

Wildlife Department
Alabama Cooperative
Extension Service
109 Duncan Hall
Auburn University, AL 36849
Phone: 334-844-4444

Alaska

Wildlife Biologist
Natural Resources
Conservation Service
949 East 36th Ave., Suite 400
Anchorage, AK 99508-4362
Phone: 907-271-2424

Wildlife Department
Alaska State Extension Services
University of Alaska
Box 756180
Fairbanks, AK 99775-6180
Phone: 907-474-7246

Wildlife Division
Alaska Department of Game
and Fish
Box 25526
Juneau, AK 99802-5526
Phone: 907-465-4100

Arizona

Wildlife Biologist
Natural Resources Conservation
3003 North Central Ave., Suite
800
Phoenix, AZ 85012-2945
Phone: 602-280-8808

Wildlife Department
Arizona State Extension Services
University of Arizona
Tucson, AZ 85721
Phone: 520-621-7209

Wildlife Division
Arizona Game and Fish
Department
2221 West Greenway Rd.
Phoenix, AZ 85023
Phone: 602-942-3000

Arkansas

Wildlife Biologist
Natural Resources Conservation
Service
Federal Office Building,
Room 5404
700 West Capitol Ave.
Little Rock, AR 72201-3228
Phone: 501-324-5445

Wildlife Department
Arkansas State Extension
Services
Box 391
Little Rock, AR 72203
Phone: 501-671-2001

Wildlife Division
Arkansas Game and Fish
Commission
#2 Natural Resources Dr.
Little Rock, AR 72205
Phone: 501-223-6305

California

Wildlife Biologist
Natural Resources Conservation
Service
2121-C Second St.
Davis, CA 95616-5475
Phone: 916-757-8215

Wildlife Department
California State Extension
Services
Cooperative Extension and
Agricultural
Experiment Station
University of California
300 Lakeside Dr., Sixth Floor
Oakland, CA 94612-3560
Phone: 415-987-0060

Wildlife Division
California Department of Game
and Fish
Box 944209
Sacramento, CA 94244-2090
Phone: 916-653-7664

Colorado

Wildlife Biologist
Natural Resources Conservation
Service
655 Parfet St., Room E 200C
Lakewood, CO 80215-5517
Phone: 303-236-2886, ext. 202

Wildlife Division
Colorado Division of Wildlife
6060 Broadway
Denver, CO 80216.
Phone: 303-291-7208

Wildlife Department
Colorado State Extension
Services
1 Administration Building
Colorado State University
Fort Collins, CO 80523
Phone: 970-491-6281

Connecticut

Wildlife Biologist
Natural Resources Conservation
Service
16 Professional Park Rd.
Storrs, CT 06268-1299
Phone: 203-487-4013

Wildlife Department
University of Connecticut
Cooperative
Extension
College of Agriculture and
Natural Resources
Box U-87
Storrs, CT 06269-4087
Phone: 203-486-2840

Wildlife Division
Connecticut Department of
Environmental
Protection
State Office Building
79 Elm St.
Hartford, CT 06106-5127
Phone: 203-566-4522

Delaware

Wildlife Biologist
Natural Resources Conservation
Service
1203 College Park Dr.,
Suite 101
Dover, DE 19904-8713
Phone: 302-678-4160

Wildlife Department
Delaware State Extension
Service
University of Delaware
133 Townsend Hall
Newark, DE 19717-1303
Phone: 302-831-2504

Wildlife Division
Delaware Division of Fish and
Wildlife
Box 1401
Dover, DE 19903
Phone: 302-739-5295

Florida

Wildlife Biologist
Natural Resources Conservation
Service
2614 N.W. 43rd St.
Gainesville, FL 32606-6611
Phone: 903-338-9525

Wildlife Department
Florida State Extension Service
University of Florida
1038 McCarty Hall
Gainesville, FL 32611-0210
Phone: 904-392-1761

Wildlife Division
Florida Game and Fresh Water
Fish
Commission
Farris Bryant Building
620 South Meridian
Tallahassee, FL 32399-1600
Phone: 904-488-2975

Georgia

Georgia Biologist
Natural Resources Conservation
Service
Federal Building, Box 13
355 East Hancock Avenue
Athens, GA 30601
Phone: 706-546-2272

Wildlife Department
Georgia State Extension
Services
The University of Georgia
College of Agricultural and
Environmental
Sciences
Athens, GA 30602-7501
Phone: 706-542-3924

Wildlife Division
Georgia State Game and Fish
Division
2070 U.S. Hwy 278 S.E.
Social Circle, GA 30279
Phone: 706-557-3020

Hawaii

Wildlife Biologist
Natural Resources Conservation
Service
Box 50004
Honolulu, HI 96850-0002
Phone: 808-541-2601

Wildlife Division
Hawaii Department of Land and
Natural Resources
Box 621
Honolulu, HI 96809
Phone: 808-587-0400

Idaho

Wildlife Biologist
Natural Resources Conservation
Service
3244 Elder St., Room 124
Boise, ID 83705
Phone: 208-378-5700

Wildlife Division
Idaho Fish and Game
Department
Box 25
Boise, ID 83707
Phone: 208-334-5159

Wildlife Department
Idaho State Extension
Services
University of Idaho
Cooperative Extension Service
System
Moscow, ID 83843
Phone: 208-885-6356

Illinois

Wildlife Biologist
Natural Resources Conservation
Service
1902 Fox Dr.
Champaign, Il 61820-7335
Phone: 217-398-5267

Wildlife Department
Illinois State Extension Services
University of Illinois
123 Mumford Hall
1301 West Gregory Dr.
Urbana, IL 61801
Phone: 217-333-5900

Wildlife Division
Illinois Department of Natural
Resources
Lincoln Tower Plaza
524 South Second St.
Springfield, IL 62701-1787
Phone: 217-785-0075

Indiana

Wildlife Biologist
Natural Resources Conservation
Service
6013 Lakeside Blvd.
Indianapolis, IN 46278-2933
Phone: 317-290-3200

Wildlife Department
Indiana State Extension
Services
Purdue University
1140 Agriculture
Administration Bldg.
West Lafayette, IN 47907-1104
Phone: 765-494-8489

Wildlife Division
Indiana Division of Game
and Fish
402 West Washington St.,
Room W-273
Indianapolis, IN 46204-2212
Phone: 317-232-4080

Iowa

Wildlife Biologist
Natural Resources Conservation
Service
693 Federal Building
210 Walnut St
Des Moines, IA 50309-2180
Phone: 515-284-6655

Wildlife Division
Iowa Department of Natural
Resources
Wallace State Office Building
East Ninth and Grand Ave.
Des Moines, IA 50319-0034
Phone: 515-281-5145

Wildlife Department
Iowa State Extension Services
Iowa State University
315 Beardshear Hall
Ames, IA 50011
Phone: 515-294-6192

Kansas

Wildlife Biologist
Natural Resources Conservation
Service
760 South Broadway
Salina, KS 67401
Phone: 913-823-4565

Wildlife Department
Kansas State Extension Services
Kansas State University
127 Call Hall
Manhattan, KS 66506
Phone: 913-532-5734

Wildlife Division
Kansas Department of Wildlife
and Parks
900 Jackson St., Suite 502
Topeka, KS 66612-1220
Phone: 913-296-2281

Kentucky

Wildlife Biologist
Natural Resources
Conservation Service
771 Corporate Dr. Suite 110
Lexington, KY 40503-5479
Phone: 606-224-7350

Wildlife Division
Kentucky Department of Fish
and Wildlife Resources
#1 Game Farm Rd.
Frankfort, KY 40601
Phone: 502-564-3400

Wildlife Department
Kentucky State Extension
Services
University of Kentucky
Lexington, KY 40546
Phone: 606-257-4302

Louisiana

Wildlife Biologist
Natural Resources Conservation
Service
3737 Government St.
Alexandria, LA 71302-3727
Phone: 318-473-7751

Wildlife Division
Louisiana Department of
Wildlife and Fisheries
Box 98000
Baton Rouge, LA 70898
Phone: 504-765-2623

Wildlife Department
Louisiana State Extension
Services
Box 25100
Baton Rouge, LA 70894-5100
Phone: 504-388-6083

Maine

Wildlife Biologist
Natural Resources Conservation
Service
5 Godfrey Dr.
Orono, ME, 04473
Phone: 207-866-7241

Wildlife Department
University of
Maine Cooperative Extension
University of Maine
234 Nutting Hall
Orono, ME 04469
Phone: 207-581-2902

Wildlife Division
Maine Department of Inland
Fisheries and Wildlife
284 State St., Station #41
Augusta, ME 04333
Phone: 207-287-5202

Maryland

Wildlife Biologist
Natural Resources Conservation
Service
John Hanson Business Center
339 Busch's Frontage Rd.,
Suite 301
Annapolis, MD 21401-5534
Phone: 410-757-0861, ext. 315

Wildlife Department
Maryland State Extension
Services
University of Maryland
1104 Symons Hall
College Park, MD 20742
Phone: 301-405-2072

Wildlife Division
Maryland Department of
Natural Resources
Tawes State Office Building
Annapolis, MD 21401
Phone: 410-260-8540

Massachusetts

Wildlife Biologist
Natural Resources Conservation
Service
451 West St.
Amherst, MA 01002-2995
Phone: 413-253-4351

Wildlife Department
Massachusetts State Extension
Services
University of Massachusetts
Holdsworth Natural Resources
Center
Amherst, MA 01003
Phone: 413-545-2665

Wildlife Division
Massachusetts Department
of Fisheries, Wildlife,
and Environmental Law
Enforcement
100 Cambridge St.
Boston, MA 02202
Phone: 617-727-3155

Michigan

Wildlife Biologist
Natural Resources Conservation
Service
1405 South Harrison Rd.,
Room 101
East Lansing, MI 48823-5243
Phone: 517-337-6701, ext. 1201

Wildlife Department
Michigan State University
Extension
10B Agriculture Hall
East Lansing, MI 48824-1039
Phone: 517-355-0240

Wildlife Division
Michigan Department of Natural
Resources
Stevens T. Mason Building
Box 30028
Lansing, MI 48909
Phone: 517-373-2329

Minnesota

Wildlife Biologist
Natural Resources Conservation
Service
600 Farm Credit Services
Building
375 Jackson St.
St. Paul MN 555101-1854
Phone: 612-290-3675

Wildlife Department
Minnesota State Extension
Services
University of Minnesota
240 Coffey Hall
1420 Eckles Ave.
St. Paul, MN 55108
Phone: 612-625-3774

Wildlife Division
Minnesota Department of
Natural Resources
500 Lafayette Rd.
St. Paul, MN 55155-4020
Phone: 612-296-2549

Mississippi

Wildlife Biologist
Natural Resources Conservation
Service
Federal Building, Suite 1321
100 Capitol Street
Jackson, MS 39269-1399
Phone: 601-965-5205

Wildlife Division
Mississippi Department of
Wildlife, Fisheries, and Parks
Box 451
Jackson, MS 39205
Phone: 601-364-2000

Wildlife Department
Mississippi State Extension
Services
Mississippi State University
Mississippi State, MS 39762
Phone: 601-325-3036

Missouri

Wildlife Biologist
Natural Resources Conservation
Service
Parkade Center, Suite 250
601 Business Loop 70 West
Columbia, MO 65203-2546
Phone: 314-876-0900

Wildlife Department
Missouri State Extension
Services
University of Missouri
309 University Hall
Columbia, MO 65211
Phone: 573-883-7754

Wildlife Division
Missouri Department of
Conservation
Box 180
Jefferson City, MO 65102-0180
Phone: 573-751-4115

Montana

Wildlife Biologist
Natural Resources Conservation
Service
Federal Building
10 East Babcock St., Room 443
Bozeman, MT 59715-4704
Phone: 406-587-6813

Wildlife Department
Montana State Extension
Services
Montana State University
Linfield Hall
Bozeman, MT 59717
Phone: 406-994-6647

Wildlife Division
Montana Department of Fish,
Wildlife, and Parks
1420 East Sixth Ave.
Helena, MT 59620
Phone: 406-444-3186

Nebraska

Wildlife Biologist
Natural Resources Conservation
Service
Federal Building Room 152
100 Centennial Mall North
Lincoln, NE 68508-3866
Phone: 402-437-5300

Wildlife Department
Nebraska State Extension
Services
University of Nebraska
Lincoln, NE 68583-0703
Phone: 402-472-2966

Wildlife Division
Nebraska Game and Parks
Commission
Box 30370
Lincoln, NE 68503
Phone: 402-471-5539

Nevada

Wildlife Biologist
Natural Resources Conservation
Service
5301 Langley Lane, Building F
Suite 201
Reno, NV 89511
Phone: 702-784-5863

Wildlife Department
Nevada State Extension
Services
University of Nevada
1000 Valley Rd.
Reno, NV 89512
Phone: 702-784-4020

Wildlife Division
Nevada Department of
Conservation and
Natural Resources
1100 Valley Rd.
Reno, NV 89512
Phone: 702-688-1599

New Hampshire

Wildlife Biologist
Natural Resources Conservation
Service
Federal Building
2 Madbury Rd.
Durham, NH 03824
Phone: 603-433-0505

Wildlife Department
University of New Hampshire
Cooperative Extension
Taylor Hall
59 College Road
Durham, NH 03824-2618
Phone: 603-862-3594

Wildlife Division
New Hampshire Fish and Game
Department
2 Hazen Dr.
Concord, NH 03301
Phone: 603-271-3422

New Jersey

Wildlife Biologist
Natural Resources Conservation
Service
1370 Hamilton St.,
Somerset, NJ 08873-3157
Phone: 908-246-1205

Wildlife Division
New Jersey Division of Fish,
Game and Wildlife
CN 400
Trenton, NJ 08625
Phone: 609-292-9410

Wildlife Department
New Jersey State Extension
Services
Rutgers State University Cook
College
Box 231
New Brunswick, NJ 08903
Phone: 732-932-9306

New Mexico

Wildlife Biologist
Natural Resources Conservation
Service
6200 Jefferson St. N.E.
Albuquerque, MN 87109
Phone: 505-761-4400

Wildlife Department
New Mexico State Extension
Services
New Mexico State University
Box 30003 Campus Box 3AG
Las Cruces, NM 88003
Phone: 505-646-3748

Wildlife Division
New Mexico Natural Resource
Department
Villagra Building
Santa Fe, NM 87503
Phone: 505-827-7911

New York

Wildlife Biologist
Natural Resources Conservation
Service
441 South Salina St., Suite 354
Syracuse, NY 13202-2450
Phone: 315-477-6504

Wildlife Division
New York Department of
Environmental Conservation
50 Wolf Rd.
Albany, NY 12233
Phone: 518-474-2121

Wildlife Department
New York State Cooperative
Extension
Cornel University
NY State College of Agriculture
and Life
Sciences and Human Ecology
276 Roberts Hall
Ithaca, NY 14853-4203
Phone: 607-255-2237

North Carolina

Wildlife Biologist
Natural Resources Conservation
Service
4405 Bland Rd., Suite 205
Raleigh, NC 27609-6293
Phone: 919-873-2102

Wildlife Department
North Carolina Cooperative
Extension Services
North Carolina State University
Box 7602
Raleigh, NC 27695
Phone: 919-55-2811

Wildlife Division
North Carolina Wildlife
Resources Commission
Archdale Building
512 North Salisbury St.
Raleigh, NC 27601-1188
Phone: 919-733-3391

North Dakota

Wildlife Biologist
Natural Resources Conservation
Service
Box 1458
Bismarck, ND 58502-1458
Phone: 701-250-4421

Wildlife Department
North Dakota State Extension
Service
North Dakota State University
Box 5437
Fargo, ND 58105
Phone: 701-231-7173

Wildlife Division
North Dakota State Game and
Fish Department
100 North Bismarck Expressway
Bismarck, ND 58501
Phone: 701-2216300

Ohio

Wildlife Biologist
Natural Resources Conservation
Service
200 North High St., Room 522
Columbus, OH 43215-2748
Phone: 614-469-6962

Wildlife Division
Ohio Division of Wildlife
1840 Belcher Dr.
Columbus, OH 43224-1329
Phone: 614-265-6300

Wildlife Department
Ohio State University Extension
Services
2120 Fyffe Rd.
Columbus, OH 43210
Phone: 614-292-4067

Oklahoma

Wildlife Biologist
Natural Resources Conservation
Service
100 USDA Agriculture Center
Building
Suite 203
Stillwater, OK 64074-2624
Phone: 405-742-1200

Wildlife Department
Oklahoma State Extension
Services
Oklahoma State University
Agricultural Hall Room 139
Stillwater, OK 74078
Phone: 405-744-5398

Wildlife Division
Oklahoma Department of
Wildlife Conservation
Box 53465
Oklahoma City, OK 73152
Phone: 405-521-3851

Oregon

Wildlife Biologist
Natural Resources Conservation
Service
101 S.W. Main St., Suite 1300
Portland, OR 97104-3221
Phone: 503-414-3201

Wildlife Department
Oregon State Extension Services
Oregon State University
Corvallis, OR 97331
Phone: 541-737-2713

Wildlife Division
Oregon Department of Fish and
Wildlife
Box 59
Portland, OR 97207
Phone: 503-229-5410 ext. 401

Pennsylvania

Wildlife Biologist
Natural Resources Conservation
Service
One Credit Union Pl., Suite 340
Wildwood Center
Harrisburg, PA 17110-2993
Phone: 717-782-2202

Wildlife Division
Pennsylvania Game Commission
2001 Elmerton Ave.
Harrisburg, PA 17110-9797
Phone: 717-787-3633

Wildlife Department
Pennsylvania State Extension
Services
Pennsylvania State University
201 Agricultural
Administration Bldg.
University Park, PA 16802-2600
Phone: 814-865-2541

Rhode Island

Wildlife Biologist
Natural Resources Conservation
Service
60 Quaker Lane, Suite 46
Warwick, RI 02886-0111
Phone: 401-828-1300

Wildlife Department
Rhode Island State Cooperative
Extension Services
University of Rhode Island
Kingston, RI 02881
Phone: 401-874-2599

Wildlife Division
Rhode Island Department of
Environmental Management
Stedman Government Center
4808 Tower Hill Rd.
Wakefield, RI 02879
Phone: 401-277-3075

South Carolina

Wildlife Biologist
Natural Resources Conservation
Service
Strom Thurmond Federal
Building
1835 Assembly St., Room 950
Columbia, SC 29201-2489
Phone: 803-765-5681

Wildlife Department
South Carolina State Extension
Services
Clemson University
Clemson, SC 29634-0310
Phone: 864-656-3382

Wildlife Division
South Carolina Department of
Natural
Resources
Rembert C. Dennis Building
Box 167
Columbia, SC 29202
Phone: 803-734-4007

South Dakota

Wildlife Biologist
Natural Resources Conservation
Service
Federal Building
200 4th St. S.W.
Huron, SD 57350
Phone: 605-352-1200

Wildlife Department
South Dakota State Extension
Services
South Dakota State University
Box 2207D
Brookings, SD 57007
Phone: 605-688-4792

Wildlife Division
South Dakota Department of
Game, Fish, and
Parks
Siqurd Anderson Building
523 East Capitol
Pierre, SD 57501-3182
Phone: 605-773-3387

Tennessee

Wildlife Biologist
Natural Resources Conservation
Service
675 U. S. Courthouse
801 Broadway St.
Nashville, TN 37203-3878
Phone: 615-736-5471

Wildlife Division
Tennessee Wildlife Resources
Agency
Ellington Agricultural Center
Box 40747
Nashville, TN 37204
Phone: 615-781-6552

Wildlife Department
Tennessee State Extension
Services
University of Tennessee
Agricultural Extension Service
Box 1071
Knoxville, TN 37901-1071
Phone: 423-974-7114

Texas

Wildlife Biologist
Natural Resources Conservation
Service
W. R. Poage Federal Building
101 South Main Street
Temple, TX 76501-7682
Phone: 817-774-1214

Wildlife Department
Texas Agricultural Extension
Service
Texas A&M University
College Station, TX 77843-7101
Phone: 409-845-7967

Wildlife Division
Texas Parks and Wildlife
Department
4200 Smith School Rd.
Austin, TX 78744
Phone: 512-389-4802

Utah

Wildlife Biologist
Natural Resources Conservation
Service
125 South State St., Room 4002
Salt Lake City, UT 84138-0350
Phone: 801-524-5050

Wildlife Division
Utah State Division of Wildlife
Resources
1596 WN Temple
Salt Lake City, UT 84116-3154
Phone: 801-538-4702

Wildlife Department
Utah State Extension Services
Utah State University
Logan, UT 84322-4900
Phone: 801-797-2201

Vermont

Wildlife Biologist
Natural Resources Conservation
Service
69 Union Street
Winooski, VT 05404-1999
Phone: 802-951-6796

Wildlife Department
University of Vermont Extension
601 Main St.
Burlington, VT 05401-3439
Phone: 802-656-2990

Wildlife Division
Vermont Fish and Game
Department
103 South Main St., 10 South
Waterbury, VT 05671-0501
Phone: 805-241-3730

Virginia

Wildlife Biologist
Natural Resources Conservation
Service
Culpepper Building
1606 Santa Rose Rd., Suite 209
Richmond, VA 23229-5014
Phone: 804-287-1691

Wildlife Department
Virginia State Extension Services
Virginia Polytechnic and State
University
Blacksburg, VA 24061-0402
Phone: 540-231-5299

Wildlife Division
Virginia Department of Game
and Inland
Fisheries
4010 West Broad St.
Richmond, VA 23230-1104
Phone: 804-367-9231

Washington

Wildlife Biologist
Natural Resources Conservation
Service
Rock Point Tower 2, Suite 450
West 316 Boone Ave.
Spokane, WA 99201-2348
Phone: 509-353-2337

Wildlife Department
Washington State Extension
Services
Washington State University
Box 646230
Pullman, WA 99164-6230
Phone: 509-335-2933

Wildlife Division
Washington Department of Fish
and Wildlife
600 Capitol Way North
Olympia, WA 98501-1091
Phone: 360-753-5710

West Virginia

Wildlife Biologist
Natural Resources Conservation
Service
75 High St., Room 301
Morgantown, WV 26505
Phone: 304-291-4153

Wildlife Department
West Virginia State Extension
Services
West Virginia University
817 Knapp Hall
Morgantown, WV 26506
Phone: 304-293-5691

Wildlife Division
West Virginia Division of
Natural Resources
1900 Kanawha Blvd. East
Charleston, WV 25305
Phone: 304-558-2771

Wisconsin

Wildlife Biologist
Natural Resources Conservation
Service
6515 Watts Rd., Suite 200
Madison, WI 53719-2726
Phone: 608-264-5341 ext. 122

Wildlife Department
University of Wisconsin
Extension
432 North Lake St.
Madison WI 53706
Phone: 608-263-2775

Wildlife Division
Wisconsin Department of
Natural Resources
Box 7921
Madison, WI 53707
Phone: 608-266-2121

Wyoming

Wildlife Biologist
Natural Resources Conservation
Service
Federal Office Bldg.
100 East B. St. Room 3124
Casper, WY 82601
Phone: 307-261-6453

State Forestry Agencies

ALABAMA

AL Forestry Commission
513 Madison Avenue
PO Box 302550
Montgomery, AL 36130-2550
t: 334-240-9304

ALASKA

AK Division of Forestry
3700 Airport Way
Fairbanks, AK 99709
t: 907-451-2666

ARIZONA

Arizona State Forestry Division
1110 W. Washington St., Suite 100
Phoenix, AZ 85007
t: 602-771.1412

ARKANSAS

AR Forestry Commission
3821 West Roosevelt Rd.
Little Rock, AR 72204-6396
t: 501-296-1941

CALIFORNIA

Dept of Forestry & Fire Protection
PO Box 944246
1416 9th Street, Room 1505
Sacramento, CA 94244-2460
t: 916-653-7772

COLORADO

CO State Forest Service
Colorado State University
Foothills Campus - 1050
Fort Collins, CO 80523-5060
t: 970-491-6303

CONNECTICUT

Division of Forestry
79 Elm Street
Hartford, CT 06106
t: 860-424-3630

DELAWARE

Delaware Forest Service
2320 S. DuPont Highway
Dover, DE 19901
t: 302-698-4548

FLORIDA

Division of Forestry
3125 Conner Boulevard
Tallahassee, FL 32399-1650
t: 850-488-4274

GEORGIA

GA Forestry Commission
PO Box 819
Macon, GA 31202-0819
t: 478-751-3480

HAWAII

Division of Forestry & Wildlife
1151 Punchbowl Street
Honolulu, HI 96813
t: 808-587-4182

IDAHO

ID Department of Lands
PO Box 83720
Boise, ID 83720-0050
t: 208-334-0242

ILLINOIS

IDNR – Forest Resources
One Natural Resources Way
Springfield, IL 62702
t: 217-785-8774

INDIANA
IDNR - Division of Forestry
402 W. Washington St. Rm W296
Indianapolis, IN 46204
t: 317-232-4116

IOWA
Department of Natural Resources
502 East 9th Street
Des Moines, IA 50319
t: 515-242-6898

KANSAS
Kansas Forest Service
2610 Claflin Road
Manhattan, KS 66502-2798
t: 785-532-3300

KENTUCKY
KY Division of Forestry
627 Comanche Trail
Frankfort, KY 40601
t: 502-564-4496

LOUISIANA
Office of Forestry
PO Box 1628
Baton Rouge, LA 70821
t: 225-952-8002

MAINE

ME Forest Service
22 State House Station
Augusta, ME 04333
t: 207-287-2791

MARYLAND

DNR – Forest Service
580 Taylor Avenue, E-1
Annapolis, MD 21401
t: 410-260-8501

MASSACHUSETTS

DCR – Div. State Parks & Rec.
251 Causeway Street
Boston, MA 02114
t: 617-626-1250

MICHIGAN

Dept. of Natural Resources
Forest, Mineral & Fire Mgmt
PO Box 30452
Lansing, MI 48909-7952
t: 517-335-7009

MINNESOTA

Division of Forestry
500 Lafayette Road
St. Paul, MN 55155-4044
t: 651-259-5284

MISSISSIPPI

MS Forestry Commission
301 N. Lamar St., Suite 300
Jackson, MS 39201
t: 601-359-2801

MISSOURI

MO Dept. of Conservation
PO Box 180
Jefferson City, MO 65102
t: 573-751-4115 ext. 3120

MONTANA

DNRC - Forestry Division
2705 Spurgin Road
Missoula, MT 59804
t: 406-542-4300

NEBRASKA
NE Forest Service
Forestry Hall
PO Box 830815
Lincoln, NE 68583-0815
t: 402-472-2944

NEVADA
Division of Forestry
2478 Fairview Drive
Carson City, NV 89701
t: 775-684-2500

NEW HAMPSHIRE
Division of Forests & Lands
PO Box 1856
172 Pembroke Rd.
Concord, NH 03302-1856
t: 603-271-2214

NEW JERSEY
State Forestry Service
PO Box 404
Trenton, NJ 08625-0404
t: 609-292-2520

NEW MEXICO
Forestry Division
PO Box 1948
Santa Fe, NM 87504-1948
t: 505-476-3328

NORTH CAROLINA
NC Division of Forest Resources
1616 Mail Service Center
Raleigh, NC 27699
t: 919-857-4844

NORTH DAKOTA
ND Forest Service
307 First Street, East
Bottineau, ND 58318-1100
t: 701-228-5422

OHIO
Division of Forestry
2045 Morse Road, Bldg. H-1
Columbus, OH 43229-6605
t: 614-265-6690

OKLAHOMA

OK Dept. of Ag. – Forestry Services
PO Box 528804
Oklahoma City, OK 73152-3864
t: 405-521-3864

OREGON

OR Department of Forestry
2600 State Street
Salem, OR 97310
t: 503-945-7211

PENNSYLVANIA

Bureau of Forestry
PO Box 8552
Harrisburg, PA 17105-8552
t: 717-787-2703

RHODE ISLAND

Division of Forest Environment
1037 Hartford Pike
North Scituate, RI 02857
t: 401-647-3367

SOUTH CAROLINA
SC Forestry Commission
5500 Broad River Road
Columbia, SC 29221-1707
t: 803-896-8800

SOUTH DAKOTA
Resource Conservation & Forestry
Foss Building
523 E. Capitol Avenue
Pierre, SD 57501
t: 605-773-3623

TENNESSEE
TN Dept of Ag. – Div. of Forestry
Box 40627 Melrose Station
Nashville, TN 37204
t: 615-837-5411

TEXAS
Texas Forest Service
301 Tarrow, Suite 364
College Station, TX 77840-7896
t: 979-458-6606

UTAH

Dept. of Natural Resources
1594 W. North Temple, Suite 3520
Salt Lake City, UT 84116-3154
t: 801-538-5389

VERMONT

Dept Forests, Parks & Recreation
103 S. Main Street
Waterbury, VT 05671-0601
t: 802-241- 3680

VIRGINIA

VA Department of Forestry
900 Natural Resources Dr., Ste 800
Charlottesville, VA 22903
t: 434-977-6555

WASHINGTON

Department of Natural Resources
PO Box 47001
Olympia, WA 98504-7001
t: 360-902-1603

WEST VIRGINIA

WV Division of Forestry
1900 Kanawha Boulevard, East
Charleston, WV 25305-0180
t: 304-558- 3446

WISCONSIN

DNR – Division of Forestry
PO Box 7921
Madison, WI 53707-7921
t: 608-264-9224

WYOMING

WY State Forestry Division
1100 West 22nd Street
Cheyenne, WY 82002
t: 307-777-7586

Wildlife Seed and Plant Sources

Seeds

Adams Briscoe Seed Co.
Box 19
Jackson, GA 30233
Phone: 770-775-7826

Haile-Dean Seed Co.
501 North Hennis Rd.
Winter Garden, FL 34787
Phone: 1-800-423-7333

BuckLunch.com
888-373-0667
www.bucklunch.com

National Wild Turkey Federation
Project HELP
Box 530
Edgefield, SC 29824
800-843-6983
www.nwtf.org

Osenbaugh Grass Seeds
RR 1, Box 44
Lucas, IA 50151
800-582-2788

Pennington Seed Co.
Box 290
Madison, GA 30650
800-277-1412

Sharp Brothers Seed Co.
396 S.W. Davis St.-Ladue
Clinton, MO 65735
800-462-8483
www.sharpseed.com

Spandle Nurseries
131 Wildlife Dr.
Claxton, GA 30417
800-553-5771
www.spandels.com

Whitetail Institute
239 Whitetail Trail
Pintlala, AL 36043
334-281-3006
www.whitetailinstitute.com

Texas Seed Co.
Drawer 599
Kenedy, TX 78119
Phone: 1-800-321-5673

Bamert Seed
Muleshoe, TX 79347
800-262-9892
www.bamertseed.com

Tacomate Seed
P. O. Box 239
Tangent, OR 97389
www.tecomateseed.com

Star Seed
Osborne, KS
800-782-7311
www.gostarseed.com

Hunter's Specialties
6000 Huntington Ct
Cedar Rapids, IA 52402
319-395-0321
www.hunterspec.com

Cooper Feed & Seed
131 Eaton St.
Lawrenceville, GA 30045
770-963-2101
www.cooperseeds.com

Evolved Harvest
3849 Plaza Tower Dr.
Baton Rouge, LA 70816
www.evolved.com

Bio-Logic
662-495-929
www.mossyoakbiologic.com

Ferry – Morse Seed Co.
601 Stephen Beale Dr.
Fulton, KY 42041
800-626-3392
www.ferry-morse.com

Hunting Cabin Packages

Original Log Cabin Homes
7677 N. Halifax Rd.
Rocky Mount, NC 27809
www.logcabinhomes.com

Pioneer Log Homes
1100 N. Beeline Hwy
Payson, AZ
928-472-8073
www.pioneerloghomesofbc.com

Appalachian Log Homes, Inc
11312 Station West Drive
Knoxville, TN 37922
1-800-726-0708
www.alhloghomes.com

Honest Abe Log Homes, Inc.
3855 Clay County Highway
Moss, Tennessee 38575
1-800-231-3695
www.honestabe.com

Jim Barna Log Systems
P. O. Box 4529
Oneida, Tn 37841-4529
Phone: (423)-569-5903, 1-800-962-4734
www.logcabins.com

Coventry Log Homes
108 S. Court St.
Woodsville, NH 03785
800-308-7505
www.coventryloghomes.com

Northeastern Log Homes, Inc./ VERMONT
P. O. Box 126
Groton, VT 05046-0126
1-800-992-6526

Northeastern Log Homes, Inc./MAINE
P. O. Box 46
Kenduskeag, ME 04450-0046
1-800-624-2797

Northeastern Log Homes, Inc./MASSACHUSETTS
1126 Southampton Rd.
Westfield, Ma. 01085-1368
1-800-528-4456

Northeastern Log Homes, Inc./KENTUCKY

P.O. Box 7966

Louisville, KY 40257-0966

1-800-451-2724

www.northeasternlog.com

The Wilderness Cabin Co.

415 Neave Court

Kelowna, BC Canada V1V 2M2

1-888-891-3111, 250-765-0535

www.wildernesscabin.com

Suwannee River Log Homes

4345 U.S. 90

Wellborn, FL 32094

www.srloghomes.com

Kuhns Brothers Log Homes

Lewisburg, Pa.

800-326-9614

www.kuhnsbros.com

Panel Concepts, Inc.

331 No. M-33

Mio, Michigan 48647

989-826-6511

www.panelconcepts.com

Ward Log Homes
P. O.Box 72
Houlton, Maine 04730
800-341-1566
www.wardloghomes.com

Cracker Style Log Homes
20253 NE 20th St.
Williston, FL 32696
352-529-2070
www.crackerstyleloghomes.com

Deep Creek Log Homes
P. O. Box 2225
Wendell, NC 27591
www.deepcreekloghomes.com

Sierra Log Homes
3650 Morrow Way
Chico, CA 95928
800-899-0680
www.cnwloghomes.com

Hunting Insurance Companies

Davis-Garvin Agency, Inc.
P. O. Box 21627
Columbia, SC 29221-9961
800-845-3163
www.davisgarvin.com

Quality Deer Management Association
Hunt Club Insurance
P.O. Box 227
Watkinsville, Ga. 30677
800-209-DEER
Web: www.qdma.com

Outdoors Insurance
Hunt Club Liability Insurance
P. O. Box 6336
Wheeling, WV 26003
866-695-9040
www.outdoorsinsurance

Forest Landowners Insurance Program
P.O. Box 410679
Kansas City, MO 64141
800- 658-7047
www.locktonrisk.com/forestlandowners/huntlease.htm

National Rifle Association Hunt Club Insurance
Kirke-Van Orsdel, Inc.

1776 West Lakes Parkway

West Des Moines, LA 50398

800-544-9820

www.nra.org

Buckmasters Liability Insurance

10360 Highway 80

East Montgomery, AL 36117

P. O. Box 244022

Montgomery, AL 36124-4002

Phone: 800-240-3337

Fax: 334-215-3535

www.buckmasters.com

Outdoor Underwriters, Inc.

140 Stoneridge Dr., Suite 265

Columbia, SC 29210

866-961-4101

www.outdoorund.com

Deer Management Organizations

Quality Deer Management Association
P. O. Box 160

Bogart, GA 30622

800-209-3337

www.qdma.com

Whitetails Unlimited
P. O. Box 720

Sturgeon Bay, WI 54235

800-274-5471

www.whitetailsunlimited.com

TROPHY SCORING ORGANIZATIONS

Boone & Crockett Club
250 Station Dr.
Missouli, MT 59801
406-542-1888
www.booneandcrockettclub.com

Pope and Young Club
273 Mill Creek Road
P. O. Box 548
Chatfield, MN 55923
(507) 867-4144
www.pope-young.org

The Longhunter Society
P. O. Box 67
Friendship, IN 47021
812-667-5131
www.nmlra.org/longhunter.asp

Safari Club International
4800 W. Gates Pass Rd.
Tucson, AZ 85745
888-486-8724
www.safariclub.org

Deer Management Tools Resources

Ben Meadows
3589 Broad Street
Atlanta, GA 30341
800-241-6401
www.benmeadows.com

Wildlife Enterprises
107 Oak Way
Kerrville, TX 78028
830-257-4538
www.wildlifeenterprises.com

Forestry Suppliers, Inc.
Box 8397
Jackson, MS 39284
800-752-8460
www.forestry-suppliers.com

Interstate Graphics, Inc.
7817 Burden Rd.
Rockford, IL 61115
800-243-3925
www.interstategraphicsinc.com

Minuteman Signs
Box 457
Pfafftown, NC 27040
207-512-8617
www.minutemansigns.com

Signs by John Voss
Box 553
Manlius, NY 13104
800-473-0698
www.vosssigns.com

Quality Deer Management Association (QDMA)
P. O. Box 160
Bogart, GA 30622
800-209-3337
www.qdma.com

Moultrie Products
150 Industrial Rd.
Alabaster, AL 35007
205-664-6700
www.moultriefeeders.com

MAPPING PROGRAMS

myTOPO.com
P. O. Box 2075
Red Lodge, MT 59068
Ph: 877-587-9004
www.mytopo.com

DeLorme
Ph: 800-569-8313
www.delorme.com

U. S. Gelogical Survey
P. O. Box 25286
Denver, CO 80225
Ph: 888-ask-usgs
www.usgs.gov

ATV FOOD PLOT ACCESSORIES

Woods-N-Water
311 North Marcus St.
Wrightsville, GA 31096
Ph: 888-440-9108
www.theplotmaster.com

Abby Mfg.
501 Co. Rd. 115
Walnut, MS 38683
888-794-4004
www.abby-usa.com

BushMaster Jr.
800 South Industrial Pkwy.
Yazoo, MS 39194
Ph: 877-647-2563
www.amcomfg.com

EarthWay Seeders
Ph: 800-294-0671
www.earthway.com

Panorama Harrow
Ph: 800-392-2386

Monroe-Tufline Mfg. Co.

P. O. Box 7755
Columbus, MS 39705
Ph: 662-328-8347
www.monroetufline.com

Kolpin Dirtworks
www.kolpinpowersports.com

Kasco
www.kascomfg.com

Frontier Implements
www.deere.com

Arctic Cat – SPEEDpoint
www.arcticcat.com

Index

Q

R